FULLY REVISED &
UPDATED EDITION

Nutrition for Life

THE AUTHORITY ON DIET
AND HEALTHY EATING
FOR THREE DECADES

CATHERINE SAXELBY

Hardie Grant

BOOKS

This fully revised and updated edition
published in 2020 by Hardie Grant Books,
an imprint of Hardie Grant Publishing
First edition published in 1986 by Reed Books

Hardie Grant Books (Melbourne)
Building 1, 658 Church Street
Richmond, Victoria 3121

Hardie Grant Books (London)
5th & 6th Floors
52–54 Southwark Street
London SE1 1UN

hardiegrantbooks.com

 A catalogue record for this
book is available from the
National Library of Australia

Nutrition for Life
ISBN 978 1 74379 522 4

10 9 8 7 6 5 4 3 2 1

Managing Editor: Marg Bowman
Design Manager: Jessica Lowe
Designer: Ella Egidy
Cover image: Michelle Moore, Stocksy
Production Manager: Todd Rechner
Production Coordinator: Mietta Yans

Colour reproduction by Splitting Image Colour Studio
Printed in China by Leo Paper Products LTD.

Contents

Acknowledgements   v

Introduction   1

1 Eat more ...
Vegetables   4
Smart carbs and whole grains   7
Good fats   11
Protein   17

2 Eat less ...
Junk food   22
Sugar   28
Caffeine   33
Salt   36
Alcohol   39

3 Hot topics today
Sweet syrups and sugar alternatives   42
Sweeteners   46
New foods with a nutrition buzz   49
Phytochemicals   58
Vitamin D and sunshine   62
Vitamin B12 and why you need it   64
Iron and fatigue   65
Diet and pregnancy   67
The omega factor   70
Probiotics and your microbiome   74
Fermented foods   76

4 Current cuisine
Cafe culture – how to treat yourself well   80
Snacking – making it healthy   80
The newest fast food   82
Eating out – healthiest cuisines   84
Vegetarian and vegan diets   88

5 Food, health and ethics
Food waste and what you can do   96
Eating seasonally and locally   97
Organic certification and practices   98
Pesticides and food irradiation   100
Hormones and GM foods   102
Edible weeds (wild food) and foraging   103
Food scares   104

6 Body matters
The healthiest way to lose weight   106
New Year's resolutions and why
    they don't last   107
Weight loss fundamentals   107
Exercise matters for weight loss   110
Cutting carbs for weight loss   113
Diet trends such as keto and vegan   115
Intermittent fasting   123
Mindful eating   124
Shame-free body zones   125
Helping overweight kids   126
Detoxing   127

7 Smart shopper
The 10 basics of a food label   130
Decoding the nutrition panel   131
Understanding the list of ingredients   133
Claims on the pack   134
Label de-coder example   137
Additives – how safe are they?   137
Streamline your shopping   141
How to use the Health Star Rating   143

8 Diets for health problems
Eat to beat...
cholesterol and heart disease   144
metabolic syndrome   146
type 2 diabetes   148
food allergy and intolerance   150
irritable bowel syndrome   153
lactose intolerance   154
coeliac disease   156
anxiety and depression   158
ageing   160
heartburn   161
gallstones   162
traveller's diarrhoea   164
a hangover   165
iron-deficiency anaemia   167
constipation   168

9 The top 20 superfoods
Catherine Saxelby's top 20 superfoods   170

Index   182

Photographic credits

The publishers would like to thank and acknowledge the following photographers and photo libraries for the use of images:

iStock: Geshas (p28); Manuta (pp36, 48); Monica Ninker (p38); Rawpixel (p98); Clark and Company (p103); brebca (p114); Adobe Stock: 5ph (p142); Unsplash: Magdalena Raczka (piv); Hermes Rivera (ppvi–vii); Bruno Nascimento (p2); Heather Barnes (p6); Rezel Apacionado (p8); Brad Stallcup (p9); Nazar Hrabovyi (p11); Alex Loup (p13); Sonnie Hiles (p15); Jonathan Borba (p16); Jez Timms (p17); Louis Hansel (p18); Jade Ashton Scully (p19); Ana Tavares (p20); Ella Olsson (p21); Joseph Gonzalez (p23); Amirali Mirhashemian (p24); Vita Marija Murenaite (p25); Katarzyna Grabowska (p27); Jade Wulfraat (p30); Heather Ford (p31); Natanja Grun (p32); Kayla Phaneuf (p34); Christine Trant (p39); Chris Ralston (p40); Brooke Lark (pp41, 120, 121); Nicole Honeywill (p43); Tania Fernandez (p44); Plush Design Studio (pp47, 59); Monika Grabkowska (pp49, 57, 66, 73, 137, 152, 169, 171, 181); Ronit Shaked (p50); Nick Sarro (p53); Jennifer Schmidt (p54); Toa Heftiba (p55); Adrienne Leonard (p56); Asoggetti (p58); Minh Pham (p62); Marine Dumay (p63); Heather Ford (p64); Vitor Pinto (p67); Hoan Vo (p69, 107); Alla Hetman (p70); Am Fl (p71); Klara Avsenik (pp76, 77); Jakub Kapusnak (p78); Nathan Dumlao (p81); Karly Gomez (p83); Edward Guk (p85); Christine Siracusa (p86); Anna Sullivan (p87); Louis Hansel (pp88, 117); Food Photographer Jennifer Pallian (p90); Edgar Castrejon (p91); Toa Heftiba (p92); Stefan Johnson (p93); Xiaolong Wong (pp94, 168); Annie Spratt (p97, 104); Orlova Maria (p100); Nicolas Dmitrichev (p102); Agence Producteurs Locaux Damien Kuhn (p105); Daniel Hjalmarsson (p108); Melissa Walker Horn (p109); Gesina Kunkel (p110); Derick McKinney (p112); Heather Gill (pp119, 167); Form (124); Georgia de Lotz (p128); Graphic Node (p132); Nikolai Chernichenko (p135); Lindsay Moe (p136); Sharon McCutcheon (p138); Hans Reniers (p140); Lex Sirikiat (p145); Deryn Macey (p147); Rachael Gorjestani (p148); Luann Hunt (p150); Nordwood Themes (p151); Kim Daniels (153); Mae Mu (p155); Shawn Fields (p156); Alex Block (p157); Ellen (p158); Luisa Schetinger (p159); Alison Marras (p160); Eduard Militaru (p161); Lindsay Moe (p162); Jennifer Schmidt (p163); Manu Schwendener (p164); Julia Kouzenkov (p166); Elle Hughes (p172); Gaelle Marcel (p173); Markus Spiske (p174); Eiliv Sonas Aceron (p175); Jenn Kosar (p176); Tetiana Bykovets (p177); Jo Sonn (p178); Carolyn V (p179); Alexander Mils (p180).

Acknowledgements

The author is grateful to the following nutrition scientists and food technologists for their help in compiling this work – as with any book, many others helped me to bring this book together, and I'd like to thank in particular:

Munaiba Khan
Manny Noakes
Dai Suter
Greg Pointing
Lisa Yates
Robyn Hodge
Leigh Julian
Chris Southwell
Nicole Senior
Sophie Feng
Susanna Morley
Caitlin Delaney
Ngaire Hobbins
Melissa Meier
Sally Marchini

How best to use this book

You don't need to read this book from cover
to cover. Just flick through, find a section
that interests you and dip in. You'll find all the
latest facts and figures here at your fingertips.

Food kilojoules and calories

All figures in this book are given in kilojoules,
the metric unit of energy measurement. With food,
one calorie equals 4.186 kilojoules (4.2, or simply
4, is close enough for a quick conversion). For
example, a slice of bread supplies 290 kilojoules
or (290 divided by 4) approximately 70 calories.

For my ever-supportive husband, David,
who believes in everything I do and
has endured many and varied regimes.
Having grown up a non-salad eater,
he recently said he now likes salad.

Introduction:
HELLO
AND
WELCOME

**Thank you for buying this book.
It means so much to me!**

> 'Health is a state of complete physical, mental and social well-being and not merely the absence of disease or infirmity.'
>
> The World Health Organization

I'm amazed at how much nutrition has changed. Every day there are new food trends popping up, such as eating insects instead of meat – and the Heart Foundation's red tick has now been replaced by the Health Star Rating. With so many changes, there's enormous confusion about the best way to eat. For instance, should I eat more fats and less carbs? Should I eat keto or raw? Should I shun gluten if I want to lose weight? On top of all this, we're eating out more and more, as well as drinking more alcohol.

In preparation for this book rewrite, I surveyed my audience of readers and asked them what topics they would like covered. Their responses fitted into three main areas. They wanted to know more about foods for:

- Anti-ageing
- Losing weight
- Having more energy in their day.

Plus they were after specific topics on controversial foods like coconut, hemp, kale and insects, and diets such as low-carb, keto and vegan. They wanted information from a credible expert such as a qualified dietitian or nutritionist – rather than a celebrity blogger or chef.

In with the new ...

This book was first published way back in 1986 as a magazine-style book priced at a tiny $5.95. Its original concept was that of a magazine where all the articles were focused on healthy eating. Like other magazines, it was originally sold through newsagents – but as time went on it moved into bookshops and became more of a traditional-looking book.

It was an instant success. A surprise to us all! It achieved sales reaching more than 400,000 over five editions and was once the most popular-selling book in Australia and New Zealand. This is the sixth edition, the most comprehensive ever produced, and it's as essential as ever.

This 2020 edition of *Nutrition for Life* has been fully updated to reflect current nutrition thinking. It is the biggest and most ambitious of all editions yet, in a fresh and attractive package, with plenty of user-friendly hacks and easy tables with the most up-to-date information on food and nutrition.

I have totally revised every section and it now covers topics like the microbiome, juice cleanses, mindful eating and the longest-lasting superfoods, as well as specific diets like FODMAPs, and others for health problems such as high cholesterol, diabetes and gastro. I also address some of the most hotly debated topics, from organic foods and pesticide residues to vegan eating and GM (genetically modified) foods.

Nutrition for Life is not a diet book. It never was. It does not have a set diet plan that everyone must eat by, nor a long list of foods to avoid. It does offer information that will allow you to get the most from your foods and answers to those confusing nutrition problems and food controversies.

Catherine

Catherine Saxelby
Accredited Nutritionist and
Accredited Practising Dietitian

'DON'T DIG YOUR GRAVE WITH YOUR OWN KNIFE AND FORK.'

OLD ENGLISH PROVERB

1 Eat more ...

Here are the basics – healthy foods that you can and should eat more of.

Vegetables

In terms of health, whatever the question, the answer is 'vegetables'. In the world of nutrition, eating your recommended five serves of vegetables each day (more if you can) is the best way to protect against most health problems, from being overweight to having cholesterol levels that are too high. Yet many of us struggle to achieve this goal. Surveys show that only 4 per cent of us eat the recommended daily intake of vegetables and legumes. In Australia, for example, at best around half of the adult population consumes half of what they're meant to.

Ideally try to eat vegetables throughout the day: at breakfast, lunch, dinner and in between. If you leave all your vegetables for dinner, it's hard to get those five serves in. For example, for snacks consider swapping chips and nuggets for vegetables instead, like carrot or celery sticks with hummus dip.

6 easy ideas to help kids reach their 5-a-day

1. Set a good example as a parent and eat your vegetables and be enthusiastic about them.
2. Pack raw vegetable sticks (carrot, celery, sugar-snap peas, cherry tomatoes) into your kids' lunch boxes for snacks during the day.
3. When it's cold, fill hungry tummies with a mug of vegetable soup or a hot corn on the cob when they come home from school.
4. Be a bit sneaky and grate vegetables into bolognaise sauce, rissoles and hamburger patties so that reluctant vegetable eaters get the nutrition they need.
5. As a fun incentive, start a star chart for your kids, on the fridge. Promise the kids a fun outing or extra play time. Get them to tick the chart when they eat a serve of veges, so they can see how they're faring.
6. If you have the space, grow a vegetable garden with your kids. Or you can grow cherry tomatoes, baby spinach or herbs in pots on a sunny windowsill or balcony.

6 easy ideas to help adults reach their 5-a-day

1. For breakfast add steamed spinach, slow-roasted tomatoes or grilled mushrooms to your eggs. Or make an omelette with a vegetable filling such as corn kernels, sliced leek, thinly sliced zucchini or capsicum.
2. For lunch add extra salad to your sandwiches. Go for variety like lettuce, tomato, grated carrot, sliced cucumber, sprouts, rocket or beetroot.
3. Enjoy a mug of homemade vegetable soup with lunch.
4. For dinner serve large portions of non-starchy vegetables such as broccoli, carrots, asparagus, bok choy or choy sum, mushrooms and brussels sprouts.
5. Enjoy a colourful stir-fry – the more colourful the vegetables you use, the more phytochemicals you get (see page 7).

What is a serve?

- 1 medium tomato
- ½ cup sweet corn kernels stripped off the cob (or canned)
- ½ cup cooked green or orange vegetables (e.g. broccoli, spinach, carrots or pumpkin)
- ½ cup dried-and-cooked or canned (preferably with no added salt) beans, peas or lentils
- ½ medium potato or other starchy vegetable (e.g. gold potato, taro or cassava)
- 1 cup green leafy vegetables or raw salad leaves

Tip: Buy in season

Aim to buy your vegetables when they are in season. They'll be the cheapest at the markets. Vegetables are at their peak nutritionally with the maximum vitamins, minerals and flavour when they are naturally ripe. Don't buy out of season because you'll pay more for produce that has most likely clocked up a lot of food miles, as often it has been flown in from another country.

6. For a snack cut up vegetable sticks such as carrots, celery or zucchini (to replace corn chips or crackers) to dip into hummus or salsa.

Frozen or fresh?

Frozen vegetables can be as nutritious as home-cooked vegetables – as long as you cook them while still frozen (do not thaw) and quickly, in as little water as possible. Remember they are already partially cooked, so they don't need more than 1 or 2 minutes in boiling water. Think of it more as a final heat, not a full cook.

Freezing (at –18°C for no more than six months) is the most nutritious and efficient way to preserve food. Freezing is superior to canning because frozen vegetables retain a lot more of the heat-sensitive vitamins that decline during canning (particularly vitamin C, thiamin and folate) and have a better texture. Yes, frozen vegetables lose *some* of these vitamins but not all. Also, frozen vegetables hardly ever have any added salt, which is a big drawback with canned vegetables.

Raw or cooked?

A mix of raw and cooked vegetables is important for good health. A salad at lunch and cooked vegetables at dinner is one easy way to achieve this.

In most instances, eating fresh raw vegetables provides you with the highest amount of nutrients that vegetables contain, especially heat-sensitive vitamins that are often lost in cooking, like vitamin C and two key B vitamins – thiamin (B1) and folate. I often recommend a salad or a green smoothie (vegetable-based juice) a day for this very reason.

However, cooking vegetables has its advantages. It makes certain nutrients able to be more easily absorbed by the body, e.g. beta-carotene and the antioxidant lycopene are absorbed better from cooked carrots or tomatoes than from raw.

Boost your nutrition with vegetables

You certainly don't have to become a vegan but eating plenty of vegetables makes good nutritional sense. Vegetables are packed with vitamins, minerals, fibre and numerous phytochemicals (antioxidants) – and have very few kilojoules.

You'll often hear the phrase '5-a-day'. This is a simple way to remember how many serves of vegetables you need to aim for. Eating your 5-a-day helps prevent heart disease, some types of cancer (in Australia 11 per cent of all cancers are thought to be related to people not eating enough vegetables and fruits), excess weight and constipation. Five serves a day can also reduce blood pressure and mental troubles like depression.

6 ways to cook healthy vegetables

1. Cut vegetables into large pieces. Do not cut them too small or soak them before cooking. This maintains as much of their nutritional value as possible, without losing important vitamins and minerals into the cooking water.
2. Avoid cooking in copper and brass pans. Some vitamins like vitamin C oxidise too readily with these metals.
3. Cook vegetables lightly. Cook them quickly, so they're still a little firm when pierced with a sharp knife. Think tender but still crisp. Whether you steam, stir-fry or microwave your vegetables, cook them for the shortest time you can.
4. Cook vegetables in only a little water. If you boil vegetables, use as little water as possible. To cut the cooking time, bring the water to the boil, then add your diced vegetables and cover. If you microwave your vegetables, you don't even need to use any water.
5. Finish with fat. Fat-soluble vitamins – A, D, E and K – need fat in order to be absorbed. So a splash of oil on your carrots or an oil-based dressing drizzled over your salad makes good nutrition sense while also tasting good.
6. Don't keep vegetables warm for long periods, say over 15 minutes, before you serve them, as the vitamins they contain will decline.

Eat the rainbow

Much like a rainbow, vegetables come in a range of beautiful vibrant colours. These colours are created by all the different vitamins, phytochemicals and other nutrients that are in vegetables.

Dark-green colours as found in spinach and broccoli are rich in chlorophyll, which purifies the blood and balances your metabolism.

The yellow-orange colour in vegetables comes from beta-carotene, alpha-carotene, xanthophyll, cryptoxanthin and related carotenoids; carotenoids are helpful for protecting vision and combating cellular damage, which may reduce the likelihood of cardiovascular events and eye disease.

Richly coloured purple foods are everywhere: purple carrots, red cabbage, red onion, eggplant (aubergine), purple corn, purple potatoes, purple broccoli and purple cauliflower. Purple foods harbour

Purple foods harbour some of the most amazing nutritional benefits possible.

some of the most amazing nutritional benefits possible. They are high in anthocyanins (see pages 53, 61) – for instance, purple carrots have up to 28 times more anthocyanins than orange carrots.

In contrast, beetroot's deep purple colour comes from plant chemicals called betalains. Like anthocyanins, betalains have antioxidant and anti-inflammatory properties. You can also find betalains in the stems of chard and rhubarb but it's the flesh and skin of beetroots that are especially rich in them.

In a class by themselves, these pigments are considered to be powerful antioxidants that can guard the body's fragile cells from the destructive effects of unstable molecules known as free radicals. Anthocyanin-rich foods should be included in a 5-a-day diet to protect against chronic diseases such as cardiovascular disease, neurodegeneration and certain cancers.

So always try to eat a rainbow of colourful vegetables – greens, yellows, oranges, purples and reds. This ensures you get a wide variety of different nutrients.

Smart carbs and whole grains

Think of white sliced supermarket bread or a hot dog bun. It's soft, easy to eat and easy to swallow; almost nothing to chew. You can probably wolf down two or three slices in a couple of minutes – and that's the problem. These modern-day carbs are too easy to eat. And overeat. They've had their fibre removed, and they've been processed and refined so they are almost too rapidly digested and absorbed into the body. They require little chewing. And they taste good. Before you know it, you've swallowed 1600 kilojoules (around 400 calories).

Then the carbs enter your bloodstream rapidly, causing your blood glucose to spike suddenly, which then triggers a corresponding surge of insulin. Insulin is a hormone that turns a 'key' in the cells of your muscles, effectively opening a door to move the glucose out of your bloodstream and into your muscles to power them with fuel. But if your muscles don't need the fuel for any activity (e.g. if you're just sitting at a desk), that unused glucose gets directed into storage – in your fat cells.

The end result is that you've eaten more kilojoules than you needed or are aware of. Modern thinking

is that we don't realise how much we actually eat – despite all the cues around us! Think of that big box of movie popcorn that doesn't leave you feeling satisfied. An hour later, you're looking around for a snack to carry you over to the next meal. Your body has had to call on more insulin than usual and another gram or two of fat has been stored.

Why you need some carbs – the right ones – in a healthy balanced diet

1. If you exercise, your muscles need carbs to work. And you must do some exercise if you're serious about losing weight.
2. Carbs balance your protein and fat intake. If you didn't eat any carbs, you'd be eating a caveman diet of meat, fish and eggs – washed down with lashings of butter, cream and mayonnaise. Hardly good for your arteries or your kidneys, which have the job of eliminating the unused protein end-products.
3. Carbs provide fibre (found mainly in whole grains and beans) and vitamin C (sourced from fruit and salads). And where do phytochemicals come from? You guessed it – vegetables, fruit, herbs and many whole grains.

A rethink on complex vs simple

Carbohydrates were once incorrectly divided into two categories – complex (starches) and simple (sugars). New research has changed this way of thinking because it proves that slow-absorbing carbohydrates can come in either sweet *or* starchy forms. Today the advice is rather to eat more 'slow' carbohydrates. Whole grains take longer to be digested and absorbed by the body and so fill you up and keep hunger at bay for longer. You don't crave a snack 20 minutes after a meal.

Why smart carbs are 'smart'

Smart carbs are:
- Nutrient-dense – they're packed full of essential vitamins, minerals and fibre
- *And* wholegrain – they contain the three key parts of the grain: the bran, germ and endosperm
- *Or* slowly absorbed – have a low GI ranking of 55 or less)
- *Or* high in fibre – great for regularity and bowel health

Choose your smart carbs

Here is a list of smart carbs to help you start to make better carb choices. The carbs closer to the top are healthier carbs and better for weight loss.

- Legumes – beans such as kidney beans, chickpeas, lentils, spilt peas
- Starchy vegetables – corn, green peas, carrots, gold potato
- Oats, old-fashioned and steel-cut
- Oat bran, rice bran
- Muesli
- Cereals – wholegrain, high fibre, bran
- Dense grainy breads – mixed grain, wholemeal, dark rye, linseed and soy
- All fruit
- Pasta, noodles – cooked al dente, not mushy
- Rice – basmati or Doongara
- Yoghurt

Further down the list comes:
- Potato – because it's high GI
- Couscous, polenta – still refined
- White bread, including tortillas and lavash flatbreads
- Cereals – refined, rolled or flaked types
- Rice – Calrose or jasmine

7 reasons to steer clear of refined carbs

White bread, white rice, peeled and/or fried potatoes, and many breakfast cereals are:

1. Refined – a percentage of their original nutrients have been milled or abraded (ground) away
2. Low in fibre
3. High in kilojoules – 100 grams of boiled white rice packs in 490 kilojoules (117 calories) while 100 grams of full-fat yoghurt has only 390 kilojoules (93 calories) and oranges a tiny 180 kilojoules (43 calories)
4. Easy to over-consume (they don't 'fill you up')
5. High GI – they are digested and absorbed quickly
6. A 'vehicle' for carrying fat – think of how much oil, cheese or cream you can add to potato mash or fried rice OR how much butter you spread onto bread
7. Carriers of 'hidden fat' – you consume lots of fat when eating biscuits, croissants, doughnuts, pastries, pies, potato chips and fries (see pages 22–6)

What about fibre?

Some carbs are classified as 'non-digested', with some of these being components of fibre, while others are a form of starch that is not digested (known as resistant starch). These are important for a healthy gastrointestinal tract – they add bulk, overcome constipation and act as food for the 'friendly' bacteria (your gut microbiome) that live happily in the large bowel.

Starches and sugars have the same kilojoule count – 16 kilojoules (4 calories) per gram. The non-digested types of carb or fibre provide none or few kilojoules, depending on whether any can actually be digested and absorbed. Typically you'll get about 8 kilojoules (2 calories) per gram from what is defined as fibre on a food label.

Why the wrong carbs make us fat

Our modern-day staples like white bread, white rice and potato are the worst carbohydrates to eat when you're trying to lose weight or eat for health, and to feed your biome (short for microbiome).

You'd do better on wholegrain or low GI (Glycaemic Index) versions of any carbohydrate – grainy bread, brown rice, jacket potato with the skin, plus pasta, legumes and starchy vegetables such as golden sweet potato, celeriac and parsnip. These carbohydrates will make you feel fuller *before* you've overeaten and 'stick with you' for longer after a meal.

Carb-free diets took carbs off the menu

Carbs are out of favour with the keto diet, which is similar to the initial stages of the Atkins diet. It forbids any sort of carbohydrate, including that in fruit and legumes, and allows unlimited quantities of meat, cheese, deli meats, fish – all eaten with butter, cream or rich sauce. The keto theory says that if you are in ketosis, you'll automatically start burning your own stores of body fat and produce 'ketones' as fuel for your brain and blood cells. Chemically this is true but you can't stay on a keto diet forever and long-term weight loss needs two weeks or longer for permanent change.

If you decide to give the keto diet a try, I suggest you 'adapt' and improve it by including (daily):
- Lots of vegetables and salad
- 1 piece of fruit
- 1–2 slices of a dense wholemeal bread or a bowl of oats or wholegrain cereal or muesli
- A 200 gram tub of yoghurt (only cheese is currently permitted)

This will only add 30–60 grams of carb to your day (still extremely low compared to the 200 plus grams usually eaten daily). But this strategy does add those healthy whole foods that are a key part of good nutrition.

How much?

Unlike protein and vitamins, there are no precise recommendations for how much carbohydrate you should eat. In fact, carbohydrate intakes can vary enormously and still be compatible with good health. Compare the high-carb traditional Japanese rice diet (where around 70 per cent of their kilojoules comes from carbs) to the almost carb-free fish diets eaten by the Inuit living in Iceland, where less than 10 per cent of their kilojoules comes from carbohydrate.

How low can you go?

If you want to lose weight or if you lead a mostly sedentary lifestyle, these are the minimum amounts of carbs that I recommend you eat daily:
- On a standard weight loss regime of 5000 kilojoules (1200 calories) a day, which is what most women aim for, don't drop below 130 grams of carbohydrate or around eight serves a day. This is the official Australian Dietary Guidelines figure for a low-carb

intake and represents 40 per cent of your total energy intake.
- For women who want to work to a higher carbohydrate intake (say if you love pasta and breads) but maintain the same weight loss level as above, aim for 165 grams a day or 10 serves. This is 55 per cent of your total – still within the guidelines for good health.
- For men, a standard weight loss regime of 7500 kilojoules (1800 calories) a day is suggested. This allows for 170 grams of carbohydrate or around 10 serves a day (40 per cent of your total intake).
- Don't forget that there are small amounts of carb in the so-called 'non-starchy' or 'free' vegetables that you eat in unlimited quantities, e.g. 100 grams of green beans has 2 grams of carbs. So does a tomato, believe it or not, while an onion has 5 grams. Not as much as from potato, but when you're consuming a lot of vegetables, it adds up.

The carb rules – the healthiest ways to cut carbs

1. Avoid the 'junk' carbs like those found in soft drinks, sweets, cakes and biscuits.
2. Swap white bread for a more grainy loaf or chewy wholemeal bread that is much more filling and nutritious.
3. Swap your breakfast cereal to one made of oats (muesli or porridge) or whole wheat (wheat-flake biscuits, wheat flakes) or bran (all-bran, bran flakes). A bowl at breakfast is convenient and healthy and will keep your bowels working well.
4. For dinner one medium potato or half a cup of cooked rice will balance your meal without overloading you with carbs. Certain vegetables contain higher carbohydrate values but are still nutritious; have a small serve of pumpkin, carrots, corn and peas.
5. Avoid fruit juice; it has had its fibre removed and is easy to over-consume. Drink water and eat the real fruit (two pieces a day) instead.

Bottom line

Cut down, don't cut out! There's no need to cut out *all* carbs from your diet. Take a look at which carbs you like to eat and decide which of those are the good ones that you want to keep. You may love bread, as I do, but don't care too much for rice or potato. Or you may simply cut down the *size* of all the carbohydrate portions you eat. In the end, make wholegrain, high fibre or low GI your carb mantra.

Good fats

Healthy fats can help protect you against heart disease, cancer, Alzheimer's and many other conditions. But while eating healthy fats is good for your heart, when it comes to your waistline, all fats have around the same number of kilojoules.

At 37 kilojoules (9 calories) per gram, fat is the most concentrated in kilojoules, supplying twice as many as carbs or protein. This was the key reason fat was restricted back in the 1990s to help slow the obesity crisis. However, people made up the difference by taking in more of the refined starches, sugars and syrups, which still kept their total intake the same as before.

Reducing the total fat you consume not only helps you shed kilograms, it can also help you live longer and be healthier. And when cooking, make sure you use the healthier oils that provide those essential nutritional benefits. Here is a list of oils from minimally processed nuts, fruit and seeds so you benefit from other naturally occurring good-for-you compounds that are found alongside the fats.

EVOO and cold-pressed oils

Oils ain't oils, as the famous slogan goes. And this is true of the oils you use every day in your kitchen.

Extra-virgin olive oil (EVOO) is the main oil you want to use. I visited a modern oil mill, and saw firsthand the large 'screw' auger that squeezes the olives to press out all the lovely oil. It's the same method the ancient Greeks and Romans used for centuries to extract the oil from the olives they grew in their hot arid climates. EVOO is a cornerstone of the famed Mediterranean diet that nutritionists the world over agree is the healthiest way to eat.

I like to buy an oil that's grown locally, is dark in colour and has a strong gutsy flavour. A good olive oil is high in monounsaturated fat including oleic acid, and in polyphenols, which give the oil its dark-green or yellowish tinge.

And don't believe the hype about not being able to cook with EVOO at high temperatures – you can. And contrary to what many people say, it actually has a higher smoke point than coconut oil. Having said that, you shouldn't let any oil get hot enough that it smokes!

Other cold-pressed oils that I recommend are macadamia, avocado and mustard seed.

Easy ways with extra-virgin olive oil:
- Splash EVOO over salads and cooked vegetables
- Instead of spreading bread with butter, serve crusty bread with a small bowl of EVOO for dipping
- Use EVOO for cooking and pan-frying
- You can make your own salad dressings ahead of time and store them in a tiny jar; they will keep for four or five days in the fridge. I like to use the traditional formula of three parts EVOO to one part lemon juice or vinegar, plus a little Dijon mustard and a few grinds of black pepper (there is enough salt in the mustard so I don't add any more). Shake and pour over your salad just before serving

One tablespoon (20 millilitres) of olive oil supplies: 18 grams fat, no protein, no sugar, no salt, no dietary fibre and 640 kilojoules (152 calories).

Note: EVOO contains squalene and plant sterols, which are analysed as 'fat' but are different to the triglycerides usually discussed in nutrition.

Avocado

Avocados, with their smooth creamy flesh, are a nutritious tree fruit that contains a significant amount

The terminology of fats

> MUFAs – monounsaturated fatty acids
> PUFAs – polyunsaturated fatty acids
> UFAs – unsaturated fatty acids
> SFAs – saturated fatty acids
> TFAs – trans fatty acids

of fat. In contrast, almost all other vegetables and fruit have virtually no fat, but instead are sources of sugars and starch.

An avocado has on average around 13 per cent total fat. This translates to 7 grams of fat per quarter of a large avocado. One quarter weighs about 50 grams. So instead of a tablespoon of butter or margarine (with its 10 grams of fat) on your toast, you can spread a quarter of an avocado and eat less fat.

The good news is that this fat is mainly in the form of monounsaturated fat, being made up of the fatty acid oleic acid. This is the same 'heart-health' fatty acid found in almonds, macadamias and olive oil. They have only a little saturated fat and contain no cholesterol, despite the myth to the contrary, which is still hard to dispel.

Despite the soft, smooth flesh, avocados are a surprisingly good source of fibre and are a good source of vitamins such as vitamin E, vitamin C and folate (a B vitamin). Plus avocados are one of the best sources of the mineral potassium, containing 40 per cent more than bananas, a well-known high-potassium food.

Because avocados don't need cooking, their vitamin C and folate – which are heat-sensitive – are not lost in preparation.

Easy ways with avocados:
- Spread mashed avocado onto crusty bread or toast instead of butter or margarine
- Peel and dice an avocado and add to any salad
- Buy a small avocado and eat a whole one for a mid-afternoon snack
- Mash a ripe avocado with lemon juice, garlic, a little chopped fresh chilli and serve as a pre-dinner dip

Half an avocado (100 grams) supplies:
1 gram protein, 13 grams fat (including 3 grams saturated fat), 4.5 grams carbohydrates (including 4 grams starch and a trace of sugars), 4 grams dietary fibre and 605 kilojoules (144 calories).

Nuts and nut butters

Nuts are a healthy high-fat food in a fat-phobic world. With around 50 per cent fat, nuts add a good dose of the healthy unsaturated fats – polyunsaturated and monounsaturated fats – to your diet. They have little saturated fats and virtually no trans fats.

The fat profile of each nut varies. They are also rich in a unique combination of nutrients such as vitamins, minerals and phytochemicals. So including a variety of nuts in your diet is a smart choice and ensures you have a good balance of the right stuff. For instance, almonds, cashews, hazelnuts, macadamias, peanuts, pecans and pistachios are higher in monounsaturated fats, whereas Brazil nuts, pine nuts and walnuts have more polyunsaturated fats. Almonds are high in calcium and beta-sitosterol while hazelnuts score well for vitamins E and B6.

All raw or roasted and unsalted nuts are healthy. Apart from their good fats, they offer protein, fibre (around 8 grams per 100 grams on average), vitamin E, the B vitamin folate, as well as a swag of minerals such as magnesium, zinc and iron.

Those who eat nuts regularly are at less risk of developing heart disease and diabetes, have healthier body weights and are likely to live longer than those who don't.

Easy ways with nuts:
- Munch on a handful of nuts (preferably unsalted) as a mid-afternoon snack
- Serve nuts instead of chips with nibbles
- Throw roasted nuts into a salad just before serving – they add great crunch and flavour
- Toss nuts through your vegetables with some olive oil and garlic
- Add nuts to your stir-fries, pastas and risottos
- Make your own trail mix – a selection of your favourite whole nuts plus larger dried fruit such as apricots and apple rings, and chocolate bits, if desired
- Make up a pesto with any nut in place of the usual pine nuts

A small handful of natural almonds (¼ cup or 30 grams or 20 almonds) supplies:
5 grams protein, 16 grams fat (including 1 gram saturated fat), 1 gram carbohydrate (including a trace of starch and 1 gram sugars), 4 grams dietary fibre and 700 kilojoules (167 calories).

Seeds

Seeds like sesame, sunflower, pumpkin (pepitas), linseeds (flaxseeds), chia and hemp add good fats. Like nuts, they can add heaps of texture and flavour to dishes, so a little goes a long way.

Like nuts, they come in at around 50 per cent fat, but have little in the way of saturated fat and more polyunsaturated and monounsaturated fats. There's not much carbohydrate or sugar but a decent hit of fibre. For instance, sesame seeds have 12 per cent, while linseeds are up at a hefty 28 per cent fibre.

You'll get plenty of potassium, a little sodium and some surprising minerals such as calcium, magnesium, phosphorus, copper, iron and zinc. Most seeds contain around 15 per cent protein – a similar level to wheat, but they're gluten free.

Linseeds are also rich in lignans, a type of plant oestrogen that lowers female oestrogen levels, helps minimise the unpleasant side effects of menopause like flushing, and has anti-tumour properties.

Apart from linseeds, most seeds need to be crushed or ground to release their full nutrition package. Research shows that the fat and minerals contained in whole seeds is not well absorbed by our bodies – the outer seed layer does not break down easily because it's designed to protect the seed inside.

So whole seeds tend to pass through you undigested, giving you their fibre and flavour, but not much more. To really benefit from their rich content of oils, minerals and vitamins, it's best to consume them ground (like the famous LSA blend, which stands for linseed, sunflower, almond) or as seed butters like tahini (sesame seed paste) or cashew butter or a blend with peanut butter. Alternatively, make sure you chew and grind them between your teeth well.

Easy ways with seeds:
- Sprinkle seeds over your cereal or muesli, but remember to chew them well to get their nutrients
- Add a tablespoon to your smoothie to boost your fibre intake
- Make a nutrient-packed topping for fruit salad or yoghurt by grinding together 1 cup of walnut pieces with ½ cup linseeds (or buy LSA – make sure it is as fresh as possible); store the topping in the refrigerator and use within two weeks.
- Add to baking, such as muffins, either sprinkle on top or mix in a tablespoon for each cup of flour
- Toast lightly in the oven on a non-stick pan and add to salads and stir-fries for a lovely extra crunch
- Choose seeded breads like soy and linseed

One tablespoon of linseeds (28 grams) supplies: 6 grams protein, 10 grams fat (including 2 grams saturated fat), 10 grams carbohydrate (including 2 grams sugars), 8 grams dietary fibre and 580 kilojoules (138 calories).

Oily fish

Oily fish include small fish such as anchovies, sardines, herring and kippers, as well as larger types like ocean tuna, Atlantic salmon, various mackerel, eel, trout, silver warehou, mullet, trevally, sand whiting and snapper.

Compared to white fish like bream, oily fish are darker in colour and stronger in flavour with a high fat content in their flesh (anywhere from 7 to 20 per cent compared to white at less than 3 per cent).

There are plenty of good reasons to eat oily fish. The greatest reason is their natural fats. They have five to six times more omega-3 than white fish, and are especially rich in two special omega-3 fatty acids: the long-chain fatty acids known as EPA and DHA. These omega-3s are especially good for your heart and blood. While these fats won't lower cholesterol, they will keep your heart rhythm steady, your blood free-flowing and your blood triglycerides down. And as the saying goes, fish is brain food. These fatty acids are good for your brain, eyes and nerves.

Oily fish are rich in vitamin A as well as vitamin D – a vitamin that is often hard to obtain from food alone. Plus they are high in protein, and full of minerals from the sea like iodine, potassium and 'prostate-protecting' zinc.

Good news. You don't have to eat these fish fresh. They are also beneficial when frozen, smoked or canned.

How much is enough?
Plan for two serves a week of oily fish.

Easy ways with oily fish:
- Enjoy delicious sardines on toast in winter
- Cook fresh salmon, tuna or mackerel with colourful vegetables for dinner
- Keep cans of tuna or salmon in the cupboard for quick lunches or snacks

A medium (140 grams) salmon fillet, grilled, supplies: 36 grams protein, 13 grams fat, no carbohydrate, no dietary fibre and 1090 kilojoules (260 calories).

Dairy and fat

Evidence now shows that full-cream dairy foods do not have adverse effects on heart disease or diabetes despite previous recommendations to stick with only skim or low-fat products.

If you like to drink a lot of milk and are watching your weight though, swap to a low-fat milk to reduce your kilojoule intake (see Dairy Comparison). The same applies to yoghurt and fresh cheeses such as cottage and ricotta. Hard cheeses such as cheddar are difficult to produce in low-fat form. (Note that low-fat and skim milk are not recommended for children less than two years old.)

Dairy comparison per 100 millilitres

(about half a glass)

Full-fat

Low-fat

Skim

Kilojoules   Fat   Sugars

The story of saturated fats

For decades, we've been told to replace the 'unhealthy' saturated fats with heart-healthy polyunsaturated fat, like sunflower oil or polyunsaturated margarine, and to limit any saturated fat that we eat to only 8 per cent of our total kilojoule intake, which translates to around 18 grams a day. It was thought that saturated fats contributed significantly to increased cholesterol, which is a risk factor for heart disease (of course, there are other causes of heart disease like smoking, high blood pressure and obesity).

But now it seems that not all saturated fatty acids are bad. Nor should we judge a food solely by its saturated fat level. Some saturated fats are neutral for cholesterol. Some raise cholesterol more than others. Choosing the right types of fats to consume is important in reducing the risk of heart disease. But this doesn't mean you can eat loads of foods high in saturated fat like coconut oil or butter.

While we wait for the science to unravel these complexities, stick to the healthy fats contained in EVOO, avocado, and nuts and seeds, and the fats we find in whole fresh foods such as eggs, fish and dairy.

Fat facts

Some fat is essential for a healthy diet because it supplies:

- Fuel for energy
- Two essential fatty acids (omega-6 linoleic acid and omega-3 alpha-linolenic acid) that our bodies can't manufacture; these are the chemical starting points for a whole range of important compounds known as eicosanoids, which include cholesterol, vitamin D and prostaglandins; prostaglandins act as powerful vasodilators and inhibit the aggregation of blood platelets
- The fat-soluble vitamins (A, D and E), and fat-soluble phytochemicals such as beta-carotene and lycopene, which helps the body absorb these vitamins
- 'Spares' protein so it can do its primary role of building and repair

Protein

From cradle to grave, protein is required throughout life to create, maintain and renew our body cells. Enzymes, antibodies, haemoglobin and other blood compounds are assembled from proteins or are proteins themselves. Protein is also needed for the turnover (the rate of change or renewal) and repair of muscles, skin and hormones, as well as the maintenance of healthy bones. Contemporary views on protein suggest that protein may help with appetite control, greater fat loss and reduced muscle loss, a boost to thermic effect (that feeling of warmth after a meal) and the lessening of cravings.

Amino acids – the building blocks

Proteins are made up of chains of amino acids. Only around 20 amino acids are found in food, but the number of combinations in which they are arranged is infinite. Nine of these amino acids are considered indispensable or essential because they cannot be made by the body and so can only be provided by food. These nine amino acids are: isoleucine, leucine, lysine, methionine, phenylalanine, threonine, tryptophan, valine and histidine.

Protein after exercise

To help control hunger and enhance muscle metabolism eat 25–30 grams of protein after you exercise.
   This translates to:
- 100 gram can of tuna or salmon
  Or
- 1 glass of milk *plus* 2 eggs, e.g. in a smoothie
  Or
- 1 plain hamburger *plus* an egg.

The remaining amino acids are inter-convertible – they can be made from these nine or from each other. When food proteins are digested, our bodies split them into their individual amino acids and then reassemble them into the types of human proteins we need.

How much protein do we need?

Generally nutritionists recommend 1 gram of protein for every kilogram of body weight. So, for example, a woman who weighs 75 kilograms would need 75 grams of protein a day. Increasingly, it is recommended that people in their later years (over 70) or who are

overweight need a higher intake of around 1.2 grams of protein for every kilogram of weight. So, that same woman would need 90 grams of protein a day for optimal health.

Any excess protein is diverted into energy (kilojoules) and, unless burned up by physical exertion, is stored as body fat. Excess protein also puts pressure on your kidneys, which have the job of removing all the nitrogen from protein.

Most people have no difficulty in obtaining sufficient protein. In fact, most of us already consume what we need, with no reports of insufficient protein intakes in adults who are a healthy weight.

High-protein low-carbohydrate diets with unlimited eggs, meat and fish can increase protein intake to 300–400 grams a day, which researchers believe may put too much of a load on the kidneys. So try to stick to around 75–100 grams a day.

> Any excess protein is diverted into energy (kilojoules) and, unless burned up by physical exertion, is stored as body fat. Excess protein also puts pressure on your kidneys, which have the job of removing all the nitrogen from protein.

Top protein-rich foods by serve

From the table on page 19, we can see that meat is the best source of protein, having around three times as much protein as eggs, milk, cheese, tofu and legumes. Meat is worth eating if you wish to raise your protein intake significantly (and its animal proteins are closer to those of humans). Fish and poultry match beef and lamb in protein content, although nothing is as protein-rich as liver, kidneys and other organ meats, which are no longer popular (not shown in table).

Daily protein intake

75 grams of protein = one average-sized piece of steak plus a wedge of cheese plus a can of tuna.

A day on a protein-rich diet

This meal plan is a good way to eat for weight loss or if you need a high intake of iron and zinc.

It supplies 100 grams of protein, which is equivalent to deriving 27 per cent of your kilojoules from protein, which is higher than the usual 15–20 per cent. It's correspondingly lower in carbohydrates (bread, cereal, potato) but doesn't eliminate them altogether.

Breakfast

2 eggs, poached, with grilled tomato halves and mushrooms, served on 1 slice of wholemeal toast spread with 1 teaspoon of butter.

Lunch

A large salad with mixed leaves, cucumber, grated carrot, tossed with vinaigrette dressing and topped with 200 grams of salmon (canned and drained) and ½ cup of white beans (canned and drained).

Snack

½ avocado or large handful of almonds or other nuts.

Dinner

3–4 grilled lamb cutlets topped with pesto, served with green peas, carrots and green beans.

Dessert

A bowl of sliced fruit topped with ½ cup of yoghurt.

Protein in foods

Listed in descending order by type

Meat sources	grams	Non-meat sources	grams
Beef fillet steak (cooked), 150 g	40	Eggs, 2 medium (poached or boiled)	100
Livers, chicken or lamb (cooked), 150 g	38	Milk, low-fat or full-fat, 250 ml glass	82
King prawns, 10 (cooked), 160 g	38	Yoghurt, fruit or natural, low-fat or full-fat, 200 g tub	76
Chicken, ½ breast (cooked), 150 g	34	Cheese, cheddar, 1 slice, 30 g	75
Fish fillet (cooked), 120 g	32	Tofu, ½ cup, firm or soft, 100 g	74
Tuna/salmon (canned and drained), 100 g	25	Chickpeas, ½ cup (canned and drained), 75 g	67
Veal schnitzel (pan-fried), 150 g	23	Lentils, ½ cup (dried then boiled), 75 g	66
Pork leg, 2 slices (baked), 125 g	23		
Hamburger, plain including bun	18		
Lamb loin chops, 2 medium (cooked), 145 g	17		

Source: Australian Food Composition Database 2019 from FSANZ.

Protein shakes and powders

Protein shakes are not the magic answer to all your health and weight woes. Protein shakes are not just bought by body builders. Now they are so popular that you can readily buy a tub at your local supermarket or service station.

Most consist of powdered forms of protein from soy, pea or dairy (whey or casein) with or without carbohydrates and other performance-enhancing ingredients like creatine, 'fat metabolisers', vitamins and minerals. When you mix them with water or milk, they turn into a milkshake or smoothie-type drink.

If you compare the protein, kilojoules and cost of a typical chocolate-flavoured protein shake (made using a cup of milk – 28–34 grams protein, or water – 19–25 grams protein) to two eggs (12 grams protein) or a glass of skim milk (10 grams protein), you quickly see that it's no between-meal snack. The protein powders have one-and-a-half to three times more protein than the two eggs or the glass of milk. Plus they are also higher in kilojoules than eggs or skim milk.

Instead of paying top dollar for protein powders, you could look to old-fashioned whole foods like dairy, eggs, fish, meat or nuts to keep you full and help with muscle building and weight loss. For the average person, it's fine to increase your protein intake moderately if you're looking for weight loss, but there's no need to overdo it.

Vegans and protein

Protein intake is particularly important for vegans, as plant proteins from grains, legumes and nuts are limited in one or two of the nine essential amino acids. Protein from wheat, for example, is low in lysine, which classically is described as the first limiting amino acid in cereals. In contrast, eggs contain heaps of lysine, which well and truly covers the body's requirement for lysine.

> Protein intake is particularly important for vegans, as plant proteins from grains, legumes and nuts are limited in one or two of the nine essential amino acids.

That said, mixtures of two plant proteins can complement each other, with one making good any deficiency of the other. For example, a dish of the grains, barley or rice (which are low in lysine) served with dried beans like chickpeas, soybeans or lentils (rich in lysine, but limiting in methionine) can provide the correct balance of all essential amino acids. You do not have to eat two plant proteins in the same meal. Simply consuming them over the day is fine.

Processed protein

CSIRO research of 200,000 people found that people with low-quality diets obtained eight times more of their protein from junk foods than people with high-quality diets. These people were also three times more likely to be obese. They derived their protein from inferior protein sources such as pies, burgers, pizza with processed meats, chicken nuggets, sausages and ice cream. Healthy meals based on superior protein sources such as fish, chicken, meat, eggs or tofu help to control appetite and reduce the urge to indulge in junk food. Bottom line: get your protein from fresh foods, as many junk foods may be high in protein but also very high in kilojoules.

2 Eat less ...

No food is entirely bad – it's more a matter of quantity and how you use it.

Junk food

Everyone knows that junk foods – sweet biscuits, cakes, pies, pasties, chips, crisps, pizza, nuggets and sugary drinks – are not healthy. We have lots of names for them; we describe them as 'extras' or 'treats'. Technically they are called 'discretionary foods'; yes, they add to life's fun and enjoyment but ideally they should be eaten only in small amounts. Which, unfortunately, we don't do!

Junk food (and beverages) do not belong to any of the five basic food groups (which contain foods such as vegetables, eggs, fish, meats, nuts, dairy and whole grains), because they are not needed for health and growth. They tend to be poor in nutrients (vitamins, minerals, protein) and high in kilojoules, and are often highly processed.

Take a serve of French fries, for example. While fries do contain some protein (being made from potatoes), they are little more than a source of starchy carbs and bad fats with too much salt. They are deep-fried in oil, which makes them high in kilojoules, and then salted, usually twice. According to the USDA, a medium order of fast-food fries contains a hefty 1533 kilojoules (365 calories). In comparison, one small baked potato contains just one-third of that at 545 kilojoules (130 calories).

Junk food – consumption by weight vs what's popular

In terms of sheer weight of food consumed, burgers, pizzas, chips, chicken nuggets and desserts like sticky date pudding or cheesecake are the foods that many of us eat in large amounts – we need to cut back on these. Not to mention beers, ciders, wines, cocktails and other alcoholic drinks also (see pages 39–40).

If you look at what's most popular, based on the percentage of people who consume them daily, you see things from a different angle, and it's sugar, soft drinks and processed meats that we regularly indulge in – these also need to be avoided.

What's wrong with junk food

In studies carried out in Brazil and the UK, junk foods are described as EDNP – 'Energy-Dense, Nutrient-Poor' – something we just don't need in our overweight, sedentary world. In other words, junk food is best described as high in kilojoules (energy) but poor in essential nutrients such as vitamins. What's more, they're very high in sugars, sodium (a measure of salt) and bad fats. If you're trying to lose weight, these are the foods to get rid of. They give you little in the way of nutrients, are easy to over-consume and are chock-full of kilojoules.

You can't eat these every day

According to surveys carried out by the Australian Bureau of Statistics, we adults eat way too much junk food. More than one-third (35 per cent) of the foods we eat is in the form of junk food, which is not good for our nutrition or our collective waistlines.

If you are overweight, on a low income, on a tight budget or not very active, then cutting them right down is even more important. Pick one serve of something you really like – and enjoy every mouthful – and ditch the rest. Otherwise aim to reduce the junk food you eat to only one-third of what you now consume.

So next time you're contemplating a doughnut, chocolate bar, soft drink or pie, think again and ask yourself: Is there something else I can buy or eat instead? Aim for a sandwich, cheese with crackers, a nut-seed slice, tub of fruit salad or tub of yoghurt. Have water or a diet drink. And for your children's lunch boxes, consider adding a tub of cut fruit or yoghurt, or a box of sultanas instead of that muesli bar.

Fast food basics

Burgers, hot chips, pizza, fried chicken, nachos and chicken nuggets washed down with fizzy drinks or thick shakes – grabbing a quick meal on the run is a way of life for many people today. But such fast foods have many negative consequences. As with French fries on the previous page, most of it is greasy, fatty and salty – with way too many kilojoules and very little in the way of vegetables or nutritional fibre. On its own, fast food doesn't make a balanced meal, even though it's often advertised as a 'complete meal'. One lettuce leaf in a burger or a side carton of creamy coleslaw doesn't add nearly enough nutritional value. Still there have been plenty of improvements over the past few years so things are looking promising. Here we discuss the best and worst fast foods.

Not just the big boys

Despite the visibility of big franchise chains like McDonald's, Subway, Oporto, Pizza Hut and KFC, more people are buying fast foods from small independent takeaway shops, e.g. fish and chips, rotisserie chicken,

The chains spend enormous sums on television advertising, offering convenience including home delivery and drive-throughs, friendly service, hygiene and freedom from cooking.

takeaway Chinese, burgers, sushi, Thai noodle dishes, meat pies and kebabs. Food courts, pop-up carts, food trucks, train stations, quick-service cafes and petrol stations are where we're increasingly buying a meal to-go.

The chains spend enormous sums on television advertising, offering convenience including home delivery and drive-throughs, friendly service, hygiene and freedom from cooking. Motivating children to eat at their chain restaurants is a primary aim of advertising and many parents worry about how this moulds their children's eating habits. Children may come to prefer French fries instead of plain potatoes, thickshakes instead of milk and sweetened buns over regular bread. They may refuse home-cooked food, but enthusiastically go out for dinner at a fast food outlet.

Regular burgers

Whether from Nando's or McDonald's, burgers are usually somewhat nutritious and one of the better fast-food choices, especially if served with lettuce, tomato, beetroot and onion.

A standard fast-food burger will set you back over 30 grams of fat (about half of it saturated) and 3000 kilojoules (around 700 calories). Upsize to a 'super' version and you'll get double or triple the kilojoules. Unless you are running marathons, you don't need them.

> A standard fast-food burger will set you back over 30 grams of fat.

Part of McDonald's success has been its limited menu, which is identical anywhere in the world. Fewer than 20 items are offered for sale, with specials available for a limited time only. New products are tried but if they do not consistently sell well, they do not remain on the menu.

Best

Stick to a standard burger with 1 meat patty, in a bun with salad.

Worst

Forget those whopper burgers with two or three meat patties interspersed with a bun. From time to time, they make an appearance for shock value. They simply provide too many kilojoules and too much fat for inactive people. Also, eat half the chips or fries they give you – they're cheap to produce so they're always served in uber amounts to give a false sense of value-for-money.

A standard hamburger supplies 3045 kilojoules (725 calories), 42.3 grams protein, 32 grams fat (including 14 grams saturated fat), 63 grams carbohydrate (including 5 grams sugars) and 1536 milligrams sodium.

Nuggets

Golden on the outside, soft chicken meat on the inside. And easily eaten with your fingers – which is why I suspect kids just love them. But don't be fooled, a nugget is not all that healthy and there are better ways to get chicken into your kids.

For a start, the amount of actual chicken in a nugget can vary from a low 40 per cent to as much as 70 per cent. Even if you read that a nugget is '100 per cent chicken', this is not correct. The nugget may well contain 100 per cent chicken breast but it's only one of maybe another 10 ingredients in the overall product. Think about how you'd make them at home – they wouldn't be all chicken, there would be the outer breadcrumb coating plus salt, onion or garlic powder, an egg to bind plus dried herbs.

Best

Frozen nuggets from the supermarket – look down the list of ingredients on the packaging and buy ones with at least 60 per cent chicken and made with a monounsaturated oil (olive or canola) and a sodium (salt) content of less than 400 milligrams per 100 grams.

Worst

Any deep-fried nuggets from a fast food chain.

6 nuggets (124 grams) supply 1325 kilojoules (315 calories), 16 grams protein, 16 grams fat (including 3 grams saturated fat), 28 grams carbohydrate (including 13 grams sugars) and 969 milligrams sodium.

Pizzas

Pizza has come a long way since it was first created in Naples in Italy, where it was simply made by adding slices of tomato, mozzarella, oregano and a little anchovy on top of a yeasted dough base and then cooked in a wood-burning oven. This was the humble *Pizza alla Napoletana* and was a staple dish of poor families.

The pizza has never been the same since it immigrated to New York at the end of the 1800s. Now it is one of the most popular fast foods in almost every country of the world and appears with a vast variety of toppings that showcase fusion cuisines. For instance, you can munch on tandoori pizza or satay pizza and even Mexican pizza with chillies and kidney beans. Its versatility and aroma when it emerges from the oven have ensured its popularity over the years.

Best

Anything on a thin crispy base. Choose the small or 'regular' size because it's very easy to eat too much pizza. Look for extra thin, dry-ish, wood fired–oven pizzas, with a light scattering of topping so you can still see the base through it, and a tangle of fresh rocket and coriander to finish it off. The kind of pizza you might buy from the window of a small street restaurant while on holiday in Italy. These are the ones to order.

Fast food vs junk food

Not all fast food can be labelled as 'junk'. Some products make a nutrient contribution, but at a price. A plain hamburger, for example, can supply about 25 per cent of the recommended intake of protein, iron and zinc for an adult man. A hamburger with cheese supplies 20 per cent of his calcium requirement as well. But it also gives him 1590 kilojoules (380 calories), 17 grams of fat and a hefty dose of salt.

Worst

Avoid those large pizzas for under $10, where they throw in a free garlic bread as well. Food overload! Also say no to super supreme pan pizza with a cheesy crust and pepperoni, salami and bacon toppings, because they pack on the fat, salt and nitrates; ditto to toppings like olives, anchovies and all that cheese.

While very generalised, avoid those greasy pizzas overladen with cheesy, processed toppings from the large pizza chains such as Pizza Hut and Dominos. They ooze fat from the huge amounts of cheese or cheese crust and salami or bacon. What's more, they contain loads of salt and they come in super-large portion sizes that only encourage you to overeat.

Four slices of pizza supreme (300 grams) supply 3132 kilojoules (746 calories), 39 grams protein, 27 grams fat (including 14 grams saturated fat), 76 grams carbohydrate (including 7 grams sugars) and 1650 milligrams sodium.

Fries and chips

There's nothing quite as enticing as the aroma of hot chips on a cold winter's day; whether they're straight-cut, crinkle-cut, curly, thin fries or thick wedges, we consume a staggering amount of chips. It's all that last-minute salt, that aroma, that ease of popping one in your mouth with your fingers. According to US market analyst Bloomberg, McDonald's alone sells 4 million kilograms of fries each day around the world.

Yet chips get the thumbs down due to their high fat content of around 15 per cent. It doesn't sound like much as a percentage but this translates to a whopping 23 grams of fat from an average bucket of hot chips. And they're an amazing vehicle for consuming excess salt.

Chips get the thumbs down due to their high fat content.

Because of the type of fats used for deep frying, the fat in chips is generally saturated fat – the type that can raise blood cholesterol and contribute to heart problems. What's so sad is that the humble potato, the raw ingredient of chips, is a nutritious food to start with, being fat-free, full of fibre and filling in its boiled or baked states.

Best
Thick wedges with the skin on.

Worst
Shoestring fries

1 medium tub of fries (105 grams) supplies 1430 kilojoules (340 calories), 5 grams protein, 18 grams fat (including 4 grams saturated fat), 38 grams carbohydrate (including 0.2 grams sugars) and 220 milligrams sodium.

Kebabs
Nutritionally the combination of flatbread, hot lamb pieces with some tabouleh and hummus makes quite a good fast-food option. The only drawback is that sometimes the meat (or chicken) is pieced together with layers of fat that are meant to melt during cooking to keep the meat moist. Apart from this – which you can't control – keep your kebab healthy by skipping the cheese and the extra creamy sauces and sour cream.

The skinny on chips

The Heart Foundation and the University of Auckland surveyed 150 fast-food outlets and found that only 17 per cent cooked chips at the right temperature and that 39 per cent of their fryer thermostats were inaccurate. If the temperature is too low, chips take longer to cook and absorb more oil. If the temperature is too high, the chips turn out dark and the oil develops off-flavours and potential carcinogens (cancer-causing compounds). The Heart Foundation says the fat count of chips can be cut back by 30 per cent if takeaway shops do these three things:

1. Cook chips at 180–185°C for about 3 minutes; and turn the thermostat down to 140°C or less when not frying to preserve the life of the oil.
2. Serve thicker chips, 12 millimetres or bigger, and don't let them thaw before cooking when using frozen chips.
3. Keep the oil clean by skimming and filtering it regularly. Use a good quality oil such as sunola, a type of sunflower oil with excellent stability for deep frying.

The problems with fast food

Fast foods encourage overeating, especially through portion sizes that have been getting bigger yet the final offering is still cheaper. What is now a standard serve of fries is double that of a decade ago. Serving sizes of soft drinks have soared from a normal 200 millilitre cup to a whopping 900 millilitre bucket today. And fast-food outlets are masters at getting you to upsize your meals for a fraction more money – think of their 'two-for-one' meal deals. It represents value for money, but it's a bargain that our waistlines don't need. In addition, overeating occurs thanks to the ways of eating, which are the opposite of what someone trying to eat mindfully should do:

- You eat with your hands – not a fork and knife.
- You eat while you walk or drive – not seated at a table.
- You chow it down quickly – no leisurely dinners.

Sugar

Sugar is a refined food, supplying no vitamins, minerals or fibre. The only nourishment it has to offer is kilojoules, making it a source of energy. It's palatable and easy to over-consume. But if you eat too much, it can lead to you being overweight. This sets the scene for other health problems such as heart disease, diabetes, pre-diabetes, fatty liver or cancer. It also plays a role in tooth decay. So you need to consider how much sugar you eat and how often you eat it.

On its own, a little sugar is not bad for you. It is unlikely to destroy the nutritional value of your whole diet and it does make low-fat, high-fibre foods taste better – think how much more appealing multigrain toast is with a spread of honey, or roast meat is with a marinade of maple syrup. You don't have to give up all sugar to be healthy. But you do need to cut down!

Hide and seek the sweet

Only about 25 per cent of the total sugar we ingest is sugar what we consciously add to foods – like tea, coffee and home baking. The remaining 75 per cent comes from the everyday packaged foods and drinks we love to consume such as cereals, muesli bars, biscuits, ice creams, desserts, chocolates, flavoured milks, juice drinks and soft drinks. At times, we don't even realise sugar is present.

This is a dramatic reversal from the last century. Up until the 1960s, most sugar was used at home to make jams, homemade biscuits, slices, bottled fruits and puddings as well as for table use to sweeten tea. Today, with the growth of convenient ready-made foods and the decline in home cooking, sugar usage at home has dropped dramatically. Despite this, our total intake has changed relatively little.

How many teaspoons of sugar?

We don't realise how much sugar we're consuming, especially when we gulp down a can of soft drink. For instance, did you realise that a:

- 375 ml can of soft drink has 10 teaspoons of sugar?
- 600 ml large cola drink has 14 teaspoons?
- 250 ml glass of orange juice has 4½ teaspoons (coming from natural fruit sugars)?
- 300 ml carton of flavoured milk has 7 teaspoons?
- 250 ml can of energy drink has 7 teaspoons?
- 600 ml bottle of sports drink has 8 teaspoons?

Sugar in foods

Food	Serve size e.g.	grams	tsp
Drinks			
Soft drink	1 large drink, 600 ml	55.1	14
Soft drink	1 can, 375 ml	40.9	10
Milkshake	350 ml	40.2	10
Shake, McDonalds, small	340 ml	38.0	9
Sports drink	1 bottle, 600 ml	33.0	8
Energy drink	1 can, 250 ml	28.2	7
Fruit juice drink, orange	1 glass, 250 ml	28.8*	7*
Flavoured milk, chocolate	1 carton, 300 ml	28.2*	7*
Cordial (made up)	1 glass, 250 ml	22.5	5.5
Fruit juice 100% orange	1 glass, 250 ml	18.5*	4.5*
Iced tea, Lipton's original	1 bottle, 250 ml	11.5	3
Plain milk	1 glass, 250 ml	12.1*	3*
Alcoholic Drinks			
Port	1 small glass, 60 ml	7.7	2
Sherry, sweet	1 small glass, 60 ml	6.8	1.5
Wine, white, sauvignon blanc	1 glass, 150 ml	0.2	0
Wine, red	1 glass, 150 ml	0.3 g	0
Sparkling wine, champagne	1 glass, 150 ml	1.5 g	0
Beer, full-strength 4-5% alcohol	1 can, 375 ml	0.4 g	0
Beer, mid-strength 3-4%	1 can, 375 ml	0 g	0
Spirits	1 shot, 30 ml	0 g	0
Cakes and Biscuits			
Cheesecake	1 wedge, 165 g	32.3	8
Lamington	1, 73 g	23.0	6
Carrot cake	1 slice, 100 g	22.1	5.5
Danish pastry	1, 100 g	16.1	4
Tim Tam	2, 38 g	15.6	4
Cupcake, iced	1, 40 g	14.6	3.5
Muesli slice	1, 78 g	14.7*	3.5*
Muffin, blueberry	1 medium, 150 g	13.3	3.5*
Butternut cookie	2, 26 g	9.6	2.5
Shortbread cream	2, 34 g	8.6	2
Doughnut, plain (cinnamon and sugar)	1, 50 g	6.6	1.5
Scotch finger	2, 36 g	6.6	1.2
Arrowroot biscuits	2, 17 g	3.6	1
Choc-chip cookie	2, 14 g	4.0	1

Food	Serve size e.g.	grams	tsp
Cereals			
Coco Pops	1 bowl, 30 g	9.1 g	2.5
Froot Loops	1 bowl, 30 g	11.4	3
Muesli, untoasted	1 bowl, 60 g	12.9*	3*
Frosties	1 bowl, 30 g	12.4	3
Nutri-Grain	1 bowl 30 g	8.4	2
Sultana Bran	1 bowl 30 g	7.4*	2*
Porridge, oat, cooked	1 bowl, 120 g	4.0	1
Corn Flakes	1 bowl, 30 g	1.3	0.5
Wheat-flake biscuits	2, 30 g	1.0	0.5
Ice creams and desserts			
Sundae, McDonalds, no topping	1, 135 g	27.0	7
Yoghurt, fruit	200 g tub	25.6*	6.5*
Paddle Pop	1, 90 g	17.8	4.5
Ice-block, water	1, 85 g	15.9	4
Ice cream, vanilla	1 scoop, 50 g	9.9	2.5
Jams, toppings and sauces			
Sweet & sour sauce	¼ cup, 80 g	30.2	7.5
Honey	1 tbsp, 28 g	23.0	6
Jam, berry	1 tbsp, 26 g	17.5*	4.5*
Marmalade	1 tbsp, 26 g	17.0*	4.5*
Chocolate topping	1 tbsp, 25 g	12.3	3
Plum sauce	1 tbsp, 20 g	9.6	2.5
Sauce, BBQ	1 tbsp, 20 g	8.0	2
Chutney, fruit	1 tbsp, 20 g	8.3*	2*
Dressing, coleslaw	1 tbsp, 20 g	5.3	1.5
Hoisin sauce	1 tbsp, 20 g	6.7	1.5
Chilli sauce	1 tbsp, 20 g	3.0	1
Sauce, tomato	1 tbsp, 20 g	4.7	1
Mayonnaise	1 tbsp, 20 g	2.9	0.5
Confectionery			
Mars Bar	1 bar, 63 g	29.3	7.5
Bounty Bar	1 bar, 45 g	19.9	5
Sesame seed bar	1 bar, 45 g	20.8	5
Milk chocolate	6 squares, 30 g	16.7	4
Hard-boiled sweets	3, 12 g	8.8	2
Jellies, jubes	2, 10 g	5.0	1.5
Caramels	2, 12 g	6.6	1.5
Muesli bar, plain or fruit	1 bar, 31 g	6.1 *	1.5*
Liquorice, black	1 strip, 13 g	4.8	1

*Also includes natural sugars

Source: Calculated from the Australian Food Composition Database 2019 at FSANZ and manufacturers' figures.

How much sugar should I eat?

The more active you are, the more sugar you can eat. You're burning off more so your overall sugar can go up. According to the World Health Organisation (WHO), 10 per cent of your daily kilojoule intake can come from 'free sugars – the sum of added sugar *plus* the sugars from honey and fruit juices'. This is a small amount that does not cause health problems but is difficult to measure. But if you're not active or need to shed weight, this free sugar is the first thing you need to reduce and avoid.

We currently drink and eat our way through approximately 60 grams of free sugars a day (equivalent to 14 teaspoons of white sugar). This includes added sugar and the natural sugars from fruit juice and honey. But this is an average, which hides great differences.

For example, a 16-year-old active boy who burns off 12,600 kilojoules (3000 calories) a day could safely tuck into some 19 teaspoons (76 grams) of sugar a day. In contrast, his mother who is mainly sedentary and who eats only 7500 kilojoules (1800 calories) a day would be able to consume 45 grams of sugar (from both the sugar she adds to food and what's already in sweetened foods). This translates to 11 level teaspoons of sugar a day – not much when you realise that one 60 gram chocolate bar has 8 teaspoons (33 grams) of sugar. So most of us have to halve what we eat now.

Tip

To work out the number of teaspoons of sugar in a product, divide the grams of sugar by 4 (there are 4 grams of sugar in each standard level teaspoon of sugar).

Sugar comes in many guises

When we talk about sugar, we normally think of white table sugar, which is sucrose. However, sugar comes in a number of forms. Here are 10 other refined sugars that you can spot on food labels:

1. Lactose (milk sugar)
2. Maltose
3. Invert sugar (preferred by pastry cooks and confectioners because it doesn't crystallise)
4. High-fructose corn syrup (HFCS), a sweetener used in the US
5. Golden syrup
6. Treacle
7. Apple juice concentrate
8. Cane sugar extract
9. Demerara sugar
10. Rapadura

How much sugar for your age, stage of life, gender and activity level?

The more energy (kilojoules) you burn, the more sugar you can eat and still be healthy. A healthy sugar intake range for adult men is 60–80 grams and for adult women is 45–65 grams. For children aged around six, a healthy sugar intake is 35–40 grams. Once they're older, bigger and more active, say around 14 years, it is 55–65 grams.

Is sugar bad for your health?

Despite recent no-sugar programs, dietary guidelines have long suggested that we eat only modest amounts of sugar and sugar-containing foods. You don't need to avoid sugar completely for good health, but it makes sense to cut back on less nutritious items like soft drinks, pastries and sweets, especially if you have concerns about your weight.

Other foods containing sugar, such as flavoured yoghurt or canned fruit, have a much better nutrition profile and give you important nutrients such as calcium, protein or fibre along with the sugar.

5 ways to cut back on sugar

1. Say goodbye to fizzy sugary drinks. Quench your thirst with water instead of soft drinks, energy drinks, sports drinks and cordial. Soft drink has approximately 10 per cent sugar and most people drink a lot of it; a 375 millilitre can contains 40 grams of sugar.
2. Cut back on sweet junk food like lollies, roll-ups, chocolate, cakes and fancy ice creams. Save these treats for special occasions and make them small.
3. Snack on fresh fruit, nuts, avocado, yoghurt or cheese and crackers instead of sweet biscuits, chocolate or chips. Sweeten your cereal with banana, chopped fresh fruit or a handful of sultanas.
4. Don't stress about the sugar from fruit yoghurt, flavoured milk, canned fruit or worry about the brown sugar on porridge or jam on toast – they're the smallest contributors and make healthy food taste good. Jam is high in sugar (65 per cent) but you only spread 2 teaspoons on your toast, so you consume a small 6 grams of sugar.
5. Juice, even the unsweetened types, still adds natural sugars from the fruit such as oranges or apples. We drink large quantities of it – a 200 millilitre glass of fresh orange juice has 20 grams of sugars and it's not that filling, being a liquid. So stick to a small half glass (125 millilitres) and buy the pulp-retained varieties for their fibre.

Sugar appears on the ingredient list of many foods but in very small quantities because it functions as a flavour balancer (like in tomato pasta sauce) or as a food for the yeast to start digesting (like in bread, kombucha or beer). These sources of sugar are negligible and do not pose any health concern.

On a label, 'sugars' means the total of what's natural (say from fruit or milk) *plus* what's added – it doesn't tell you how much sugar has actually been added. You need to run your eye down the ingredient list and see if some form of added sugar is near the top of the list (see page 133).

Where the sugar comes from

Foods containing sugar	grams	tsp
1 bowl of cereal	10	2.5
1 muesli slice	17	4
2 cups of tea with sugar	8	2
1 scoop ice cream	10	2.5
Total	45	11

On a label, 'sugars' means the total of what's natural (say from fruit or milk) *plus* what's added – it doesn't tell you how much sugar has actually been added.

Be sugar savvy

Sugar is a problem in our national diet, but it's not *the* problem. We definitely need to cut it back, but we don't need to completely eliminate it from our diet. The goal is to keep our intake under 12 teaspoons a day. Be more aware of how and where we consume sugar by reading the label and making smart food choices about what we drink and eat throughout the day.

Caffeine

Coffee is a drink with history, flavour and attitude. From espressos to flat whites, coffee is the great social beverage that is accessible in a variety of ways all around the world. The practice of drinking coffee spread from the East to Europe in the 1500s and coffee houses (or cafes in France) were established in the late 1600s.

The biggest contribution that coffee makes to our diet is through caffeine. Caffeine is a methylxanthine compound that acts on the central nervous system, speeding up the heartbeat and rate of breathing, dilating blood vessels and relaxing the smooth muscles found in the walls of organs. It boosts alertness and concentration and masks fatigue – key reasons for its enduring popularity in our fast-paced world.

How much is okay?

Most of us can handle around 300 to 400 milligrams of caffeine a day without problems. This translates to four or five cups of instant coffee or three shots of espresso (however you prefer it), although it's very variable.

How much is too much?

Surprisingly, some people never notice any side effects from drinking too much coffee. Other people get warning signs from caffeine habituation such as:

· Insomnia
· Upset stomach
· Rapid heart rate (palpitations or tachycardia)
· An overactive mind
· Increased anxiety and shakes ('coffee jitters')
· Frequent urination.

If you've got any of these symptoms and you're a big coffee drinker, you can be fairly sure it means you're having too much caffeine.

Types of coffee

Here's a run down on all those fancy coffee types and how much actual coffee you're getting; handy when you're trying to cut back on caffeine and wondering which coffee gives the least buzz:

Black Coffees

Espresso or short black
A single shot of coffee that is extracted in around 30 seconds by forcing near-boiling water through ground coffee under pressure, and is served in a small cup. A well-made espresso is characterised by a dark, golden crema and a smooth aftertaste. Being just coffee and water, it is the simplest form of coffee.

An espresso shot is the basis of all other coffees. It is usually 30 millilitres but some baristas like to be more generous with 45 millilitres.

Long black (Americano)
A long black is an espresso shot pulled on top of a cup of boiling water.

Lungo
An extra-long extraction that allows somewhere around twice as much water as normal to pass through the ground coffee, usually with a single shot of espresso.

Ristretto
Meaning 'restricted' in Italian, a ristretto is normally only the first 15 millilitres of extraction and is therefore 'restricted' in the amount of coffee extracted to better capture the sweetest, most intense characters of the coffee beans.

Milky Coffees

Cappuccino
Arguably the most popular way to drink coffee in Australia; a single shot of espresso makes up one-third, followed with one-third steamed milk and one-third thick frothed milk, and a glamorous sprinkle of chocolate on top. It was named after the Capuchin monk's white and brown long, flowing hoods.

Caffe latte
Now mostly known simply as a latte. It's a shot of espresso with three times the amount of creamy, steamed milk. Be aware that the word *latte* on its own in Italian means 'milk', so be careful to use the full name when ordering one in Rome. A trained barista often creates artistic designs in the froth.

Flat white
Very similar to the latte and popular in Australia and New Zealand where it was invented, thanks to the waves of Italian migrants who settled here after World War II. This is ideal for those who enjoy the strength of the latte but not the froth that comes with it (I'm one of them). Like a latte, the drink is prepared with one shot of espresso and steamed hot milk.

Macchiato

A shot of espresso with just a dash of hot milk added. It comes from the Italian word *macchiato*, which means 'to stain' or 'spot'. It's for the coffee lover who wants a strong espresso but with a little something to take away the edge or slightly soften the coffee. Traditionally it's served in a demitasse glass.

Affogato

A tall glass filled with ice cream, with a double shot of espresso poured over and topped with cream and shaved chocolate. Flavoured syrups such as caramel, vanilla or hazelnut, or a nip of liqueur can be added.

Piccolo

Piccolo means 'small', and this baby coffee appeals to those who don't want a huge volume of liquid. Usually it's a double shot of espresso served in a small glass.

Mocha

Equal portions of espresso, unsweetened hot chocolate and frothed milk. This coffee is sweeter but not as intense in coffee flavour. It's more of a transition drink from the sweetness preferred by teenagers to the full-strength coffee craved by adults.

Frappé

Think of a big cold milkshake made with coffee and you've got the frappé. Popular in coffee chains where it's sold in huge buckets and adds heaps of kilojoules. It's coffee mixed with sugar, milk and ice and/or ice cream, whizzed until thick and foamy and served in a long glass with a flourish of whipped cream (even more kilojoules).

Vienna

A double shot of espresso served in a tall glass, topped with a really big swirl of whipped cream and dusted with chocolate powder – not good for the waistline.

What are the downsides of too much caffeine?

According to the Mayo Clinic, caffeine can cause a short but dramatic increase in your blood pressure, even if you don't have high blood pressure. Why it does this no one knows for sure. So cutting back is important, especially if you already have high blood pressure, are overweight or over 70.

1. Caffeine increases the amount of acid produced by the stomach, which can irritate the stomach lining or worsen an existing ulcer.

2. If you're pregnant, it's probably wise to limit caffeine to less than 200 milligrams a day (less than three espresso coffees a day) or none at all. Earlier reports of caffeine causing birth defects or low birth weight or miscarriage have not been supported at moderate levels, but such effects/risks have not been safely ruled out with higher caffeine consumption.

3. Drinking coffee as an unfiltered brew – such as Turkish, Greek or plunger coffee (French press) – can raise cholesterol. Studies from the Netherlands reveal that unfiltered coffees are rich in sediment that contains substances known as diterpenes, which are found in oil droplets and fragments of beans floating in the coffee. The researchers concluded that drinking five cups a day could send cholesterol up by 1 millimole per litre, which is significant when the ideal level is 5.5 or less.

What are the upsides for caffeine?

On the positive side, there are promising reports that coffee consumption may help slow Parkinson's disease in older men and possibly decrease the risk of type 2 diabetes. A space to watch over the next few years.

Caffeine in drinks

Product	Caffeine (mg)
Coffee	
1 cup decaffeinated (250 ml)	2–5
1 cup instant coffee (250 ml)	60–80
1 shot espresso (30 ml)	60–80
1 cup cappuccino, latte, flat white – 1 shot espresso (30 ml) and topped with hot steamed or frothed milk	60–80
1 shot of Turkish coffee (30 ml)	60–80
1 cup percolated/plunger/drip (250 ml); anything that uses ground coffee, e.g. coffee machines, percolators, plungers, French press and drip paper filters	60–120
1 long black – 2 shots espresso, (60 ml)	80–120
Tea	
1 cup peppermint/chamomile herbal infusion (250 ml)	0
1 cup rooibos – African red tea (250 ml)	0
1 cup decaf tea (250 ml)	2–5
1 cup tea from leaf or teabag (250 ml)	10–50
Drinks	
1 can cola soft drink, decaffeinated (375 ml)	0
1 cup hot cocoa (250 ml)	5–20
1 can cola soft drink, diet and sweetened (375 ml)	35–45
1 carton coffee-flavoured milk (300 ml)	40
1 can energy drink (250 ml)	80
Over the counter stimulants	
No Doze	100

How to cut down

Don't go 'cold turkey' because you'll only trigger caffeine withdrawal – throbbing headaches, tiredness, yawning and lethargy – which can last for a couple of days but is bad enough to send you screaming back for caffeine. The trick is to cut back gradually to allow your body to adapt. Here's how you can do it.

1. Cut out one cup of coffee or one can of caffeinated energy drink each day. Start on a weekend or on holidays when you aren't under the pressures of work. Begin by dropping an afternoon or evening caffeine hit. Plan to have your last coffee by 4 pm so the caffeine can work itself out of your system before bedtime.

2. Aim to cut your overall intake by half long-term, or until you have reached a level that you're comfortable with and don't have sleepless nights or shaky hands. You don't have to give up coffee entirely, just enough to reduce the side effects, depending on your sensitivity.

3. A common goal is to keep cutting back until you drink no more than three cups of instant coffee or one or two espresso shots a day.

Coffee alternatives

Decaf

Decaffeinated coffee is made by removing the caffeine from green beans before roasting them. It is used to make either black or white coffees. One removal method uses a well-tested solvent, methylene chloride, but then the problem arises of how to remove all traces of the solvent. Another method is to use water to dissolve out the caffeine but it's more expensive. Whichever method is used, there is some loss of flavour and aroma. If you drink a milky coffee, it's probably still pleasant but coffee aficionados will not find it to their taste.

Guarana and caffeine

Don't be fooled by guarana. It's just another plant that's a source of caffeine. Yes, it's natural but so are coffee beans and tea leaves. Yerba maté is another drink that's high in caffeine.

Dandelion and roasted root coffee substitutes

Coffee substitutes are useful for people who are affected by caffeine's over-stimulating effects. They are made from roasted, malted grains like barley, wheat or rye, or from roasted chicory or root vegetables (dandelion, beetroot or carrot) with molasses or maltodextrin added. The roasted ingredients are steeped and the liquor separated and concentrated under vacuum before drying. Some coffee substitutes are high in fibre. If you like your coffee weak with milk, I think you'll find these fine, but not if you're a lover of espresso. Examples are dandelion tea (also called dandelion coffee), Caro, Ecco, Cafix and Pero.

Salt

Here's a quick winter's lunch: a bowl of canned soup accompanied by a slice of buttered toast topped with melted cheese. Sounds simple enough. But this typical meal has more salt than you need for the whole day. And that's the problem. Salt, a common ingredient in foods, is everywhere and often our taste buds don't even recognise foods as being salty.

Salt is a compound called sodium chloride, of which about 40 per cent is sodium. Salt is the main source of sodium in the average diet. In tiny amounts, sodium is an essential mineral. Our bodies need it to regulate the water balance, maintain blood volume, control muscle and nerve function and to regulate our body temperature.

In the large amounts that we now consume, however, sodium has an adverse effect on our health. It attracts and retains fluid inside the body, causing fluid retention. This can lead to a weight gain of up to 1 kilogram, which strains the heart and makes it pump extra fluid through the arteries. The arteries thicken, reducing blood flow, which raises blood pressure.

Excess sodium can worsen kidney function in patients with renal disease and cause calcium loss via the urine; so it contributes to brittle bones (osteoporosis) in later life. Research suggests that too much salt can also cause asthma to worsen. Cutting back on your salt intake will make a big difference to high blood pressure and any condition where fluid retention is a symptom, such as heart failure, cirrhosis of the liver and Meniere's syndrome. Not forgetting kidney problems and brittle bones.

What to aim for

People can survive on less than 200 milligrams of sodium a day, but the average Western diet supplies 2300–4600 milligrams per day (equivalent to 6–12 grams of salt), which is 10–20 times more sodium than the 200 milligrams we actually need. The recommended daily maximum intake for sodium is 2300 milligrams, a little more than the amount in a teaspoon or 6 grams of salt.

Here's what the claims on packaging mean

No-added-salt, salt-free or unsalted foods must not contain any added salt or any ingredient with salt. Think of canned beans, canned vegetables, peanut butter, tomato paste and canned sardines. Most mineral and soda waters (despite the name) are fairly low in sodium.

Low-salt foods must not contain more than 120 milligrams of sodium per 100 grams. Some foods, such as butter and margarine, have their sodium expressed in terms of salt. This figure of 120 milligrams of sodium per 100 grams is equivalent to 0.3 per cent salt.

Salt-reduced foods generally have 25–30 per cent less salt than their regular counterparts. Many butters, margarines, sauces, cereals, cracker biscuits and soy sauces fall into this category.

Salt – one ingredient, many uses

Salt is one of the most widely used ingredients. It is used not only to flavour foods but also to preserve foods. Here are three foods that traditionally have relied on salt for their production:

Bacon needs salt to bind water to the proteins of raw pork, producing a juicy rasher that is moist and tender. Salt also helps stop the growth of bad bacteria such as salmonella.

Cheese manufacture relies on salt to create the right environment for each cheese culture to grow. Blue cheeses, for example, are produced from a bacteria culture called *Penicillium roqueforti*, which only grows when 4–5 per cent salt is mixed with the curds. Cheddar is made with 2–3 per cent salt, while ricotta has none.

Bread requires 2 per cent salt to slow the rate of fermentation of the yeast and prevent mould growing in humid weather.

Types of salts

Table salt
Table salt is found in most salt shakers. It is a finely ground salt with small, even-sized crystals, typically created from rock salt. It usually contains an anti-caking agent like sodium aluminosilicate (554) or magnesium carbonate (504) to keep it free flowing, even in high humidity.

Iodised salt
This looks the same as table salt but has a minute amount of iodine added, either in the form of potassium or sodium iodate,* or iodide. The iodine is added to help prevent iodine deficiency, which can

lead to thyroid problems such as goitre. This is the salt I prefer for cooking at home. Research shows that our iodine intake has been dropping in recent years, which has implications for a slowing down of the functioning of the thyroid hormone and for normal brain development in babies and young children.
* The salt acts as a carrier for iodine.

Sea salt
With its large uneven flakes or crystals, sea salt looks 'natural' and is favoured by chefs, but it's still a form of salt (sodium chloride) and will not lower your overall salt intake by any significant amount. It's made by evaporating seawater and has 99 per cent of the sodium of table salt. The other 1 per cent consists of minerals like magnesium, potassium and zinc, which are found naturally in seawater. Many claims have been made about the health benefits of sea salt but none have been scientifically validated.

Rock salt and river salt
These are more gourmet and claim they are better for you, but they have essentially the same salt content as table salt. They appear to produce a more intense salty flavour because the salt is in large chunks. Some come in pink, red or grey colours due to the presence of natural minerals. A popular example is Murray River Pink salt, but there are Himalayan and Maldon salts also.

Celery salt, vegetable salt and garlic salt
These are also no better than table salt in terms of reducing your sodium intake. They still contain some 70 per cent salt with dried ground celery, vegetables or garlic making up the remaining 30 per cent. It's a reduction in salt intake, but it's hardly a big one.

Chicken salt
Most people love a sprinkle of chicken salt on their chips or roast chicken but really it's all about the flavour. There's a bit of chicken essence and the rest is just good ol' salt.

Cooking salt
Cooking salt has the same salt content as table salt but it occurs in coarse chunks and most have added iodine. It is sold in larger quantities and used for more industrial-sized jobs like mass-roasting potatoes on a bed of salt or getting stains out of carpet.

Whether you opt for table salt or sea salt, there's little difference in the sodium content by weight, and they all need to be kept to a minimum. The key difference is taste, texture and iodine content.

So ... is one better?

Whether you opt for table salt or sea salt, there's little difference in the sodium content by weight, and they all need to be kept to a minimum. The key difference is taste, texture and iodine content. Many chefs prefer to use the coarser gourmet and sea salt chunks. If you opt for a quarter teaspoon of a coarse-grained salt like sea salt, you'll find that less fits onto a spoon so you'll get less sodium. But that's about it when it comes to benefits.

How to reduce your salt intake in 7 easy ways

1. Buy salt-reduced foods and those made with no-added salt whenever you can. This will have the biggest impact on reducing your salt intake. Key foods to choose carefully (because they contribute to so much of our salt intake) are bread, cheese, butter or margarine, processed meats, takeaway foods and sauces (even though they may not taste salty).
2. Cut salty foods such as olives, anchovies, pretzels, potato crisps, corn chips and salted nuts from your diet. These perpetuate a craving for saltiness and create a noticeable thirst, which explains why they are often served as appetisers with pre-dinner drinks.
3. Gradually add less salt to your meals at the table. This will help re-educate your palate and will reduce your total sodium intake by 15 per cent.
4. Use potassium chloride – a salt substitute – for the first two weeks. Like salt, it's a white crystalline powder that can be shaken over food. Some people detect a metallic aftertaste that they find unpleasant. However, most people discontinue it after a few weeks because they lose the desire for saltiness. If you have heart or kidney problems, check with your doctor in case you retain potassium.

How salt creeps in

Unprocessed foods contain little salt, but the more processed foods are, the more salt they contain.

Low	mg	Medium	mg	High	mg
Pork fillet, cooked 100 g	72	Ham, ½ cup shaved (50 g)	778	Bacon, grilled 2 rashers (50 g)	1108
Rice boiled, no added salt 1 cup (100 g)	3	Fried rice, 1 cup (100 g)	369	Seasoned rice 1 cup (100 g)	630
Tomato, 1 raw (100 g)	6	Canned tomatoes ½ cup (100 g)	78	Tomato sauce 2 tablespoons (28 g)	271
Potato, 1 baked (200 g)	34	Hot potato chips 1 bucket (180 g)	324	Potato crisps 1 packet (100 g)	460

5. Initially, cook recipes with half the quantity of salt, reducing further over time. Do not add any salt if you use salted ingredients such as bacon, stock, soy sauce, oyster sauce, fish sauce, hoisin sauce, steak sauce or cheese.

6. Add flavour with herbs, spices and aromatic ingredients like lemon juice, orange rind, mustard powder and wine. They substantially enhance flavour when you cut out salt. Also use plenty of chilli, onions, garlic and shallots.

Potassium is a complementary mineral to sodium.

7. Eat more fresh rather than processed foods. Fresh vegetables, dried and fresh fruit, fish, meat, rice and pasta cooked without salt have little sodium and plenty of potassium. Potassium is a complementary mineral to sodium that can protect against sodium's harmful effects. It is needed for nerve function and fluid balance.

> Do not add salt to food for your baby or children because their kidneys are unable to remove the sodium.

Alcohol

A refreshing beer on a hot day or a glass of red wine with dinner is something many of us enjoy. In modest quantities, alcohol provides pleasure and helps people to relax.

But having excess alcohol is detrimental to health in many ways and increases our chances of becoming overweight, as it is a concentrated source of kilojoules. At 29 kilojoules per gram, pure alcohol has almost twice that of carbohydrate or protein – two nutrients where there is often debate on how much to eat for weight loss.

Pros

Here are the positives from a glass of your favourite tipple:

1. Studies show that people who drink moderately are less likely to suffer heart attacks. Alcohol appears to work by raising HDL-cholesterol – the type that protects against heart disease.

2. Moderate social drinkers live longer than total abstainers or those who consume three or more drinks a day.

3. Alcohol encourages social networks such as a visit to a club or pub where one can meet up with friends.

6. It works as a diuretic, forcing the kidneys to produce more urine, and thus overworking them.
7. It interferes with sexual function, especially in males. Alcohol lowers the level of the male sex hormone, causing loss of libido, decreased sperm production and occasionally impotence.
8. It amplifies the effects of a long list of medications such as sedatives, anti-depressants and anti-anxiety medications, and certain painkillers. Often the medication packs carry a warning and it is essential to heed it, especially if driving or operating machinery.

Nutrition in alcohol

Alcoholic drinks score low in nutrition, despite the fact that their raw ingredients – like grapes (to make wine) or malted grains (beer) – are quite nutritious. Thiamin, for example, is present in grains but in the manufacture of beer it is destroyed, or concentrated in the yeast and lost from the beer when it is clarified and the sediment removed. Varying amounts of minerals, such as potassium and iron, are present in the end-products – red wines and dark beers can carry substantial amounts of iron – but there is little else apart from sugars and alcohol.

Alcohol should be strictly limited by anyone wanting to lose weight. Alcohol can be used in cooking, however, because the heat evaporates much of it, leaving an enhanced flavour with few fattening kilojoules.

How much?

Latest medical advice is that both men and women should stick to a maximum of two drinks a day. More than this is potentially hazardous to health, bringing with it a high risk of mental and physical damage. Pregnant women should not drink at all, especially during the first three months of pregnancy, because there is a risk of birth defects.

Alcohol and the liver

Alcohol is metabolised mainly by the liver, where it is converted to acetaldehyde and enters the body's biochemical pathways. A small amount of alcohol is removed by the kidneys, and in sweat and breath (which explains why alcohol can be detected by breathalysers). It takes the body about one hour to eliminate the alcohol from a single glass of wine or spirits, and about 12 hours to eliminate half a bottle of spirits.

Cons

Here are the negatives of excessive alcohol consumption:
1. It inflames the lining of the stomach, intestine and pancreas.
2. It increases the excretion of the mineral zinc and magnesium. Zinc is concentrated in semen and the prostate gland, and is required for full maturation of the sexual organs in adolescents.
3. It prevents the proper absorption of B vitamins and in addition depletes them from the body, as B vitamins are required for the metabolism of alcohol. At the extreme, long-term excess alcohol consumption can lead to Wernicke-Korsakoff syndrome, a disturbance in mental functioning caused by lack of thiamin (vitamin B1).
4. It can lead to cirrhosis of the liver (although not all alcoholics develop this).
5. It can cause a hangover with symptoms including a pounding headache, a drier-than-dry mouth, loss of balance, nausea and fatigue the morning after over-indulging.

3 Hot topics today

How can you tell if it's hype or hope for better health? In an era of 'fake news', it's often hard to tell what's right and what's a myth. Here I examine the trends that are taking off.

Sweet syrups and sugar alternatives

Everyone knows sugar is bad for us but what about those other sweet alternatives like honey or agave? Are they any 'healthier' than sugar? Do they deserve a place in your everyday eating? Here's a rundown on the most popular, listed from best to worst.

Sweet syrups

Syrups such as honey, maple syrup, golden syrup, rice malt syrup and agave are refined sugars. They are about one-third water, so they appear to contain less sugar than the crystals. They are mostly mixtures of glucose and fructose with some sucrose (see page 45).

Honey

A generally thick amber liquid made by honey bees (*Apis mellifera*) using the nectar from flowers, honey has been 'nature's sweetener' for centuries. Nutritionally its true advantages are minor, which I know will disappoint many. Honey does contain B vitamins and minerals but the quantities are tiny and not significant nutritionally. Many people believe that raw honey – with its flecks of bee pollen and fragments of honeycomb – is more wholesome but there is no hard evidence to suggest that honey is better for you than sugar. Ultimately, it's still 'sugar' in another form.

Studies have confirmed that honey can have a higher level of phytochemicals (antioxidants) (see pages 58–61), which gives it an edge over sugar. Colour is a good guide – darker honey has more phytochemicals than lighter coloured honey, according to a recent study of 42 commercial honeys sold in Australia including floral, regional, organic, generic, pure and manuka honeys.

Generally manuka honey from tea trees has the highest phytochemical content. However, they are quite variable and do not consistently score high. It probably depends on the regions from which they come, which has a tremendous impact on their flavour and composition.

Although honey is the most natural of all syrups, and my preference, it can't replace sugar in every cooking situation.

Maple syrup

Maple syrup is the sap that comes from the maple tree (*Acer saccharum*) after it's been concentrated and refined. It's a mix of sugars – anywhere from 90 to 100 per cent sucrose and 0 to 10 per cent glucose or fructose. There are also traces of organic acids, vitamins and some mineral material in maple syrup, with manganese, potassium, iron and calcium being the most prevalent minerals. Despite these traces, it has little food value. Make sure you buy the expensive 100 per cent Canadian maple syrup, not the cheaper maple-flavoured syrup, which has an inferior flavour and is made from a nasty mix of sugar, corn syrup, molasses, caramel colouring, alcohol, vanilla extract, flavours and a sulphite-based preservative.

Birch syrup

Birch syrup comes from tapping the sap from birch trees (*Betula papyrifera*) and is produced in much the same way as maple syrup. The watery sap is reduced by evaporators or reverse osmosis machines until it reaches a sugar content of 66 per cent or higher to allow it to be classified as a syrup. Many varieties of trees are used, depending on which country the syrup is from.

It's not as sweet as maple syrup, so it's used more as a glaze for meat rather than a pancake topping. Unlike maple syrup, the sugar in birch syrup is mainly fructose (about 50 per cent) and glucose (about 40 per cent) but it is low in sucrose.

It takes a lot more sap to make birch syrup because the trees are less productive (you need around 100 litres of sap per litre of syrup) than maple trees (around 40 litres of sap per litre of syrup), so it's more expensive.

Agave

Agave syrup has been consumed for thousands of years in Mexico and Central America. It is produced from the blue agave succulent (sp. *Agave*), a large, spiky plant that resembles a cactus but is actually related to the aloes such as aloe vera. Its sweet sap is first extracted from the core of the plant (called the 'pina'), then filtered and heated or treated with enzymes, and concentrated until it becomes a thick syrupy liquid. It tastes like honey with overtones of

> It tastes like honey with overtones of caramel and burnt sugar.

caramel and burnt sugar. I find it runnier than honey, with a similar viscosity and colour to maple syrup. It is high in fructose, so has a low Glycaemic Index (GI). You can't eat it as if it were a 'free food' with zero carbs – you still need to limit your intake of it.

Rice malt syrup

Rice malt syrup, or brown rice syrup, is popular as a sweetener and is used as a substitute for sugar in everything from raw bliss balls to alternative versions of dessert. It's also sought after as a vegan substitute for honey and for its composition, which is largely glucose based. For comparison, sugar is half glucose and half fructose.

A traditional sweetener used in both Japan and China, rice malt syrup contains little fructose, being a mixture of simple glucose, maltose (two glucose units joined together) and maltotriose (three glucose units joined together). While you may see claims that rice malt syrup has a low GI of only 25, this is not the case. In fact, it has an extremely high GI of 98, according to the Sydney University Testing Lab. This is almost the same as pure glucose, which is the maximum on the scale with its high GI of 100.

Nutritionally it's similar to honey or golden syrup. Rice malt syrup may contain tiny amounts of minerals like calcium and potassium but nothing substantial.

Taste-wise, it has none of the depth of flavour you would find in honey or golden syrup.

Golden syrup

Golden syrup is derived from molasses, which is the residual syrup left over from the milling of sugar cane. Golden syrup is a mix of three sugars – sucrose, glucose and fructose – but because it contains more water and less sucrose than white table sugar, it is not as sweet. It is a concentrated sugar syrup with a distinctive flavour and golden colour. I've had a jar in my kitchen for years – I only use it to make Anzac biscuits every once in a while and for adding moistness to my Christmas cake.

Treacle

Treacle is a viscous, dark-brown liquid that has a stronger flavour and aroma than golden syrup. Like golden syrup, some of the sucrose sugar is broken down to its glucose and fructose components during production. This process stops crystals from forming and thus creates a stable semi-liquid product.

Molasses

Molasses is the dark, sticky liquid that is left behind after the raw sugar crystallises during sugar milling. It's a mixture of 36–38 per cent sucrose, 10–13 per cent glucose plus fructose combined and 24–30 per cent water. It also has a few minerals such as magnesium and potassium and traces of B vitamins. From time to time, blackstrap molasses has been promoted as a 'health food' but the quantities of B vitamins present are very small. It tastes very strong and is not terribly sweet or attractive. Surprisingly it has a higher sodium (salt) content, which contributes to its not-so-nice flavour.

Bottom line for syrups

Despite all the hype, there's nothing special nutritionally about any of these sweet syrups, even though some have a few minerals or claim to have less fructose or to be organic or are marketed as 'natural'.

The syrups are more expensive than sugar – maple syrup or agave costs $9 or more for a slim 250 millilitre bottle. If they're sweet, they still need to be counted on a diabetic diet or for weight loss.

They're all similar in terms of sugar content and kilojoules – 1 level tablespoon (30 grams) of honey or any other sweet syrup supplies approximately 360 kilojoules (85 calories) and 22–25 grams of carbohydrates (of which all are sugars). And none are superior to white sugar.

Alternatives to sugar

Panela

Technically, panela is partially refined, non-centrifugal sugar. All this means is that the sweet cane juice has been boiled to evaporate its water and create a thick darkish syrup that is then poured into blocks so the last vestiges of water can evaporate. Panela is brown because it has retained its molasses content and may have a few more vitamins and minerals than white sugar but kilojoule-wise it's the same as sugar. Claims of 'organic' or 'Fair Trade' on the packaging simply give it a health halo.

It's around 78 per cent sucrose with some 4 per cent glucose and 4 per cent fructose, so it is similar to ordinary sugar, which means that it will likely have a similar GI of around 65. As with other brown sugars, the molasses content may contribute a few vitamins and minerals not found in regular granulated white sugar but the amounts are way too small to count towards your recommended daily intake.

Although panela looks homemade, it's not any healthier than ordinary sugar.

Fructose
Often known as 'fruit sugar', fructose is found in almost all fruits. It has a low GI of around 20 and is possibly less satisfying than other sugars. Fructose should not be confused with high-fructose corn syrup – a mix of 50 per cent fructose and 50 per cent glucose with a high GI of 89.

Fructose contains the same kilojoules as sugar but, being slightly sweeter, can be used in smaller quantities to achieve the same degree of sweetness, which is why food manufacturers love to add it to their products because they don't need as much and can cut costs.

Now marketed as a 'natural cane sugar–free' sugar replacement, you can buy pure fructose powder (brand names like Fruisana and Sweetaddin) but it's expensive and limited in its uses. It can't be used for baking or browning, for instance.

Some research suggests that fructose is a potential cause of weight gain because it is metabolised differently to glucose, and so it doesn't trigger the hormones that regulate appetite and food intake. This means that fructose is much more likely to be converted into body fat.

What's more, fructose bypasses the rate-limiting step of glycolysis and is not regulated by the hormone insulin, so it is easily transported into the body's cells.

Fructose has other known negative side effects, such as abdominal discomfort. Part of the reason is that it is absorbed more slowly in the intestinal tract than glucose, sucrose or maltose so hangs around for longer. Excess fructose is stored by the liver as triglycerides of fat, which can lead to non-alcoholic fatty liver disease and insulin resistance. But this all depends on how much you consume and whether there's any glucose present (there usually is). Say, if you eat fruit, you usually eat a mixture of fructose with glucose.

Glucose
Glucose (also sold as dextrose) is a white crystalline powder with a GI at the maximum of 100. It is the standard by which other sugars and carbohydrates are ranked. A GI of 100 means that glucose is rapidly absorbed into the bloodstream and stimulates a fast insulin response.

Glucose powder is not as sweet as regular white sugar, so it is often fed to invalids because they can take in more carbs to help recovery without being put off by the excessive cloying sweetness of sugar.

Glucose is the simplest form of sugar. It is also your body's primary source of energy. Dextrose (the other name for glucose) is often marketed to athletes as a source of instant energy. ('Dextrose' is used so they don't associate it with glucose or sugar!) Like glucose jelly beans, it will quickly raise blood glucose levels and replenish blood glucose.

Coconut sugar
Coconut sugar (also known as coconut sap sugar or evaporated coconut nectar) is produced from the fresh sap that oozes from the cut flower buds of the coconut palm (*Cocos nucifera*).

What surprises me is that this sugar is not derived from the coconut itself. The sap is collected or 'tapped' each day from the flowers, boiled in large shallow pans to evaporate the water and then concentrated by drying to remove any residual moisture.

It is 95 per cent sugars (sucrose plus fructose and glucose). Many food products incorrectly claim that coconut sugar has a low GI of 35, but testing by the SUGIRS service at the University of Sydney reported it to be higher, at 54, which means it only just sneaks in to the low GI category (where the cut-off is 55 or less).

Bottom line for sugar alternatives
Sugar is sugar, whether white or brown, raw or unrefined. All sugars are pretty much the same.

Sugar alternatives are not 'healthier' than refined cane sugar, even though some contain a few minerals or claim to have a lower GI or to be 'more natural'. Also, they all still need to be counted on a diabetic diet or for weight loss. For a truly 'sugar-free' product, you'd have to use the kilojoule-free sweeteners such as aspartame (see page 46), stevia (see page 47) or monk fruit (see pages 47–8).

Sweeteners

Sweeteners and sugar substitutes can be useful for dieters wishing to satisfy a sweet tooth without adding kilojoules, and for people with diabetes who still crave something sweet. In addition, they do not cause tooth decay, unlike more 'natural' sugars.

But are they all that helpful in *losing* weight? Well, it depends on the individual. Some research suggests that dieters make up the kilojoule deficit in other ways during meals, thus negating the savings from a sugar-free sweetener. Adding a sweetener to your morning coffee then tucking into a pastry is not a winning trade-off! The big problem is that sweeteners maintain your cravings for sweet drinks and foods.

Sweeteners under scrutiny

Despite the negative hype about brain cancer and mental problems (see aspartame, below), all sweeteners have passed stringent testing to ensure they are safe to consume.

Studies of long-term heavy users of sweeteners, such as older people with diabetes, report no higher frequency of brain or kidney cancers. But having said that, no one should have too much of any chemical sweetener. Sweeteners keep your taste buds craving that sweet taste, which you should aim to lose.

As with most things in nutrition, it's all about the quantity. If you have one diet soft drink every day or second day that's fine, as is popping a sweetener into 2 or 3 cups of tea or coffee a day. But guzzling a litre or more of diet drink a day isn't a wise strategy.

Should you use a sweetener?

Here is a rundown of the most popular sweeteners:

Non-nutritive or intense sweeteners

Acesulfame K (Acesulfame potassium or Ace K)
A sweetener that supplies no kilojoules and remains stable after heating, it offers a huge advantage over older sweeteners like saccharin and also over aspartame. Its long-term safety has been established and it does not contribute to tooth decay. Often it is used in combination with other sweeteners such as aspartame to create a pleasant sweetness equal to sugar.
Trade names: Sunnett, Sweet One
Additive code: 950

Aspartame
A sweetener that supplies no kilojoules but is one of the most complained-about additives.

Labels on food containing this intense sweetener must indicate that the food contains the amino acid phenylalanine, as it can affect people with the rare genetic disorder phenylketonuria (PKU). PKU is characterised by a deficiency in an enzyme needed to break down phenylalanine (a by-product of aspartame) in the body to another amino acid named tyrosine. When this enzyme is deficient, phenylalanine accumulates and causes problems.

Rumours that aspartame causes brain tumours and Alzheimer's disease are groundless. It is one of the most studied additives, with an established safety record. It is 200 times sweeter than sugar, but its sweetness deteriorates after heating, so it is only suitable for cold applications such as in soft drinks, chewing gum and yoghurts.
Trade names: Equal, Nutrasweet
Additive code: 951

Sweeteners made from sugar

Sucralose

A sweetener made from sugar with over 600 times the sweetness of sugar but supplying no kilojoules. Sucralose has a high-quality sugar-like taste and can be used in cooking and baking, unlike other sweeteners. This means it is used in a wide variety of products including diet drinks, low-fat yoghurts, baking mixes, protein powders, table-top sweetener, breakfast cereals and salad dressings. It is non-toxic and non-carcinogenic.
Trade name: Splenda
Additive code: 955

Sugar alcohols

Erythritol

A sugar alcohol used to sweeten diet foods such as confectionery, erythritol has around 70 per cent of the sweetness of sugar. It can also be used as a humectant and texturiser where it functions as a food additive to enhance taste and texture.

Erythritol has been part of the human diet for thousands of years. It is present in fruits such as pears, melons and grapes, as well as mushrooms and fermentation-derived foods such as wine, soy sauce and cheese. Since 1990, erythritol has been commercially produced and added to foods and beverages to provide sweetness.

Erythritol is a white crystalline odourless powder

Compare what you'll save

with a clean sweet taste that is similar to sucrose. Its low kilojoule value and high digestive tolerance distinguishes it from other polyols such as sorbitol and xylitol. It has approximately 10 per cent the kilojoules of other polyols and 5 per cent the kilojoules of sucrose.

Because erythritol is rapidly absorbed by the small intestine and then rapidly eliminated through urine within 24 hours, laxative side effects associated with excessive consumption are unlikely.
Trade names: Natvia, Pyure, Wisdom Natural
Additive code: 968

Sorbitol

A sugar alcohol from the genus of *Sorbus* trees used to sweeten diabetic foods such as jam and chocolate, as well as children's multi-vitamins, pharmaceutical syrups, ophthalmic goods and many cosmetics. It is the alcohol form of sucrose. Sorbitol is also more slowly absorbed than sugar and has little effect on blood glucose levels. Because it supplies the same kilojoules as sugar, it is of little benefit for weight loss (unlike kilojoule-free sweeteners such as aspartame) but is fine for those with diabetes if you don't need to lose weight. Sorbitol does not cause tooth decay but if consumed in large amounts it may cause flatulence, diarrhoea and abdominal distension.
Trade names: Sorbogem and Sorbo
Additive code: 420

Xylitol

A sugar alcohol used in combination with an intense sweetener such as aspartame to produce sugar-free sweets, chewing gum and toothpaste. It can also function as a humectant, helping to maintain the texture and moistness of chewy foods. Like sorbitol, it does not cause tooth decay but high doses may have

a laxative effect. Take care not to leave any xylitol-containing foods around if you have a dog because it's toxic to them; just a few pieces of chewing gum can kill a small dog. Xylitol has a white and crystalline appearance much like normal sugar. It is produced by a process that turns a plant fibre called xylan into this sugar alternative.
Trade names: Nirvana, Lotus, Naturally Sweet
Additive code: 967

New-age 'natural' sweeteners

Stevia

A natural sweetener derived from the leaves of *Stevia rebaudiana* – a shrub common in Paraguay where for hundreds of years it has been valued for its sweetening properties and called 'honey leaf'. First discovered in Western research in 1899, the stevia leaf is 30 times sweeter than sugar but contains no kilojoules. Used extensively for many years in Japan, Korea and China to sweeten confectionery and beverages, it is now a popular sweetener because it is viewed as more natural than other sweeteners, and has fewer side effects. Commonly the steviol glycosides are combined with an intense sweetener like erythritol to provide a more balanced sweetness.
Trade names: Natvia, SweetLeaf, SteviaSweet, Truvia, PureVia
Additive code: 960

Monk fruit (or luo han guo)

Monk fruit extract is derived from the fruit of *Siraitia grosvenorii*, a perennial vine native to southern

China, where it is consumed as an everyday food and used in traditional Chinese medicine. Monk fruit is known for its characteristic intensely sweet taste. The fruit derives its intense sweetness from its naturally occurring glucose and fructose, as well as its high-intensity triterpene compounds known as mogrosides.

Because of the sweet mogrosides, monk fruit extract is approximately 20 times sweeter than other fruit juices. It has a very clean flavour profile with no lingering bitterness. This makes the extract an obvious

Currently monk fruit can only be used as a food and drink flavouring.

solution for replacing sugar in beverages.

Currently monk fruit can only be used as a food and drink flavouring. But you could soon see it on supermarket shelves as a table sweetener, made for use as a teaspoon-for-teaspoon equivalent to white sugar.
Trade names: In The Raw, Lakanto, MoreLife, Raw Earth
Additive code: none yet

Older sweeteners

Saccharin
A sweetener that supplies no kilojoules. Discovered way back in 1879, saccharin is 500 times sweeter than sugar, but often has a bitter, metallic aftertaste. In very high doses, saccharin has caused tumours in the bladders of experimental animals. The equivalent consumption by humans would be much higher than is presently consumed. Authorities in the UK, USA and Australia regard it as safe.
Trade names: Sugarless, Sugarine
Additive code: 954

Cyclamate
A sweetener that supplies no kilojoules, cyclamate is useful in low-kilojoule foods because it has no aftertaste. It is 30 times as sweet as sugar. Large amounts of cyclamate fed to rats have caused bladder cancer (resulting in its ban from sale in the USA in 1970) but the effect on humans is questionable. Subsequent studies have not found cyclamate to be carcinogenic but it has remained under a cloud and is hardly used today.
Trade names: none at retail
Additive code: 952

Trend alert: new foods with a nutrition buzz

Here's a preview of the latest 'health foods'. Should you be adding these so-called 'magical superfoods' to your daily diet?

Turmeric

In traditional Ayurverdic Indian medicine, turmeric (*Curcuma longa*), the bright orange-yellow spice used to make curries, is believed to help digestion. In Western medicine, it is being studied for its possible ability to inhibit cancer growth and lower whole-body low-grade inflammation that plays a role in damaging brain cells and the heart.

Shoppers are mostly familiar with the dried powdered form of turmeric and its unforgettable colour. But you can also purchase it fresh as a root; it looks quite similar to a smaller rhizome or root of ginger. But once it is cut open, you quickly realise that its flesh is a vibrant orange colour and is very different from the softer colour of cut ginger. Not only has turmeric been used throughout history as a culinary spice and herbal medicine, but it works as a fabric dye too.

Studies on turmeric originally focused on its anti-inflammatory benefits and ability to decrease the risk of cancer. Now studies are looking at its potential for improving cognitive (brain) function, blood sugar balance and kidney function, as well as lessening the severity associated with certain forms of arthritis and chronic digestive problems like Crohn's disease and ulcerative colitis.

Whole turmeric – sliced or grated – or ground turmeric spice are likely to provide you with a different set of benefits than its more widely studied constituent curcumin, which can be as high as 5 per cent in whole turmeric. That's because turmeric includes three closely related curcuminoids: curcumin, demethoxycurcumin and bisdemethoxycurcumin. But it also contains over 30 volatile oils like tumerone, germacrone, atlantone and zingiberene. These different substances all have their own unique health benefits. For example, tumerone is an aromatic compound that has been reported as having an effect on the neural cells of the brain, so the growth of nerve cells was enhanced.

Turmeric or curcumin has been studied in over 120 clinical trials for various human diseases, but the conclusions have either been uncertain or negative. In other words, turmeric had no effect or – worse still – an adverse effect on the prevention of illnesses.

Matcha

Matcha is essentially green tea leaves (*Camillia sinensis*) that have been ground to a powder. The best grade leaf is used in the famous Japanese tea ceremony; while the matcha in ice creams and cakes is usually made from a lower grade leaf.

Matcha is cultivated and processed differently from ordinary green tea so it develops a more intense flavour. When you consume matcha, you are drinking the whole leaf as opposed to drinking the steeping liquid as with other teas. Because of this, you get more of the polyphenols, but you also get larger doses of any contaminants such as lead, which can be found in teas grown in countries where pollution is high and pesticide residues are present. You also get a larger hit of caffeine than you would in ordinary green tea.

All sorts of health claims are made for one of the polyphenols in matcha known as EGCG (epigallocatechin gallate) but these are based on early stages of laboratory animal studies. However, there can also be harmful side effects from over-consumption, including liver damage.

Hemp

Hemp has recently been approved for consumption in Australia, although it has been used as food for centuries in other cultures. These hemp food products are derived from low-THC hemp seeds, which don't contain the psychoactive substances associated with cannabis. Industrial hemp is a distinct variety of *Cannabis sativa L.*, meaning it won't make you high. Low-THC hemp products available in Australia include whole hemp seeds, hemp flakes, hemp oil, hemp protein (the part left over after the oil is extracted) and hemp flour (ground hemp seeds).

Hemp seeds can be eaten whole because they don't need soaking, crushing or cooking. Typically around half its content is fat; its contribution to plant omega-3s such as alpha-linolenic acid (ALA) is outstanding. Hemp provides important vitamins including vitamin E and B group vitamins (such as folate and thiamin), along with minerals like phosphorus, potassium, magnesium and iron, and has less than 2 per cent carbohydrates.

Hemp seeds can be used in burgers, breads and cereal; they can even be used for making mylk. Hemp oil works well in salad dressings.

Kale

Kale (*Brassica oleracea*) has been touted as the uber-vegetable for the past five years. With its grey-green leaves, it is an unusual *Brassica* that looks like a cross between curly silverbeet and an unopened cabbage. It is handy because it grows well in winter, when most other vegetables do not.

The most popular type is the curly-leaf kale but you can also get lacinato and dinosaur kale or black cabbage, better known as either 'cavolo nero' or Tuscan kale.

The claims for kale's health-giving properties are amazing. It is supposed to lower your risk of cancer, aid in weight loss, help preserve your eye health, detoxify your body, be good for fortifying your bones and improve the appearance and health of your hair and skin. It supposedly has powerful anti-inflammatory properties that can protect your DNA. Plus it can help to fight depression.

Nutritionally kale is up there with the rest – but it's not that much higher. Like other vegetables, it is rich in fibre and potassium. If consumed raw, say in a salad or smoothie, it provides a lot of folate and the vitamins C and K. It is also a good source of calcium and iron, which is unusual for a vegetable. But what's really impressive is its content of beta-carotene – the carotenoid that is converted by the body into vitamin A as needed – as well as its lutein–zeaxanthin content, which is also in silverbeet and baby spinach leaves. You need lutein–zeaxanthin for good eyesight.

Despite all these amazing claims, kale has not yet been proven to be either better or worse than silverbeet or cabbage. Although it is a great alternative.

Kale has not yet been proven to be either better or worse than silverbeet or cabbage.

Activated charcoal

Activated charcoal is one of the latest trends. As well as charcoal lattes, breads and pastas, there are even toothpastes that supposedly whiten your teeth with a single brushing! A black food colour, identified by the additive code number 153, is also prepared from charcoal.

Activated charcoal is formed by heating wood or other vegetable matter, like coconut shells, in the absence of oxygen. All water and other compounds are burnt off, leaving only charcoal, sometimes called vegetable black or activated vegetable carbon.

The charcoal has thousands of tiny holes in its structure that attract other substances. This is why it has been used for many years to treat poisonings because it absorbs any toxic substances swallowed and prevents them from being absorbed into the body through the digestive tract. It is also commonly used in water filters to remove contaminants.

With the modern fad for 'detox', activated charcoal has risen to prominence as an ingredient that the makers claim is 'detoxifying'. It really is a fad and a questionable one given that we are told not to burn our meat on the barbecue because the char may cause cancer.

My dentist advised against using a greyish charcoal toothpaste because it is too abrasive and will abrade the top layer of your tooth enamel. Yes, your teeth will look whiter but it can cause long-term damage to them.

Raw treats

Think bliss balls, raw cheesecake slices and vegan cacao bars. You think they're somehow healthier, with less sugar and uncooked ingredients, but this isn't always true.

Made from nuts and dried fruits such as dates, prunes, sultanas or goji berries, raw treats are still high in sugars, even if they claim to be sugar-free. The sweetener can be rice malt syrup or coconut sugar but generally there's still some form of sugar and it has to be counted as such for weight-loss diets.

> Often you simply eat twice as much because you mistakenly think they're healthier.

Raw treats score well for fibre and have less refined sugar than packaged sweets. But they can still be high in sugars and have a really high kilojoule count from the coconut oil, dried fruits and nuts. Often you simply eat twice as much because you mistakenly think they're healthier. And they can be expensive to buy thanks to the expensive ingredients.

Coconut oil

Coconut oil is available as conventional or virgin. Conventional coconut oil, also known as copra oil, is used to make the gooey centres of chocolates, coffee whiteners and movie theatre popcorn. It is made from dried coconut that is pulverised, cooked and treated with chemicals such as hexane to produce a bleached, refined oil. It looks opaque, off-white in colour and has no aroma.

Virgin coconut oil is made by a milder extraction procedure from fresh coconut flesh. It is supposedly cold-pressed or expeller-pressed, which is gentler but the process still uses some heat. Apart from being less damaged, there's little difference between virgin (cold-pressed) and conventional coconut oil because both contain the same high level of saturated fat.

Forget the amazing claims about coconut oil (that it aids weight loss, lowers blood sugar, fends off germs, boosts the immune system). It's not a superfood. It's not even a whole food (a coconut where you eat the whole white flesh is). One tablespoon (10 grams) of coconut oil will set you back 370 kilojoules (88 calories) and 10 grams of fat (of which 9 grams are saturated).

Coconut sugar

(See also page 45)
Coconut sugar is the foodie ingredient of the decade, being touted as the next big thing in natural sweeteners. It looks like a chunky brown sugar and you'll see a bowl of it in trendy cafes to spoon into your turmeric lattes.

It is 100 per cent carbohydrate (around 95 per cent of which are sugars). Despite all the hype, coconut sugar is no superfood! It's not even that healthy.

Panela

(See also pages 44–5)
Panela is soft brown, sand-like crystals. It is traditionally the most commonly used sugar in Latin America and the Caribbean. It's partially refined and still retains some of its molasses content, which gives it that characteristic brown colour. It's no healthier than ordinary sugar and has the same number of kilojoules – 1 level teaspoon contains 67 kilojoules (16 calories). It can contribute to weight gain if consumed in excess amounts.

Rice malt syrup

(See also pages 42–3)
Rice malt syrup is produced commercially by using enzymes to break down the starches in white or brown rice. Disappointingly, it has a one-dimensional flavour plus it tastes about half as sweet as honey. Everyone is looking for a sweet healthier alternative to sugar but rice malt syrup isn't it!

Ginger

Ginger (*Zingiber officinale*) is an underground stem, which is dried and sold as capsules or tablets. It can also be consumed as crystalline ginger pieces, as a tea, a dried spice or as the fresh root. Ginger was used in China over 2500 years ago and continues to be popular as a flavouring.

Ginger is widely regarded as a 'stomach settler'. Ginger tablets are taken to overcome nausea, settle motion sickness or reduce morning sickness symptoms during pregnancy. In Asian medicine, ginger has a reputation as an anti-vomiting agent as well as a digestive aid and diuretic. Claims have also been made that ginger can alleviate arthritis, treat migraine, hangovers and peptic ulcers, and lower cholesterol. But these remain scientifically unproven.

Early work in the 1980s showed ginger to be more effective than standard anti-nausea medicine in overcoming motion sickness in 36 undergraduate students who were highly susceptible to nausea. More recent studies have also had positive outcomes, while others showed no effect. Overall, scientific evidence remains hopeful but inconclusive.

Ginger owes its alleged therapeutic activity to its oil, which has been found to possess cardiotonic, analgesic, anti-tussive (anti-cough) and sedative properties when administered to animals. Ginger also contains a number of components such as camphene, zingiberene, zingerone, eucalyptol, citral and some phenols, which can all be considered beneficial and part of the whole ginger 'health package'. Ginger is generally regarded as safe to consume and unlikely to pose any threats to health.

Purple foods

Purple-coloured foods such as eggplant, radicchio, blueberries, blackberries, black rice, cranberry juice, purple carrots, plums, pomegranates and grapes are rich in anthocyanins. And you want to be eating more of these.

These are powerful antioxidants that can guard the body's cells from the destructive effects of unstable molecules known as free radicals. Anthocyanins also carry antibacterial properties, so they fight off the bad bacteria or stop them 'sticking' to internal organs. There are up to 28 times more anthocyanins in purple carrots than there are in orange ones.

Other purple foods are: purple wheat, purple corn, purple potatoes, purple cabbage, figs, passionfruit, red cabbage and Spanish onion.

In contrast, beetroot's deep purple colour comes from different plant chemicals called betalains. Like anthocyanins, betalains have antioxidant and anti-inflammatory properties. You can also find betalains in the stems of ruby chard and rhubarb, but it's the flesh and skin of beetroots which are especially rich in them.

Amaranth

Just as we finally learn to pronounce quinoa ('kin-wah'), other whole grains are taking centre stage, like amaranth – a grain crop native to Peru. Although technically not a 'true' grain, it's classified as a 'pseudo-cereal' thanks to its sought-after nutritional

profile and its uses being similar to 'true' cereal grains. So why add it to your diet? Amaranth (*Amaranthus caudatus*) is gluten-free and a protein powerhouse. You also get lysine, an essential amino acid that's missing or negligible in many other grains. Lysine is not made by the body so must be obtained from food. It's needed for the creation of body proteins (see page 17). It's high in fibre and has been shown to be beneficial in lowering cholesterol. Its light texture and nutty flavour make it a versatile ingredient that can be added to soups, salads, stir-fries and cereals. Amaranth flour can also be used in baking and in making pancakes.

Teff

Teff (*Eragrostis tef*) is an ancient grain, minute in size (less than 1 millimetre in diameter – like a poppy seed) but packed with nutrition. You may have eaten it at an Ethiopian restaurant in the traditional injera sourdough flatbread that is as thin as a crepe yet spongy like a pikelet. It functions as an edible plate and you tear it and use it instead of cutlery to scoop up delicious spicy stews.

An easy-to-grow grain, teff seeds range in colour from dark reddish-brown (red teff) to ivory (white teff). It cooks quickly, using less fuel than other grains. A gluten-free grain with a mild flavour, it's high in

Cauliflower

Cauliflower (*Brassica oleraceae* var. *botrytis*) is the darling of the moment, the vegetable du jour! This versatile and high-fibre vegetable has many ardent followers who not only adore its flavour and texture as a vegetable, or in soup, but also love it as a low-carb swap for potato, a pizza base or couscous.

I like to serve it as either cauliflower rice or cauliflower mash. For the rice you can pulse the cauliflower raw in the blender to break it into tiny bits, then 'steam' it in a wok or large pot with the cover on, stirring occasionally to prevent sticking, then serve. Or, for the mash, cook the cauliflower first, then coarsely mash it with a potato masher.

For a smoother cauliflower mash, make as above but finish off by pureeing the cooked cauliflower with a handheld stick blender until it looks like mashed potato. Add milk and butter, stir or mash well again to combine. The dish mimics both the texture and appearance of mashed potatoes.

With only 128 kilojoules (30 calories) for a cup of boiled and drained cauliflower and less than 3 grams of carbs, it's definitely worth adding to your family's menu.

Insects

Insects are nutritious and can be farmed in a very sustainable way. With their slightly nutty flavour and versatility as an ingredient, they are set to become a bigger part of our diet. The most common commercially farmed insects in Australia are crickets and mealworms.

As a general rule, insects have an excellent level of quality protein, monounsaturated and polyunsaturated fats, fibre and micronutrients like copper, manganese, phosphorus, magnesium, iron, calcium, potassium, riboflavin and zinc. All of which are easily absorbed by the body.

Having said that, many people simply do not like to taste an insect (or know it's there), so for now they're probably best served up disguised or as a part replacement for meat protein in burgers and meatloaf.

Ground crickets that look just like flour is one such product that is perfect for adding an insect-kick to smoothies or baked foods, or to enrich a slow-cooked vegetable casserole. The cricket powder can be used in both sweet and savoury dishes to add a protein and micronutrient boost. Once you try it, you will quickly accept the taste and presence of insects.

fibre and adds variety to gluten-free cooking. All teff products are wholegrain because the kernel is simply too small to mill easily. Mostly it's simply ground between two stones so the nutritious bran and germ is taken up into the flour.

Teff is most often eaten as a porridge. When cooked, it has a 'stickiness' that allows it to be easily formed into patties or cakes, and then fried like squares of polenta. It's handy as a thickener in soups and stews in much the same way as red lentils. And you can toss some uncooked teff grains into your baking, just like adding a handful of nuts or seeds for crunch and texture.

Many of Ethiopia's famed long-distance runners attribute their stamina to teff. Compared to other grains, it stands out for its levels of protein, calcium and iron (it has over twice as much iron as wheat, barley or rice). It boasts a high concentration of B vitamins, notably thiamin and B6, along with minerals, manganese and copper.

Linseeds

Linseeds or flaxseeds (*Linum usitatissimum*) are one of the two richest plant sources of a key fatty acid called alpha-linolenic acid (ALA) – an omega-3 fatty acid and a building block of the longer-length fats found in fish. The other is hemp seeds.

Small shiny seeds that are brown in colour, linseeds have been used to reduce the chances of heart disease, lower blood pressure and reduce the unpleasant effects of the menopause, such as flushing and night sweats.

Linseeds are also a good source of two other nutrients that contribute to its effects: dietary fibre (present at a huge 28 per cent) and a unique class of phytoestrogens called lignans. These phytoestrogens are a group of natural plant compounds that mimic the main female hormone oestrogen and are able to bind to the same receptors as our own oestrogens. The other key types of isoflavones (high in soy and other legumes) and coumestans (high in sprouts).

You only need one or two tablespoons a day to boost your intake of all these nutrients. Probably the easiest way to consume linseeds is by grinding them either in a pestle and mortar or a coffee grinder. Then you can add a sprinkle to your cereal or yoghurt, or throw some into a smoothie.

Alternatively, you can buy LSA mix, which is an acronym for linseeds, sunflower seeds and almonds that have been ground together, and has a pleasant nutty flavour. Most LSA mixes are half linseed, with the remainder sunflower and almonds. For vegans, linseeds are a useful way to consume unsaturated fats, omega-3 oils, B vitamins, protein and natural fibre.

Chia

For centuries, the chia plant (*Salvia hispanica*) has been growing in its natural habitat of Central and South America. It was a highly valued oilseed crop of the Mayans, Aztecs and Southwest Native Americans. They used it as a staple food because of its energy and sustenance properties. Then it took off in mainstream supermarkets in the Western world.

Chia seeds look like tiny sesame seeds and can be black, white or grey. They are sold in a packet, unprocessed. They have a neutral flavour and the growers say you can sprinkle them over or add them to just about anything – muesli, smoothies or yoghurt – without disturbing the final taste. When combined with water they form a thick gel which makes them a sought-after binding and setting agent, similar to gelatine. Each seed absorbs water and becomes a small globule of jelly, just like soft tapioca balls. This can be

added to smoothies or desserts (it's quite tasteless) so you get the beneficial soluble fibre. The only negative is that each chia seed retains a tiny fragment of hull (high in cellulose) so when you swallow it, you don't get a smooth, soft, pleasant jelly texture. You get the jelly plus lots of tiny bits of 'grit'.

Chia seeds contain 15 per cent protein, 6 per cent carbohydrate, 38 per cent fibre and 30 per cent fat as well as a variety of vitamins, minerals and trace elements including folate, phosphorus, iron, manganese, copper and potassium. Like almonds and sesame seeds, they have a surprisingly high calcium content (255 milligrams per 100 grams compared to 120 milligrams per 100 grams for milk), but how well this is absorbed by our bodies is debatable. The same can be said for the magnesium, iron, zinc and copper also present in chia seeds.

> Like almonds and sesame seeds, chia seeds have a surprisingly high calcium content.

Chickpeas

Roundish and nutty-tasting, chickpeas (*Cicer arietinum*) are one of the most popular legumes. Also known as garbanzo beans, you can throw a handful into salads, soups and curries, or puree them into that famous hummus dip along with garlic, lemon juice and tahini (sesame seed paste).

Like all legumes, chickpeas offer substantial amounts of protein – which makes them very useful to vegetarians – as well as a good dose of B vitamins, especially niacin, and significant amounts of fibre. Their fibre is of the soluble type which researchers have found helps remove cholesterol from the body (in a similar way to oat bran). They have a low GI of 28, which means their carbohydrate is slow to digest so it benefits dieters, people with diabetes and athletes who need endurance energy.

Chickpeas also give us potassium and manganese (an activator for many enzymes in the body), along with useful quantities of iron, zinc and calcium; although, these are not as well absorbed as the iron from meat or the calcium from dairy. If you avoid chickpeas because of flatulence, try soaking them overnight, discarding the water and adding fresh water for cooking. Chickpeas are a great addition to your kitchen pantry.

Pea protein

You're going to see more and more products made with pea protein powder or isolate. It's proving useful for vegans and for people with dairy intolerances or allergies who can't eat whey protein from milk.

Pea protein is a complete protein. This means that it has all nine of the essential amino acids which your body can't make and which you have to get from your diet. But while pea protein has around 9 per cent leucine, which is good for building muscle, it is low in methionine, which you would need to get from other sources in your diet.

Pea protein is made by drying peas (*Pisum sativum*) and then grinding them into a flour. This flour is then mixed with water to remove the fibre and starch, leaving the pea protein isolate. Due to the way it is made, pea protein isolate doesn't contain the anti-nutrients that peas themselves contain and that prevent absorption of nutrients in the gut.

> Due to the way it is made, pea protein isolate doesn't contain the anti-nutrients that peas themselves contain and that prevent absorption of nutrients in the gut.

Beetroot

This colourful vegetable has become one of the latest health food fads. Yes, it is good for you, but maybe not in the form of a beetroot latte. Beetroot contains nitrates which get converted to nitric oxide in the body. Nitric oxide relaxes blood vessels and can lower blood pressure. Research has shown that this effect happens even in people whose hypertension doesn't respond to the usual blood pressure–lowering drugs.

It should be noted that leafy green vegetables also contain nitrates and so if you heed the saying, 'Eat the rainbow', this can also help to lower your blood pressure.

Beetroot is available as a freeze-dried powder, no doubt for use in lattes and smoothies, but my preference would be to eat the whole beetroot. It contains fibre as well as the other nutrients and is a versatile vegetable that can be used in smoothies, grated raw into salads or cooked – either steamed or roasted – as an accompaniment to a main meal protein such as meat or fish.

Collagen

Collagen is found in the connective tissues – ligaments, cartilage, muscles, tendons and skin – as well as in the bones of all animals. It is a protein and thus a source of amino acids. Collagen supplements are usually collagen that has been hydrolyzed so that it has been broken down into its constituent peptides. This makes it easier to absorb and use. Collagen can be bought in the form of supplements sold as collagen hydrolysates or peptides but good quality bone broths are excellent homemade sources of collagen.

There are three types of collagen. Type I is the most abundant in your body, followed by Type III and then Type II. Types I and III are most beneficial for skin health and elasticity, and reducing the signs of ageing. Type II collagen, is found in the cartilage of your joints and is the type taken by people with degenerative joint problems such as osteoarthritis. If you take Type II collagen, then it is recommended that you take it separately from the other types to aid with its absorption.

There are other claims made about collagen such as benefitting hair, nails and gut health, but the research is not clear. Better-quality trials are needed.

Phytochemicals

A daily diet high in phytochemicals is good insurance for your health and well-being. Phytochemicals can help protect you from the two main killer diseases of Western countries – cancer and heart disease – as well as holding back the ageing process and protecting your eyes from cataracts and macular degeneration. You don't need to take a pill to get your phytochemicals. In fact, the best way to get all of them is simply by eating lots of vegetables, fruits, spices, herbs and teas.

What are phytochemicals?

Phytochemicals are molecules that act as the body's defence network to protect cells and genetic material from damage. They were once called antioxidants but now nutritionists realise that they do a lot more than just preventing oxidation (see page 59).

> Phytochemicals are either produced in the body or obtained from the food we eat.

Like vitamins, there are numerous different phytochemicals, each of which acts in different ways and on different parts of the body.

Phytochemicals are either produced in the body or obtained from the food we eat. The three best-known phytochemicals (once called the ACE antioxidants) are beta-carotene (the precursor to vitamin A), vitamin C and vitamin E but there are others and it's worth looking at them in detail:

Beta-carotene

The precursor to vitamin A in the body, beta-carotene is the best known and most abundant of the carotenoids – a large group of compounds responsible for the yellow and orange colours in fresh produce. Beta-carotene deactivates free radicals, improves immune capacity and inhibits the early stages of tumour development.

Studies of smokers revealed that those with low blood levels of vitamin A suffered more lung cancer. It was reported that beta-carotene can reduce the likelihood of lung cancer for smokers, lowering the risk from 50 times greater to only 15 times greater than non-smokers. However, several major trials of beta-carotene supplementation in the USA and in Finland have failed to show any benefit and in fact have turned up an increase in lung cancer rates for those subjects taking the highest dose of beta-carotene. Two large well-publicised trials had to be stopped because the subjects on supplements fared worse than the controls.

Vitamin C

Vitamin C's main job as a phytochemical is to regenerate vitamin E, but it also inhibits the formation of carcinogenic nitrosamines in the stomach. It has consistently been shown to reduce cancers of the digestive tract (oesophagus, stomach and pancreas).

Vitamin E

Vitamin E prevents LDL cholesterol from oxidation. It is the major phytochemical in all cell membranes, where it maintains the stability of the fatty acids in the phospholipid layer.

Selenium

Selenium works in combination with vitamins C and E. It enhances immune response and effects DNA repair, which can prevent cancer initiation and growth. It is a key component of the enzyme glutathione peroxidase, which 'neutralises' peroxides before they can attack cell membranes.

Zinc

Zinc is part of the enzyme superoxide dismutase, an important defence system as it prevents free radicals from forming peroxides such as hydrogen peroxide.

Copper, manganese and others

Copper and manganese are often components of key enzymes, such as the enzyme superoxide dismutase mentioned above, catalase and glutathione peroxidase. These act as anti-inflammation agents and can prevent pre-cancerous cell damage.

Phytochemicals vs antioxidants

The scientific world no longer uses the term 'antioxidants' to describe these compounds because they do other things besides preventing oxidation. Preventing oxidation inhibits the production of free radicals, which are highly reactive compounds that can damage the cellular structure throughout your body. Antioxidants were often called free radical scavengers, meaning they destroyed free radicals and neutralised 'bad' compounds in the body.

In contrast, the term phytochemicals means compounds that come from plants (phyto = plant). They usually have some biological activity but it's not always a helpful one. Some phytochemicals are anti-nutrients; some of these, like lectins, can prevent you absorbing nutrients from your food. Lectins are found in a variety of plants – beans, lentils, tomatoes, eggplants – but usually only cause problems when ingested raw. Other phytochemicals have beneficial and protective effects.

Many – but not all – phytochemicals are polyphenols. Polyphenols are a large diverse group of compounds, which share the attribute of having more than one phenol unit or building block. They include flavonoids, catechins, isoflavonoids, lignans and anthocyanins. At times, you may hear the name 'phenolic compounds', which is used interchangeably.

Key examples of phenolic compounds are the resveratrol in red wine, ECGC in tea, capsaicin in chilli and paprika, thymol in thyme, cinnamic acid in cinnamon, polyphenols from extra-virgin olive oil and rosmarinic acid in rosemary, thyme, oregano, sage and peppermint.

6 easy ways to boost your phytochemical intake

Even if you take a supplement, you still need to eat a variety of phytochemical-rich foods. Try these:

1. Eat plenty of fruit. Eat it as snacks, in smoothies, with yoghurt or ice cream, with meat and poultry. All fruit gives you phytochemicals but the richest sources are citrus fruit, berries and kiwifruit.
2. Eat large helpings of vegetables and salads. Go for vegetable soups, cook two or three vegetables with dinner, have salad with your sandwiches, munch on raw vegetables with dips or cheese.
3. Eat by the rainbow. The more colourful your fruit and vegetables are, the more phytochemicals you're getting. Choose red onion over white, dark-green lettuces over pale iceberg, blue–red berries over pale pears or apples, etc. Variety is essential.
4. Use herbs and spices liberally. Many everyday kitchen herbs are rich in phytochemicals and can double or triple your intake. The most widely researched are cloves, rosemary, turmeric, ginger, oregano, aniseed, cumin, caraway seeds, nutmeg and cinnamon. But there's no reason to dismiss the others.
5. Drink tea instead of coffee.
6. Have a glass of red wine with your meal rather than white wine. Red wine has 9–10 times the grape phytochemicals of white wine.

The power of plants

Phytochemicals in food

Over the last few years, researchers have discovered a huge number of naturally occurring, biologically active phytochemicals in foods – substances that were previously 'ignored' or dismissed as having no real purpose. You won't find many of them in supplements.

Phytochemical	Best food sources	Known role
Carotenoids (includes beta-carotene, lycopene, alpha-carotene, lutein, zeaxanthin and beta-cryptoxanthin)	Yellow-orange fruit and vegetables: oranges, apricots, rockmelon, pumpkin, carrots, sweet potato. Green vegetables: spinach, silverbeet and Asian greens	• Work as antioxidants • Protect against cancer • Enhance immune function
Lycopene (a carotenoid)	Tomatoes and tomato products (puree, sauce, paste), ruby grapefruit, watermelon	• Decreases risk of prostate cancer
Lutein and zeaxanthin (two carotenoids)	Occur together in spinach, silverbeet, dark-green lettuces and other yellow-orange and green vegetables and fruit. Commercially extracted from marigold.	• Protect the macula of the eye from degeneration, a leading cause of vision loss in older adults
Flavonoids (includes quercetin, kaempferol)	Wine, grapes, apples, tea, onions and berries; small amounts in most other vegetables and fruit	• Work as antioxidants • Reduce the risk of heart disease by minimising the oxidation of LDL cholesterol
Catechins	Green tea, black tea, matcha	• Decrease blood pressure • Keep the blood free-flowing • May help protect against heart disease, skin cancer and stomach cancer
Isoflavones (phytoestrogens includes genistein, diadzein and biochanin)	Soybeans, tofu, soy milk, other beans, peas and lentils	• Once thought to relieve hot flushes and menopausal symptoms but the studies have not been convincing • Help prevent osteoporosis • Can interfere with oestrogen synthesis • May reduce the risk of breast cancer
Lignans	Linseeds, most oilseeds (but not in the oil), sesame seeds, seaweed, brans, whole grains, beans, vegetables and fruit	• Similar to isoflavones above

Phytochemical	Best food sources	Known role
Anthocyanins	Blue and purple fruits and vegetables: cranberries, raspberries, blueberries, blackberries, grapes, pomegranate, eggplant, purple carrots and cocoa	• Work as antioxidants • Have a mild antibacterial effect
Indoles and isothiocyanates (such as sulphorophane)	Cruciferous vegetables: kale, broccoli, cabbage, cauliflower, brussels sprouts and turnips	• Trigger the appearance of enzymes which block carcinogens from working • Reduce tumour development
Allicin and related sulphur-compounds	Garlic, onion, leeks and chives	• Antibacterial and anti-viral effects • Help neutralise carcinogens • Stimulate enzymes such as glutathione transferase • Thin the blood, which may protect against heart disease
Terpenes (including limonene)	Citrus fruit: orange, lemon, grapefruit Also mushrooms, caraway seeds, ginger, cumin seeds and cruciferous vegetables	• Block development of cancer tumours in mammary tissues in animals • Reduce the size of skin cancers in animals
Saponins	Barley, oats, soybeans, chickpeas, lentils, alfalfa sprouts, peanuts, liquorice and spinach	• May slow DNA replication in cancer cells that are multiplying
Curcumin	Turmeric and mustard	• Anti-inflammatory agent • May block cancer-causing substances
Ellagic acid	Grapes, strawberries, raspberries and apples	• Reduces the activity of carcinogens
Phytates	Dried beans, brans and whole grains	• Anti-cancer agents • May block absorption of zinc into the body (but at high intakes and without fermentation of whole grains)
Coumarins	Parsley, parsnips, cucumbers, angelica, carrots, celery, liquorice root, whole grains, brans and citrus fruit	• Inhibit the growth of cancers

Vitamin D deficiency

About one-third of us now have a deficiency of vitamin D. This is pretty high in countries like Australia and New Zealand where there's plenty of sunshine most of the year.

Some also attribute this increase in vitamin D deficiency to the over-success of the 'Slip, Slop, Slap' government campaign that started in the 1980s that aimed to prevent skin damage by blocking harmful UV rays with broad-spectrum sunscreens, hats with brims and shirts at the beach.

It's hardly surprising that vitamin D deficiency is more common in the winter months, when many of us cover up, travel to and from work in the dark, and stay in the office during the day because it's too cold to go outside.

It's hardly surprising that vitamin D deficiency is more common in the winter months.

But it's also likely in these groups:
- People with skin conditions where avoidance of sunlight is advised
- People with naturally dark skin
- Babies born to mothers who themselves are vitamin D deficient
- People with little or no sun exposure such as veiled women, the elderly who never go outdoors due to ill health and those in institutional care.
- People who are obese, as fat stores 'lock' the body's vitamin D and prevent it from being used by the body

These individuals listed above may need a vitamin D supplement to achieve adequate levels. Speak to your doctor for more advice.

Foods for vitamin D

Only a few foods naturally contain vitamin D so it's often difficult to get enough from diet alone. This is one of the main reasons for the popularity of cod liver oil in European countries where sunlight is limited. Most people in Australia only get around 25 per cent of their vitamin D from food, with the rest needing to come from exposure to sunshine. Because vitamin D is fat-soluble, the food sources for vitamin D are foods that carry fats such as:
- Cod liver oil (not fish oil, which has some but not as much as cod liver oil)

Vitamin D and sunshine

Formed by the action of sunlight on the skin, vitamin D is also known chemically as cholecalciferol or vitamin D3 and has long been known as the 'bone vitamin' (more below). But being a cross between a vitamin and a hormone, it actually does a lot more for our immune system and overall health than we ever realised. How can you get enough vitamin D yet avoid too much sun?

Vitamin D and your bones

Vitamin D was first discovered in the 1920s as a result of the search for a cure for rickets – a disease that causes softening of the bones in children. Vitamin D works by improving the absorption of calcium and phosphorus into the body, so it helps to ensure strong bones and teeth as well as maintaining healthy nerve and muscle function.

Vitamin D occurs in two forms: one is produced on the skin (vitamin D3 or cholecalciferol) while the other is found in a limited range of foods (vitamin D2 or ergocalciferol).

Vitamin D can be made from sunlight on the skin. The UV rays from sunshine are essential for the reaction. In theory our bodies should be able to make the vitamin D from regular exposure to the sun. But we don't.

- Oily fish such as salmon, trout, sardines, mackerel (both fresh and canned)
- Egg yolks
- Foods fortified with vitamin D such as table margarine, specialty milks (e.g. Anlene), some plant mylks (check the labels)
- Liver
- Butter
- Cheese

Mushrooms for D

Mushrooms have an ability to produce their own vitamin D after exposure to UV light and this gets passed on to us when we eat them! Mushrooms are an abundant source of ergosterol, which can readily be converted to ergocalciferol through the action of sunlight.

Studies in Australia, which determined that exposing mushrooms to just seconds of pulsed UV light post-harvest, showed that this brief amount of light can allow them to produce an average of 26 micrograms of vitamin D2 in one 100 gram serve (equal to 3 button mushrooms). The recommended daily intake is 5–15 micrograms, so you can see that mushrooms give us a significant hit.

Later research has shown that you can actually DIY this process by placing ordinary, store-bought mushrooms in direct sunlight for one hour before eating them. Yep, it's that simple!

Working with the sun

Exposing your arms, face and hands for 10 minutes a day every second day is generally all that's needed to make enough vitamin D but this varies depending on your skin type and where you live.

For example, people with moderately fair skin living in Sydney would need 6–8 minutes of exposure to sunshine in summer on the arms but a lengthier 16 minutes in winter at midday.

The same person living in Hobart at a lower latitude would need 7–9 minutes in summer but a longer 29 minutes in winter at midday. People with olive or darker skin need 3 to 6 times longer exposure.

Deliberate exposure to sunlight between 10 am and 2 pm in the summer months is not advised. If sun exposure is not possible, then a supplement dose of at least 10 micrograms (400 IU) of vitamin D as cholecalciferol per day is recommended.

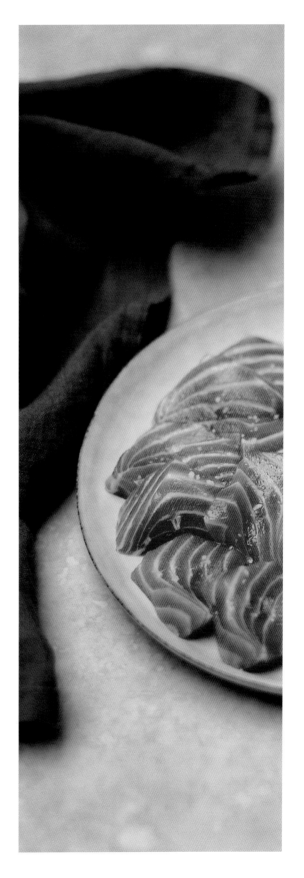

Vitamin B12 and why you need it

Vitamin B12 (cyanocobalamin) plays a vital role in metabolising food, manufacturing red blood cells, transporting and storing folate (a related B vitamin) and maintaining a healthy nervous system. B12 is essential for the synthesis of our DNA, our genetic material (and ultimately cell division), and for maintaining the integrity of the myelin sheath surrounding our nerves. It's pretty important.

An aid to absorption?

A substance called 'intrinsic factor', secreted by the stomach, enables us to absorb vitamin B12 from food. People can be B12 deficient, even though their diet has plenty of vitamin B12–rich foods, because of stomach problems or a lack of intrinsic factor. In such cases, regular injections of B12 once a year can correct the deficiency, which would otherwise lead to a serious type of anaemia called pernicious (or megaloblastic) anaemia, fatigue and blood problems.

The best vitamin B12-rich foods

So where can you get your B12? The best foods for vitamin B12 are almost exclusively animal foods such as meats, fish, seafood, poultry, eggs, cheese and milk.

Here's how animal food stacks up for this vitamin: green mussels (100 grams, about 4 = 20 micrograms), oysters (120 grams, 1 dozen = 18 micrograms), canned sardines (100 grams = 14 micrograms), salmon grilled (150 grams = 3 micrograms), chicken breast grilled (200 grams = 1 microgram), milk (1 cup = 1.5 micrograms), eggs (2 whole = 2.2 micrograms), soft white cheese (50 grams = 0.7 micrograms). As a comparison, a small grilled steak weighing 150 grams has 4.5 micrograms of vitamin B12.

Vitamin B12 is produced by bacteria in the large intestines.

Vitamin B12 is produced by bacteria in the large intestines of animals, including humans, if the gut bacteria (biome) have everything in the right concentrations and types. Plus you can have anywhere from three to five years of B12 stores in the liver before you run out.

Plant foods (legumes, grains, nuts, vegetables) are generally not a source of vitamin B12. So B12 is a nutrient of concern for vegetarians and particularly for vegans who choose an entirely plant-based diet.

Vegetarians who eat eggs and dairy (cheese, yoghurt, milk) are fine because they can obtain adequate amounts of B12 from these sources. Vegans require vitamin B12-fortified foods, e.g. soy milk, yeast spread, vegetarian sausages or rissoles, to top up their B12 supply. Check the labels on foods. Alternatively a B12 supplement is a good idea.

How much do you need?

Each day, adults need about 2.4 micrograms of B12. This rises a little to 2.6–2.8 micrograms for pregnant or breastfeeding women. You can get this amount easily from two eggs.

Running short – pregnancy and childhood

Generally deficiency isn't a problem except during pregnancy, while breastfeeding and during early childhood when demand is high. So women should ensure they eat an adequate amount of vitamin B12 to provide for their developing baby.

An infant born to a vegan mother is at high risk of deficiency if the mother's vitamin B12 intake is not adequate *and* her stores in the liver are low.

In infants, visible signs of vitamin B12 deficiency may include involuntary motor movements, dystrophy, weakness, muscle wasting, loss of tendon reflexes, psychomotor regression, shrinking and loss of growth of the brain, and blood disorders.

Small amounts (say from B12-fortified milk or cultivated mushrooms) taken each day appear to be more effective than infrequent large doses, such as intramuscular injections, given once a year.

Do mushrooms count?

B12 in mushrooms has been an on-again/off-again debate over the years but groundbreaking research at the University of Western Sydney in 2009 revealed that there is a modest amount of active B12 in mushrooms.

They found that one serve of mushrooms (100 grams or 3 button mushrooms) has almost 5 per cent of the daily adult requirement of vitamin B12. What's more, the vitamin B12 in mushrooms is the active form and not a pseudo-vitamin B12 which is inactive in humans.

So, if the mushrooms are farm-cultivated, they do add a modest quantity of vitamin B12, which is often difficult for strict vegetarians to obtain. Unusually, it is the same type of bio-available B12 as found in meats and seafood (meaning that it can be used by our bodies).

What about the B12 in fermented foods?

Claims have been made that plant sources like seaweed and algae, or fermented foods such as tempeh or kimchi contain vitamin B12. Usually this is a form of the vitamin that's inactive and unable to be absorbed by our bodies. These are claims that some of the fermented vegetables have low levels of B12, but this generally comes from the wild bacteria or yeasts that grow on them. Unless you can see good proof, treat these claims with caution.

Iron and fatigue

If you're tired all the time with little energy, it's worth paying a visit to your doctor for a blood test to check whether you have iron-deficiency anaemia. Lack of energy, poor stamina, pale skin, an inability to concentrate, frequent headaches, greater susceptibility to infections and feeling the cold often are other telltale signs. Because it is not life-threatening and because it mainly affects women and young children, iron deficiency never receives the attention it deserves.

Who could be deficient?

Here are the six groups of people who are commonly iron deficient. Do you fit into one of these?

1. Women are much more likely to have iron-deficiency anaemia than men. Women's needs for iron are almost double that of men's due to their monthly blood loss through menstruation (especially for women who have heavy periods).
2. Teenage girls require more iron to meet the demands of rapid growth and the onset of menstruation. Unhappily, many of them have low iron intakes because they eat poorly, saying 'No' to meals and then snacking on unhealthy foods.
3. Vegetarians tend to have lower iron levels than meat eaters. Although there is abundant iron in green vegetables and cereal grains, it is not well absorbed by our bodies. (See tips on page 89 for the best ways to get iron when you don't eat meat).
4. Young children under the age of two are at risk because they are growing fast and can be fussy eaters. In children, signs of iron deficiency are delayed psychomotor development and poor capacity for exercise. Babies who had a low birth weight or were pre-term are the ones to watch.
5. Poor absorbers – you can be at risk if, for some reason, your body can't absorb iron efficiently. For example, many people with coeliac or Crohn's

disease don't absorb the iron (and calcium) they ingest because the inner lining of their bowel is inflamed and/or atrophied (shrunk in size).

6. Athletes can miss out on iron because the heavy pounding of running or exercising can prematurely destroy blood cells (known as haemolysis). Greater muscle mass means more myoglobin is created, which further raises iron needs. 'Sports anaemia' is well documented in professional female athletes and can affect their capacity to train to peak levels.

Sources of iron

Red meat is, without a doubt, the best food source of iron because the iron occurs as 'haem iron', which is the most similar to our iron and is most easily absorbed by our bodies. Generally, the redder the meat, the richer it is in iron. So enjoy that steak or lamb chop or kangaroo burger. Don't forget chicken livers or the dark meat from turkey. Even if you only eat meat occasionally (which I recommend), small amounts such as a few strips of beef in a vegetable stir-fry can also improve your iron absorption from

Something in meat (known simply as the meat factor) boosts the absorption of iron.

the vegetables in that dish. Something in meat (known simply as the meat factor) boosts the absorption of iron from vegetables and grains, a key reason why I believe meat is useful.

Best ways to get iron when you don't eat meat

The iron in grains, vegetables, legumes, nuts and eggs, known as non-haem iron, is not absorbed as well as the iron from meat. To ensure you're getting adequate iron on a meat-free or low-meat diet, it pays to add a food rich in vitamin C to enhance the uptake of non-haem iron. Include foods like a squeeze of lemon juice, a side salad, a small glass of orange juice, capsicum, tomato, berries, kiwifruit or broccoli or other vitamin C–rich vegetables with your meal.

Take care with your food combos – oxalic acid inhibits the absorption of non-haem iron, so avoid eating large amounts of spinach and the *Brassicas* (broccoli, brussels sprouts, cabbage – but not bok choy or kale), sorrel or parsley at the same time as you're aiming to get iron.

Iron tips and tricks

- Calcium in dairy and plant mylks can decrease

iron absorption by 50 per cent. So drink milk at a different time to when you eat your meals.
- Limit coffee and tea to between meals because they decrease iron intake by 75 per cent. Tea is a well recognised inhibitor of iron thanks to its flavonoids, and coffee is also, due to the phytates it contains.
- Relative to water, orange juice doubles iron intake.

Iron supplements

An iron supplement can help but it is wise to choose carefully. The most common form of iron in supplements is slow-release ferrous sulphate, but this tends to cause constipation, dark stools, nausea or upset tummy when taken daily.

Ferrous gluconate, ferrous fumarate and chelated forms of iron are more readily absorbed and may cause fewer problems. All, however, are non-haem forms of iron that are subject to the same poor availability as that in vegetables.

My tips:
- Take an iron supplement on an empty stomach, i.e. before breakfast, because any food can slow absorption by up to 50 per cent.
- Take the supplement every second day because this is less likely to produce unpleasant side effects.

Diet and pregnancy

Much has changed since the days when a pregnant woman was encouraged to eat for two and avoid any undue 'stress' or exertion. Here's plain-talking food advice for that special time of your life.

Eating for you, not for two

While it is important to gain the right amount of weight during pregnancy, the old advice of eating for two is not the way to do it. The extra kilojoules needed for your developing baby don't really become significant until the last trimester when they add up to only 800 kilojoules (190 calories) extra a day – which translates to an extra slice of bread plus a glass of milk.

Count the weeks, not the kilojoules

Put dieting aside for the next nine months. Pregnancy is not the time to skimp on kilojoules, even if you need to shed a little excess. Gaining anywhere from 10 to 14 kilograms is vital for your baby's growth and development. The weight is made up of the weight of the foetus, increased blood volume, weight of the placenta plus a little extra body fat.

Avoid getting constipated

Constipation is a common complaint during pregnancy, so keep your fibre and fluid intake high. Best foods to maintain regularity are those high in insoluble fibre such as bran cereals, wholegrain breads and corn kernels. But many swear by a serve of legumes (lentils, beans, peas) along with prunes or prune juice plus a daily walk.

Build bone

If you don't have enough calcium during pregnancy, the store of calcium in your own bones will be 'drained' for your baby's developing bones and teeth. Keep your bones safe from osteoporosis by making sure you get four serves of calcium-rich foods a day like milk or calcium-rich plant mylks, yoghurt and cheeses.

Get plenty of brain food

Essential omega-3 fats are vital for your baby's brain, nervous tissues and eyes. So include oily fish, seafood such as mussels and oysters, lean meat, omega-enriched eggs and linseeds or hemp hearts (the seeds with husks removed) regularly in your diet.

Low intakes of fish and seafood during pregnancy can increase the risk of pre-term delivery and low birth weight, according to a study from Denmark. Surveying over 8000 pregnant women through their network of antenatal clinics, Danish researchers determined how often they ate fish. Frequency of pre-term deliveries fell from 7.1 per cent in the women who never ate fish to 1.9 per cent in those who ate fish at least once a week.

Cut back on caffeine

Although the occasional latte or cappuccino is unlikely to do harm, they are probably best limited to once or twice a week (see also page 34).

Folate

Folate is a B vitamin required for baby's proper neural tube and spinal cord development. You need another 200 micrograms of folate in the first three months of pregnancy. Ensure your folate needs are met with

> Folate is a B vitamin required for baby's proper neural tube and spinal cord development.

folate-rich foods such as leafy vegetables, avocados, wholemeal bread, fortified breakfast cereals, nuts (almonds, hazelnuts, peanuts, walnuts), yeast extract (Vegemite, Marmite) and oranges or orange juice. If you opt for a supplement, look for one with at least 400 micrograms of folate.

Iron it out

Iron-rich foods will keep your energy levels up and help build baby's iron stores. Red meat is the best source of easily absorbed iron, with lesser amounts found in chicken and fish.

Say No to alcohol

Avoid alcohol during pregnancy and while breastfeeding. Alcohol increases your risk of miscarriage, having a still birth or a premature birth, as well as the risk of foetal alcohol syndrome. There is no safe intake of alcohol at all. Both regular and binge drinking are harmful. Alcohol passes from the blood via the placenta and to your unborn baby. It can affect the development of baby's brain and spinal cord. Choose zero-alcohol drinks like soda and lime, alcohol-free cocktails, ginger beer or other non-alcoholic options.

Steer clear of Listeria

Listeria bacteria are found widely in nature but they can be present in higher concentrations in uncooked foods or cooked foods that have been kept for more than a day, even with refrigeration.

You can take precautions to avoid listeria by:
- Following standard food hygiene by washing and drying your hands before cooking and eating
- Eating only well washed and freshly prepared food
- Reheating foods until they're 'steaming' hot
- Refrigerating leftovers immediately and not keeping them longer than a day

Lower your risk for Listeria

Here are some high-risk foods to avoid and the safe foods to replace them with.

High-risk foods	Replace with safer alternatives
Cold meats purchased pre-sliced or packaged from delis, supermarkets and sandwich bars	Home-cooked meats used within a day of cooking
Takeaway cold cooked chicken	Home-cooked chicken or hot takeaway whole chicken – not chicken pieces
Pâté	No alternative
Pre-prepared or pre-packaged salads	Freshly prepared homemade salads which have been washed well
Raw, smoked or ready-to-eat cold cooked seafood	All freshly cooked seafood used within a day of cooking
Soft, semi-soft and surface ripened cheeses, both pre-packaged and deli bought (brie, camembert, ricotta, feta, blue)	Hard and processed pre-packaged cheeses (cheddar, tasty, cottage cheese, cream cheese)
Soft-serve ice cream	Packaged ice cream

Fish and mercury

It's good to eat fish when pregnant and when breastfeeding. It's a valuable source of protein, minerals, vitamin B12 and those omega-3 fatty acids – which are important for the development of baby's brain, eyes and nerves, before and after birth. Generally, you should try to eat two to three serves per week of any fish or seafood, with the exception of fish that contain high levels of mercury.

Mercury is a risk to unborn babies, as it can damage the brain and nervous system.

The presence of mercury in fish is a worry. Mercury is a risk to unborn babies, as it can damage the brain and nervous system, bringing about delays in later development in children. The good news is that there are only four types of fish that accumulate high levels of mercury, as they are long-living and scavengers, and which you need to limit. These are:

- Catfish and orange roughy (deep sea perch) – you can eat one serve per *week* of these fish, and no other fish that week
- Shark (flake) and billfish (a collective word that includes swordfish and marlin) – you can eat one serve per *fortnight* of these fish, and no other fish that fortnight

Remember a serve equals around 150 grams raw weight, which is roughly the same as 2 frozen crumbed fish portions.

All other fish species are safe to eat. Just make sure they are cooked thoroughly and you eat them while hot. Fish with low mercury levels include:

- Anchovy
- Bream
- Garfish
- Herring
- Mackerel
- Mullet
- Salmon, all types, fresh and canned
- Sardines, fresh and canned
- Silver warehou
- Snapper
- Trevally
- Trout
- Tuna, canned
- Whiting

Canned fish and seafood

All prawns, lobsters and bugs, squid and octopus are low in mercury.

Canned tuna is also fine. It has lower mercury levels than fresh tuna because tuna used for canning are smaller species that are caught when less than 1 year old.

Fish oil capsules are not a major source of mercury and are safe to consume.

The omega factor

I'm a big fan of omega-3 fatty acids because, thanks to their role at the cellular level, they work on so many different parts of the body, from your blood to your skin and your eyes.

Why are they called omega-3?

These unique fatty acids have a carbon–carbon double bond located after the *third* carbon atom from the methyl end of the carbon chain (hence the 'three' in their name). And that word omega? The end carbon is also called the omega carbon.

Here's how they keep you healthy

Omega-3 fats:

1. Keep your heart and blood in top shape

- They slow the build-up of fatty material on the inner walls of blood vessels (atherosclerosis), which allows the blood to flow more freely, especially through small blood vessels.
- They prevent the platelets in the blood from 'clumping' together and, like aspirin, reduce the chance of a blood clot.
- They counter irregular or chaotic beating of the heart known as cardiac arrhythmia – if cardiac arrhythmia is severe enough, it can precipitate death.
- They drop the level of blood triglycerides – another blood fat like cholesterol.
- They make the arteries more 'elastic' and thus more able to 'flex' in and out with pressure.
- They help reduce high blood pressure modestly by decreasing the production of constrictor

rather than of dilator substances and by reducing inflammation.

So basically, as you can see, if you eat a lot of omega-3s, you're less likely to have heart and blood troubles such as a stroke or heart attack.

2. Maintain your brain power

Omega-3s are a crucial part of the cells in our brains, nerves and eyes, so they work to keep you mentally sharp (fish truly is brain food!).

- Babies need omega-3s for their brains to grow properly – their brains triple in size in the first year of life. So pregnant and breastfeeding mums *must* get a steady supply of omega-3s for the sake of their baby's health.
- Fats make up over 50 per cent of the brain, and DocosaHexaenoic Acid (DHA) – a long-chain omega-3 fatty acid – is the most abundant. DHA enhances nerve signal transmission in the brain.
- That same DHA plays a key role in the development of babies' brains. It is abundant in breast milk. Many cultures have traditionally fed fish to new mothers to boost the nutrients in their milk.

3. Help manage mental illness

Omega-3 supplements are increasingly recommended to manage mental problems such as depression, anxiety and schizophrenia.

Preliminary research shows encouraging results of omega-3 supplementation on children with learning difficulties such as dyslexia, dyspraxia and attention deficit hyperactivity disorder (ADHD). An American study of ADHD boys found they all had some shortfalls of essential fatty acids. Blood samples showed that the

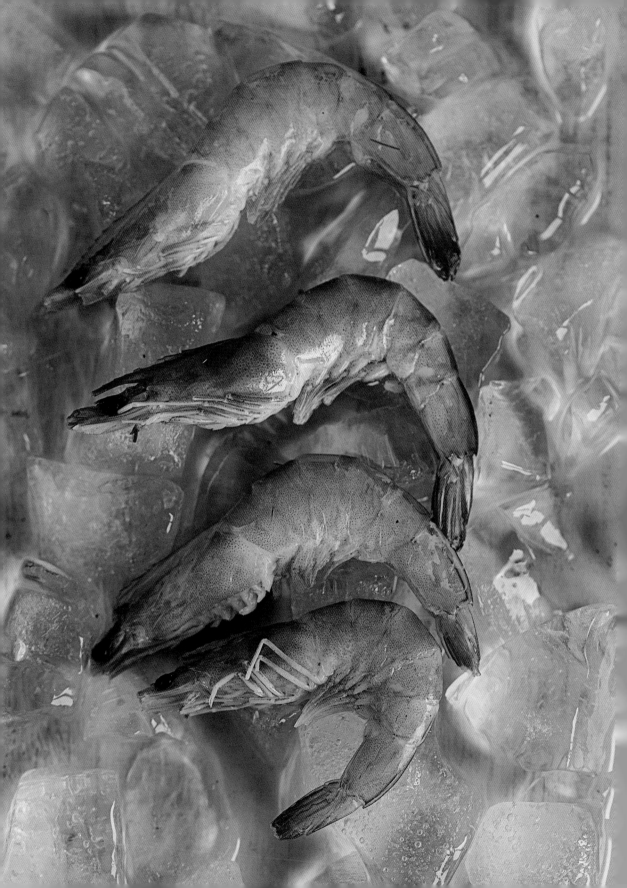

problem was not a lack of fatty acids from their food, but that the hyperactive boys couldn't convert dietary fatty acids into the long-chain types required for brain and eye function. The boys with the most intrusive behaviours – impulsiveness, hyperactivity, temper tantrums, sleep problems – had the lowest levels of DHA.

4. Decrease inflammation

Omega-3s can help people suffering from illnesses with an inflammatory or immune component like psoriasis, eczema, inflammatory bowel disease (Crohn's) and chronic obstructive pulmonary disease (COPD).

Studies of rheumatoid arthritis sufferers whose diets have been supplemented with fish oil have shown improvements in the nagging symptoms of tender swollen joints, morning stiffness and poor grip strength. In some of these studies, the dose of anti-inflammatory drugs was decreased as a result of these improvements, which meant fewer side effects.

However, the doses of omega-3s needed are large and need to come from fish oil capsules (more than 12 a day) or a high dose of liquid fish oil rather than fish. Not all the studies have been favourable, which makes it difficult to draw any firm conclusions at the moment. However, they can't hurt.

5. Maintain healthy eyesight

Omega-3s are recommended for older people to prevent macular degeneration and preserve eyesight – the lens of the eye is particularly sensitive to any nutrient deficiency. Omega-3s have thus become the ultimate anti-ageing nutrient. In one USA study, eating more than two serves of oily fish a week was associated with a 39 per cent reduced risk of age-related macular degeneration.

6. Manage diabetes

Omega-3s can benefit people with diabetes, who often have raised blood triglyceride levels and high blood pressure, clotting and circulation problems. Research carried out at the University of Wollongong in Australia shows that omega-3s appear to offer protection against insulin resistance – the more omega-3s incorporated into the cell membranes of the body's muscles, the lower the insulin resistance.

Richest foods for omega-3s

If you eat oily fish, it's relatively easy to obtain the long-chain or marine omega-3s. Fish is high in those important omega-3 fats, which mainly come from the larger oily fish from cold waters like Atlantic salmon, ocean tuna, rainbow trout, various mackerels like the blue mackerel, kingfish, silver perch and blue-eye trevalla. Other fish such as the familiar bream, flathead, morwong, mulloway, many mullets, barramundi and gemfish are good sources, as is seafood such as mussels, oysters, prawns, squid and scallops.

Most convenient are the canned salmon (pink and red), smoked salmon, canned sardines and some varieties of canned tuna (look for brands that say 'high in omega-3' on the label). Not forgetting anchovies, either in a can or a jar.

Top 20 foods for omega-3s

The table gives you the best 20 foods for long-chain omega-3 fatty acids in milligrams per serve as consumed – all figures are for cooked and drained portions unless otherwise stated.

Food	Omega-3s (mg per serve*)
Super rich, between 2000 and 4000 mg	
Salmon, 1 fillet, 150 g	3967
Rainbow trout, 1 fillet, 150 g	3061
Rich, under 2000 mg	
Bream, 1 fillet, 150 g	1989
Eel, 1 piece, 150 g	1912
Mussels, blue, 12, 288 g	1765
Swordfish, 1 fillet, 150 g	1655
Salmon, sashimi style, raw, 90 g	1432
Oysters, raw, 12, 300 g	1428
Canned salmon, pink, 1 can, 105 g	1310
Canned salmon, red, 1 can, 105 g	1233
Mullet, 1 fillet, 150 g	1128
Smoked salmon, 100 g pack	1000
Excellent, under 1000 mg	
Canned mackerel, 60 g	948
Gemfish, 1 fillet, 150 g	829
Herring, pickled, 1 fillet, 50 g	797
Sashimi, raw, 90 g	740
Lamb's fry (liver), 100 g	659
Prawns, 12, 420 g	646
Fish fingers, 3 fingers, 75 g	567
Recommended Dietary Intake	500

* Serve size varies but generally it's 150 grams for a fish fillet and 90 or 100 grams for seafood. *Source*: From Australian Food Composition Database 2019 at FSANZ.

How much?

Everybody should eat around 500 milligrams a day of the long-chain omega-3s. You'll get this by eating:

- A 150 gram serve of a super-rich food source *once a week*, such as a fillet of fresh salmon or trout
- *Or* a 150 gram serve of a rich food source *twice a week*, such as a small can of sardines or a fillet of bream
- *Or* a 150 gram serve of an excellent food source *every second day*, such as a fillet of gemfish or a tray of sashimi

Fish oil is very safe, even at high doses. It is almost free of mercury.

Alternatively, take two fish oil capsules a day so you get about 600 milligrams. Fish oil is very safe, even at high doses. It is almost free of mercury and complements the blood-thinning medications (Warfarin or Heparin) that many heart patients must take.

Richest sources of plant omega-3s

While plant-sourced omega-3 fatty acids are similar to the long-chain types, they are slightly different. They also do different things in the body, so it is important that both types are included in your diet. You need 1 gram (1000 milligrams) a day of omega-3s from plant sources such as:

- Hemp oil
- Hemp seeds and hemp hearts
- Linseed oil
- Linseeds and ground linseeds
- Chia
- Walnuts, pecans
- Canola oil
- Soybean oil
- Wheatgerm
- Wheatgerm oil

How much?

- Aim for 2–3 teaspoons of ground linseeds, chia seeds or LSA (linseed, sunflower and almond meal) a day
- *Or* eat a small handful of walnuts or pecans (30 grams, around 15 halves) for a snack
- *Or* add 1 teaspoon of flaxseed oil or hemp oil to a salad.

Probiotics and your microbiome

Every day there seems to be a new study showing the importance of a healthy microbiome to your overall health and well-being. There's no doubt about it – the digestive system, aka the gut, is pivotal to a healthy metabolism, a healthy brain and a healthy immune system. Think of it as 'inner harmony' for your digestion. But what is a microbiome and how do you keep it healthy?

The benefits of having a healthy biome

A balanced, happy and well-functioning gut:

1. Produces substances that make your internal environment unwelcoming for salmonella, rotavirus and other potentially harmful microbes
2. Maintains the integrity of the gut barrier to keep unwanted microbes and toxins from entering the body (prevents 'leaky gut')
3. Enhances the immune response – around 70–80 per cent of the body's immune cells are in the gut
4. Keeps the cells of the wall of the bowel healthy and helps them recognise and eliminate the DNA mutations that can contribute to colorectal cancer
5. Promotes fluid and electrolyte uptake in the large bowel
6. Produces vitamin K, vitamin B12 and folate
7. Shortens episodes of diarrhoea, including traveller's and toddler diarrhoea
8. Aids digestion
9. Regulates bowel movements and eases constipation and flatulence (bloating)
10. Reduces and in some cases reverses irritable bowel syndrome and Crohn's disease
11. Digests the lactose from milk – useful for the lactose intolerant
12. Deactivates harmful enzymes in the intestine

Long-living Bulgarians

The idea of consuming good bacteria for health is not new. It dates back to the early 20th century when a Russian scientist, Dr Élie Metchnikoff (1845–1919), suggested that the long lifespan of Bulgarian peasants was due to their consumption of yoghurt fermented with *Lactobacillus* (the main bacteria used in yoghurt-making). Metchnikoff believed the *Lactobacilli* exerted an important influence on intestinal health.

Later the word 'probiotic' was coined to describe these 'good bacteria'. Derived from Greek, it simply means 'for life' or 'for health'. Probiotics were initially applied to yoghurt bacteria because scientists were trying to test Metchnikoff's theory. But while yoghurt cultures make great yoghurt, they are not always the ideal bacteria to treat an intestinal disorder. Today the term probiotics encompasses what we get from other fermented foods such as sauerkraut, kimchi and kombucha.

Your microbiome vs the gut

Our intestine is host to more than 500 species and subspecies of bacteria (both helpful and harmful), viruses, moulds and fungi. Collectively they are known as the human microbiome. A microbiome is short for microbial biome and means that community of microbes and their genetic material that lives happily within the human gut. Colloquially, the terms microbiome and gut are used interchangeably.

What do these microbes do?

While these tiny microbes can be found everywhere from our skin and mouths to our genitals, the ones most under the microscope so-to-speak are those found in our gut.

The microbiome is typically made up of a healthy balance of 'good' and 'bad' bacteria. Much research is aimed at determining which microbes are which, what their functions are and what effects they have, not just on the gut, but on the body as a whole.

If the balance tips and the bad bugs start to multiply (due to stress, gastro, taking antibiotics, diarrhoea, or travelling where the water or food may not be safe), our digestive system suffers and so do we.

One way in which this happens is through the over 100 million neurons in the gut that form what is called the enteric system – a sort of second brain. These neurons 'communicate' with the microbiome, which can then affect your behaviour and feelings including eating habits, cravings and moods. There is also some evidence that making a positive change to the microbiome may reduce anxiety and depression.

Examples of 'bad' bacteria in the microbiome

As mentioned, the microbiome is home to both good and bad bacteria. An imbalance between the good and bad bacteria can lead to various health issues. For example, *Helicobacter pylori* is the bacteria responsible for the formation of ulcers. Other bad bacteria include *E. coli, Serratia marcescens* and *Candida tropicalis* – a threesome found in higher concentrations in the guts of people with Crohn's disease: while this connection has only recently been discovered, it holds out the promise of more effective treatments for a disease that is both debilitating and painful.

So what about prebiotics?

There also is ongoing research into the possibility that some members of the *Clostridia* family may play a role in psychological disorders such as autism spectrum disorder. Much more research is needed before this is confirmed but it highlights the importance of having a healthy microbiome for both your physical and psychological health.

Probiotics – meet the 'good guys'

Probiotics refers to special live bacteria in food that, if consumed in large enough numbers, can help us stay healthy by improving the balance of the bacteria in our intestines.

You'll be familiar with those 'friendly bacteria' from yoghurt drinks or probiotic capsules we take to stabilise the resident bacteria in our gut, restoring our natural balance of 'good' bacteria. However, these are just the tip of the probiotic iceberg.

Becoming increasingly mainstream are the fermented probiotics like kombucha, kefir (water and milk varieties) and fermented vegies such as sauerkraut and kimchi; plus Camembert, blue cheese and other mould-containing cheeses, buttermilk, and true sourdough bread. These all carry low levels of good bacteria.

These 'good guys' set up a symbiotic relationship with us whereby we feed them and they help us digest our food and generally keep us healthy. The take-home message seems to be that the greater the variety of bacteria we have in our guts, the healthier we will be. Plus if we get the right balance, then the whole system works.

Certain probiotics have solid evidence to show they can shorten episodes of diarrhoea in adults and children, replace good bacteria that have been killed off by a course of antibiotics and reduce the bacteria *H. pylori*, responsible for stomach ulcers. The two most widely studied and well documented probiotics are currently *Lactobacillus GG* (in Vaalia probiotic yoghurt) and *Lactobacillus casei Shirota* (in Yakult) but there are many more.

Resistant starch

Another prebiotic is resistant starch (see also page 9), which is an insoluble fibre that is considered gut health gold. It generates by-products that protect the cells in your gut and can help prevent colon cancer. Research from Spain published in *Clinical Nutrition* studied the effects of inulin and resistant starch in rats. The research indicates that these two fibres can be synergistic and produce better results in combination than either one on its own.

What does this mean for you on a day-to-day basis?

1. Limit the amount of bad bacteria you ingest. That means making sure you wash your hands before preparing food and eating. And ensure you follow food safety guidelines.
2. Eat probiotic foods to enrich your gut microbiome. These include yoghurts, kefir, kombucha, kimchi, sauerkraut, miso, tempeh and other fermented foods.
3. Aim to increase the diversity of your good bacteria by eating a fibre-rich diet full of the prebiotic foods that the 'good guys' love. If onions, garlic and whole grains don't agree with you, there are other low-FODMAP options (see page 153).
4. Take it slowly. Don't change from a low-fibre to a high-fibre diet overnight. You'll end up with bloating and stomach pains. Make the change gradually. Eat one extra high-fibre food a day. The same goes for the probiotic foods. Don't suddenly start consuming vast quantities or you could end up with bloating and loose motions.

Fermented foods

Originally popular among raw-food enthusiasts, fermented foods like kombucha and sauerkraut are enjoying a moment in the spotlight. They've been around for centuries but they have only recently been recognised for their health-giving qualities. Are fermented foods the magic elixir of life that the wellness gurus make out? Should you start eating them? And which one is best?

If you want to add fermented food to your diet, the simplest way to start is to make your own sauerkraut at home – it's quicker and easier than making kefir, yoghurt or sourdough; to start making these, you need a starter or a 'mother' and you have to feed it regularly to keep it alive. You don't have to feed regularly when you make sauerkraut – it's much simpler to make and a batch lasts a while.

Kombucha

Kombucha (pronounced kom-boo-chah) is a slightly sweet, slightly acidic, fermented beverage made from a base of tea, generally black tea but occasionally green or herbal tisanes. It is made from water, tea, sugar (the substrate for the fermentation), bacteria and yeast – an infusion of tea leaves is mixed with a SCOBY (which stands for a 'symbiotic culture of bacteria and yeast'). This tea fungus or 'mother' ferments the sugar and yields acetic acid (which gives it that characteristic sharp taste), carbonic acid and carbon dioxide gas (which adds the bubbles).

Yes, you start with sugar but it largely disappears during the making of kombucha. Ideally all you're left with is a tiny 1 per cent of sugar or less. In half a glass or 125 millilitres, that's only 1.25 grams or about ¼ teaspoon of sugar, which is hardly anything. In contrast, half a glass of soft drink has around 12 grams or 3 level teaspoons of sugar.

Does kombucha really stack up as that 'something special'? The short answer is 'not really'. The long answer? Well, you *may* ingest some friendly bacteria to help your gut function but no one knows for sure. It's been drunk to assist gut function for centuries in Japan, China, Russia and Germany but there's not a huge amount of research into its health benefits. To my way of thinking, its greatest advantage is its lower sugar content to that of regular soft drinks, combined with its refreshment value as a tart yet effervescent drink.

How do I make kombucha at home?

To make one batch of about 2 litres, here's the simplest method. You'll need:

- 2 litres tap water
- 5 black or green teabags or 2 level teaspoons (10 grams) tea leaves
- ½ cup (110 grams) sugar
- 1 pancake of SCOBY

Boil the tap water. Pour it over the teabags or tea leaves in a large jug. Add the sugar and stir to dissolve. Leave for about 30 minutes to brew, and then allow it to cool to room temperature. Remove the teabags or sieve the liquid to remove the tea leaves.

Pour the cool brewed tea into a large, clean sterilised glass jar and add the SCOBY. Ideally you can get this from a friend or maybe at a local health food shop. Cover the jar with cheesecloth or paper towels and secure with a rubber band or string.

Leave to brew for a week or more in a cool, dark place at room temperature. Over the next few days, the newly formed 'daughter' culture will start to float and form a thin gel-like membrane across the surface of the SCOBY. This is the new fungus that grows over the old one that began the original fermentation.

Soon, the tea will start to smell fermented and you should see tiny gas bubbles. This is what you want. Smell or taste it each day. The kombucha will become less sweet the longer it is brewed.

When ready, remove the SCOBY with a little of the liquid and store it in the refrigerator for a future batch. Pour the kombucha into bottles, close and refrigerate. To serve, just pour into glasses. Flavour with fruit like lemon slices, berries or slices of ginger root.

Benefits of drinking kombucha

With around 1 per cent sugar, kombucha is much lower in sugar and kilojoules than other sweet drinks such as juices (a range of 8–14 per cent sugars) or iced teas (a range of 5–6 per cent sugars). This means less kilojoules. So, half a glass (125 millilitres) of kombucha has only 75 kilojoules (18 calories) while the same amount of iced lemon tea has 380 kilojoules (90 calories).

Devotees of kombucha claim that it can stimulate the immune system, prevent cancer, improve digestion, prevent heart disease and boost liver function. It may do all this but there's scant scientific research to support these health claims.

Homemade or bottled?

You can buy bottled kombucha, both pasteurised and unpasteurised, in various flavours everywhere. Make sure it's been refrigerated. The downside is that kombucha's probiotics do not survive the pasteurisation process, and drinking it unpasteurised, if it was not produced in sanitary conditions, may pose a food safety threat, especially for those who are pregnant or have compromised immune systems. So be careful where you buy it.

The bottom line

Drink it if you enjoy the tart, not-too-sweet flavour of kombucha. If you get good at making it, kombucha may help your digestion. Or it may not. Either way, it's a pleasant drink with way less sugar than iced teas or juices.

Kefir

Kefir (pronounced 'keh-feer') is a fermented drink. It's most usually made from milk though it can also be made from water, almond milk or coconut water. It contains a wide variety of beneficial microorganisms that may help keep your gut healthy. In other words, it's a probiotic drink.

Where can you get it?

If you're lucky you may be able to buy it bottled but it can be hard to buy commercially. The alternative is to make your own. There are heaps of instructions

on the internet but you need kefir grains to start your fermentation; these cost around $20 or you may be able to find someone who has some spare that they can give you because the grains multiply easily. You can make it in a clean glass jar or you can buy a purpose-designed jar with a sieve in the lid.

The kefir process

The first time you ferment, the kefir grains can take a while to 'wake up'. So once you've added some milk to your grains and screwed the lid on tightly, you can leave it for anywhere between 24 and 48 hours. You're not supposed to let it sit in direct sunlight, so put it in a dark cupboard or just cover it with a clean tea towel and sit it on the countertop. Swirl the contents of the jar occasionally because this helps the fermentation process.

Once the contents are thicker, or even separated, it's ready. If it's separated, just stir it before straining to remove the kefir grains. You can now do a second fermentation, if you wish, without the grains. This is supposed to increase the level of B vitamins and reduce the lactose after 6–12 hours (taste it from time to time so that it doesn't become too sour). Then keep it in the fridge.

How much should you consume?

If you're not used to taking probiotics, start slowly with only 1 tablespoon of kefir per day. If you don't notice any problems (such as tummy upsets) then you can increase gradually over time until you get to a glass or 250 millitres per day.

It populates your gut with beneficial flora – the good guys – and helps restrict the growth of, and/or kill, the bad guys. Beneficial bacteria produce a compound called butyrate which protects against colon cancer. In addition, kefir is supposed to promote a healthy immune system.

What does it taste like?

Kefir has a pleasant taste, like a mild yoghurt, but not as acidic. You can add it to smoothies and other recipes in place of yoghurt.

The bottom line

It's cheaper than buying probiotic pills, has a wider range of beneficial bacteria, contains much less sugar than those yoghurt drinks from the supermarket and is easy to make.

Sauerkraut

Sauerkraut is the German word for sour cabbage. It is cabbage that's been pickled and fermented and is made by adding salt to shredded cabbage, after which the bacteria start to grow and ferment the cabbage, producing the lactic acid which gives sauerkraut its distinctive sour taste. In the days before refrigeration, it was an excellent way to preserve cabbage for the long winter months.

You can ferment many other vegetables too such as red cabbage, cauliflower, carrots, broccoli, all sorts of string beans, cucumbers, onions, radishes or beetroots. Or add these to your sauerkraut fermentation.

During the fermentation process, live bacteria are produced and these probiotics are what give sauerkraut most of its health benefits. These probiotics are important for digestive health, and while more research is needed into the exact types of probiotics found in sauerkraut, we do know that they top up the good bacteria and can help to combat inflammation.

What's in sauerkraut

Sauerkraut contains high levels of glucosinolates – compounds demonstrated to have anti-cancer activity. They occur naturally in fresh cabbage and other cruciferous vegetables such as broccoli, brussels sprouts and kale.

Sauerkraut also contains enzymes that help the body to break down food into smaller and more easily digestible molecules which in turn helps the body to absorb more nutrients.

You receive a good amount of dietary fibre from sauerkraut and it contains some vitamin C and K, as well as the minerals potassium and phosphorus, and has few kilojoules.

Sadly sauerkraut is high in sodium (salt), and the same can be said for other pickled foods like cucumbers and onions. Just ½ cup (a 50 gram serve) provides approximately one-tenth of your recommended intake of sodium for an adult, so it quickly adds up if you eat sauerkraut regularly.

There are other limitations. Due to its high concentrations of tyramine, sauerkraut appears on the lists of foods to be restricted on a MAOI diet (Monoamine Oxidase Inhibitor). However, the concentration of tyramine shows a broad variation, making it hard to predict how the one you swallow will act.

Sauerkraut also shows high concentrations of histamine. It has been suggested that histamine in food is a major cause of food intolerance. So be warned, it may cause some unwanted reactions, in particular in high-risk populations, such as depressive or allergic individuals.

Homemade vs canned or jarred

Sauerkraut that is canned or bought in a jar or heated for a long time before eating has little or no friendly bacteria – they've been destroyed by the heat. These pre-packaged sauerkraut products have no influence on health – even though they look and taste the same as raw unpasteurised types. If you're buying sauerkraut, make sure to choose unpasteurised brands (they should be in the refrigerator aisle) – or make your own. Pasteurisation kills all the helpful bacteria.

The bottom line

Eat small amounts, regularly. Small doses of sauerkraut, say 1 tablespoon (7–10 grams) a day, seems fine and can have a good effect on digestion with less constipation. Mix it into salad or serve it with a burger or toasted sandwich. My mother used to mix it with fresh sliced cabbage and caraway seeds for a nice side salad.

Kimchi

Kimchi is a traditional Korean side dish consisting of salted and fermented vegetables, which is mainly served as an accompaniment with every meal.

The most commonly used vegetables are cabbage and long Korean radishes, with a variety of seasonings including chilli, spring onions, garlic, ginger and *jeotal* (salted seafood). There are literally dozens of varieties of kimchi made with different vegetables. Its warm and spicy flavour makes even the simplest dishes come alive.

Like sauerkraut, pickling of vegetables was an ideal method of preservation prior to refrigerators. In Korea, kimchi was made during the winter by fermenting vegetables, and burying them in the ground in traditional brown ceramic pots called onggi.

Like other fermented foods, kimchi contains a high concentration of fibre.

Like other fermented foods, kimchi contains a high concentration of fibre, while being low in kilojoules. One serving also provides over 50 per cent of the daily recommended amount of vitamin C and beta-carotene. Like sauerkraut, unfortunately, it is also high in salt.

4 Current cuisine

We are all eating out more often and choosing a full meal or a quick snack from the many outlets and pop-up carts around.

Cafe culture

Do you like to indulge in something sweet with your coffee? A treat once a week is not a big deal and should be eaten and enjoyed. But if you're snacking every day, then you need to take stock and choose healthier alternatives. Here are some tips to cope with the cafe culture overload:

- Say 'no' to croissants or pain au chocolat, and 'yes' to toasted sourdough or raisin toast with the spread (butter/margarine/ricotta/honey/jam) on the side so you can add your own.
- Opt for nut breads and banana breads, but ask for no spread. Often these breads – which are more like cakes – are tasty enough without the addition of butter.
- Try a muesli slice instead of a slice of cake. A good source of whole grains and dried fruit, these slices fill you up and have some nutritional benefit, but be careful, there are still hidden sugars added to 'glue' the grains and nuts together.
- Try a wholemeal muffin. They have a slightly higher fibre content, but you still need to watch portion sizes. Fruit muffins such as blueberry or raspberry muffins are a healthier choice than the chocolate ones.
- Protein balls and raw treats can be a better choice thanks to their small size. And they're sweet enough to satisfy.
- Not really hungry but craving something sweet? Try a sweeter coffee like a caramel or hazelnut blend, which has fewer kilojoules than a great big muffin.
- Don't fall for the coffee and cake discount! It looks like a good deal – $5 for a coffee and a slice of cake when the coffee alone costs $4 – but remember, you're not saving money. If you only wanted a coffee, then you're spending more than you intended *and* that cake is going straight to your hips to account for later!

Snacking – making it healthy

Snacks are a real problem in the modern diet. Most of us can fix a healthy breakfast, order a salad for lunch and cook a grill or stir-fry for dinner. But those in-between snacks play havoc with our total food intake and turn healthy eating into an excess of fatty, sugary and salty junk food like chocolate bars, muffins, doughnuts, lollies and biscuits or bags of crisps, corn chips, pizza, fries and savoury crackers.

The problem with modern snacks

Most modern-day snacks are a nutrition disaster and one of the main reasons why many of us are gaining weight. We graze, but not on anything healthy and not on anything moderate in portion size. Most popular snacks:

1. Are a mini-meal with too many kilojoules and too much sugar and salt. So if you're not very active physically, you'll quickly pile on the weight.
2. Are 'processed' and don't contribute the essential nutrients we need for health.
3. Are digested quickly – and soon you're hungry again.
4. Are easy to over-consume thanks to their size and their sheer deliciousness. For the cost, they are simply too generous! Think of those bottomless buckets of movie popcorn, jumbo bags of potato chips, family blocks of chocolate that somehow get eaten, and giant tubs of ice cream.
5. Encourage mindless eating while watching a movie or sitting in front of the computer. When questioned, most of us fail to recall what we eat between meals. We 'forget' the muffin with our morning coffee, the pack of crisps on the drive home or the nibbles before dinner because we weren't paying attention to what we were eating.

Choosing healthy snacks

Snacks should be small in size and lower in kilojoules, fat, salt and added sugar than meals. Your aim is to have a snack that satisfies your hunger until your next meal. Try one of these:

5 snacks to keep in your desk drawer

1. Snack packs of almonds, walnuts or unsalted mixed nuts
2. Small cans of tuna flavoured with chilli, lemon or tomato
3. Nut bars
4. A trail-mix pack of mixed nuts, seeds and dried fruit
5. Fresh fruit such as an apple or banana

5 snacks to keep in your work fridge

1. A tub of yoghurt
2. A small avocado
3. A slice or wedge of cheese
4. Vegetable or tomato juice
5. Raisin loaf to toast

How to identify a healthy snack

Not all snacks are completely 'bad'. Here are four nutrition numbers that can help you to classify a snack as 'healthy'. Use these to judge a bar, muffin, biscuit, drink or anything else bought in a packet. Alternatively buy snacks with 4 Stars or higher on the Health Star Rating system (see page 143). A healthy snack has:

- Less than 600 kilojoules (150 calories) per serve *and*
- Less than 3 grams of saturated fat per serve *and*
- Less than 200 milligrams of sodium (salt) per serve *and*
- Less than 15 grams of sugars per serve.

Plus if they are wholegrain or high-fibre or supply important nutrients such as calcium, iron or protein, that's a bonus.

Why doughnuts aren't the best snack

Two cinnamon doughnuts pile on 20 grams of fat and over 2000 kilojoules (500 calories), which is one-third of the day's recommended intake for the average sedentary woman. And most of that fat is industrial fat, the type that clogs arteries and thickens your waistline.

Size makes a BIG difference

Use these five tips to help you downsize the portions of your sweet treats.

1. Choose a small cupcake or a friand rather than a supersized muffin. They'll often be just what you need, and they won't make you feel overfull and regretful afterwards.
2. Double your treat by sharing it with a friend. Halving a slice of cake with a friend will halve your intake while still allowing you to enjoy something sweet as well as some quality time with someone you like.
3. If you're alone, ask for the muffin to be cut in half, with half placed in a paper bag for later.
4. Cafes often serve massive wedges of cakes (to justify the price) so don't feel you have to eat the whole thing. The portions are way more than you actually need or want. Don't be shy about asking for any uneaten cake to be put into a bag.
5. If your heart's really set on that sweet something, make sure you enjoy it. Eat mindfully and savour every mouthful. Don't just stuff it in your mouth while you write that report and then find yourself surprised that the whole thing is gone and you didn't really remember a single bite!

Create a portion

The newest fast food

Salad bars

Salad bars are a welcome addition to the food-court scene. It's so good to have healthier fast food options that actually provide valuable nutrition (the opposite of most fast food). Of course, some items are better than others.

Delicious, fresh and nutritious, a salad bar is perfect for that quick lunch on the run. Salad bars offer more than just takeaway or made-to-order salads. They offer freshly made sandwiches to go, wraps, filled rolls, pasta salads and, in winter, soups. The Sumo Salad chain has been around for a long time, making salads more accessible, but now you have a choice of many other ready-made salad bars. Examples include Soul Origin, Saladworks or Fresh&Co, Chop't and Simply Salads.

Having a big salad at lunch is a win–win for both your weight and your gut health. A salad bowl contains the lowest kilojoule count of all fast food. Replacing bread or chips with leafy greens like spinach and rocket – which are naturally low in kilojoules and high in fibre – ensures you are kept full for the rest of the afternoon without needing a snack around 3.30 pm.

Here are some tips for ordering a healthy salad:

- If you have a choice, choose a simple vinaigrette or olive oil dressing – these contain good fats, unlike creamy sauces, which are laden with saturated fats.
- Use dressing sparingly – ask for a drizzle. The salad doesn't need to be drowned to enjoy the taste, and you save yourself unnecessary kilojoules.
- Some salads – like chicken pesto penne – come already dressed, but most are not pre-dressed. If your salad already has a dressing, don't add another. One is enough.
- Keep pasta salads small in size. Too much of a good thing can lead to your undoing.
- Combine your pasta salad with two leaf salads and a legume salad in the one container. This will ensure a small amount of pasta salad, increases the fibre of

Snacking to stay healthy

Under 600 kilojoules (150 calories)

20 almonds
14 cashews
1 egg, boiled or poached on 1 slice of bread (no butter or margarine)
vegetable sticks (1 carrot, 2 celery stalks, ½ capsicum) dipped in tomato salsa
1 corn on the cob, cooked (no butter)
1 cup (250 ml) reduced-fat milk with 2 teaspoons of malt powder, e.g. Milo, Horlicks, Aktavite
2 cheese sticks
200 g tub of non-fat yoghurt
1 slice of fruit bread spread with butter or margarine
1 crumpet with jam
1 pikelet with honey
1 fruit scone
19 rice crackers
1 small breakfast cereal bar
1 small can of baked beans
1 muesli bar
⅓ Danish pastry
2 small scoops of vanilla ice cream
3 icy poles
31 smarties
6 small squares of chocolate
8 marshmallows
7 twists/1 cup (40 g) pretzels
1 cup (34 g) or 10 corn chips
¼ individual meat pie
4 mini or 1 big sushi rolls
1 glass (250 ml) of soft drink (not the full 375 ml can)

the dish to keep you feeling full longer and reduces the kilojoules. Win–win–win.

- Ensure your salad contains a protein source such as poached chicken, tuna, egg or beef. Proteins help your body regulate blood glucose, which will help to maintain your concentration levels well beyond 3.30-itis. Another healthy protein is legumes (chickpeas, lentils and beans). These plant-based proteins are lower in kilojoules, higher in fibre and still provide the essential protein and nutrients our bodies need.
- Share large portions with a friend. Or eat half now, half later.

Filled wraps and baguette sandwiches

Wraps are often assumed to be healthier than sandwiches but there's really not much difference. A crusty baguette looks delicious filled with ham, chicken, tuna, roast beef, lean roast lamb or egg with lots of salad and makes a good lunch for busy workers. Look for grainy, rye or wholemeal bread with the most salad filling.

Virtually a crust with no soft crumb, toasted Turkish bread makes a crisp or toasted base. Healthy toppings include chicken or tuna with chargrilled vegetables like zucchini, eggplant, capsicum, as well as ham, avocado and tomato. Take care with melted cheese because it can pack in a lot of fat.

Sushi and California rolls

What could be faster to eat than a couple of sushi rolls? They're pre-made, easily placed into a paper bag, portable and easy to eat with your hands – and hardly ever get messy. Whether you buy sushi from a sushi outlet or an eatery with a moving conveyor-belt (where they count the empty plates at the end), these seaweed-wrapped rice rolls filled with tuna, prawns, salmon, egg, cucumber or avocado make a quick, light, healthy option for that lunchtime rush. They give you protein, vegetables and rice in one compact roll.

This healthy choice, however, can quickly become energy-, carbohydrate- and fat-heavy. Tempura sushi rolls, as well as additional fillings like mayonnaise and cream cheese, significantly increase the unhealthy fat and kilojoule content of your meal. Plus, depending on how many rolls you eat, you could be having the equivalent of 3–4 slices of bread in terms of carbs and kilojoules! This translates to 45–60 grams of carbohydrate, which is equal to ¾ to 1 cup of rice.

- Opt for 1–2 sushi rolls filled with lean proteins such as raw salmon or tuna, and vegetables such as avocado, cucumber or carrot.
- Avoid anything with 'katsu' or 'tempura' in the name; these versions of sushi include fried foods.
- Add a side of seaweed salad or edamame (young soybeans) to boost your fibre and vegetable intake.
- Some sushi outlets offer rice paper rolls, a lower carbohydrate alternative to the traditional sushi roll; they often have more vegetables too.
- Swap a white rice sushi roll for a brown rice sushi roll.

Go easy with the little fishes of soy sauce; soy sauce is packed full of salt – 1 tablespoon contains one-third of our daily recommended intake – so limit your intake to one soy-sauce fish per meal, which is roughly 200 milligrams of sodium per serve.

Ultra-processed foods

Many snacks are ultra-processed foods (UPFs) that are convenient: portable, cheap, shelf-stable and mess-free. Think about such ready-to-eat items as chips, fries, biscuits, chocolates, sweets, nuggets, energy bars and carbonated sweet drinks. They taste so good it's hard not to finish them once you open them. They are easy to overeat and hit all our bliss points. There is no need for cutlery or crockery, or for you to have any cooking skills.

UPFs have been blamed for obesity. Studies show that UPFs damage the nutritional integrity of diets and increase the risk of diseases such as diabetes and heart disease. They lack 'soul' and connection to raw ingredients. Generally they are high in added sugar and added salt, with bad fats and numerous undesirable flavours, colours and preservatives. Watch out for them.

Eating out – healthiest cuisines

Thai? Italian? Chinese? Nepalese? What's the healthiest cuisine to choose when you eat out? Here are four of the healthier choices.

Japanese

The traditional Japanese diet comes close to the perfect diet. And it's delicious too with foods like sashimi, salmon tataki, chicken teriyaki, beef yakitori, fine noodles in broth, edamame and seafood udon broth.

With its emphasis on vegetables, seafood, broth, plain rice, green tea and seaweed, it is a semi-vegetarian diet but with less fat, less sugar and more phytochemicals than a typical Western diet. It also has none of the rich desserts, heavy pastries and thick sauces of European cuisines.

Unique to Japan is the dietary recommendation that we consume at least 30 different foods daily. While other countries stress variety (especially when it comes to vegetables and fruit), only Japan has gone so far as to quantify an actual number to aim for.

It seems that people who eat this wide variety of foods are healthier, have a reduced risk of heart disease and diabetes and live longer. And they're more likely to meet their nutrient needs, particularly important for people over fifty. It's estimated that the average Australian eats only 15–18 different foods

per week, well below what the Japanese suggest.

There is also that famous Japanese saying '*Hara hachi bu*', which means 'Eat until you get 80 per cent full'. It is a great self-imposed habit that seems responsible for the low rates of obesity in the country. They teach it to their children from a young age.

The single bad aspect of the Japanese diet is the saltiness, a consequence of the days of salted foods combined with an acquired taste for saltiness. Salty sauces such as soy sauce, teriyaki sauce or oyster sauce take the place of salt and impart a wonderful flavour. But don't overdo them because they can send your salt intake sky high, which sets the scene for high blood pressure and stomach cancer – two health concerns prevalent in certain provinces of Japan such as Akita and Yamagata.

You'd think that with white rice a feature of almost all meals, the nutritional value of Japanese cuisine would be diminished, but it isn't. Yes it's plain boiled rice, which is low in nutrition but it is without any salt. Rice is also a lower fat and lower kilojoule alternative to the usual higher fat, higher kilojoule carbohydrates such as creamy mashed potato, fries, cheesy rolls and crusty bread.

Generally you can't go wrong with lots of a staple like rice or noodles with lightly cooked vegetables; some seafood, fish, tofu, chicken or meat; lots of fresh herbs like coriander or mint; and topped with shallots, bamboo shoots or sprouts. Start with a serve of sashimi dipped in ginger and wasabi – you won't eat better fish than this.

Say No to:

- Fried starters like spring rolls or tonkatsu
- Battered deep-fried foods like prawn tempura and fried gyoza (dumplings)
- Miso soup – a sodium bomb
- Salty sauces over everything

Middle Eastern

We've all heard of the Mediterranean diet, the traditional way of eating in southern Italy and Greece, which is based on olive oil, pasta, bread, vegetables, seafood, garlic and tomatoes. It has been shown to be associated with living longer, fewer heart troubles, less dementia and less cancer. But it also applies to other countries around the Mediterranean Sea such as Turkey, Lebanon, Israel, Egypt, Libya, Algeria and Morocco. Collectively these are all considered Middle Eastern.

At its core Middle Eastern cuisine features healthy olive oil, as well as foods made from sesame seeds (another culinary staple) – like the wonderful hummus and tahini – and sesame oil.

In place of the Italian pasta and bread, Middle Eastern countries serve dolma, kebabs, koftes, rice pilafs – and vegetables (eggplants, peppers, tomatoes or zucchinis) filled with mince stuffing or a mixture of

rice and onion with various spices for non-meat eaters. Spices like cinnamon, pepper, thyme and cumin are a dominant feature of this cuisine, as well as garlic (always welcome in the sauces or yoghurts) and a wide array of nuts.

Turkish savoury pastries known as boureks, always flaky and delicious, come in many varieties, most popularly filled with minced meat or spinach and cheese. Boureks can be rolled and served for breakfast, lunch, dinner or as a snack.

Say No to:
- Fried boureks
- Honey-rich syrupy sweets such as baklava with their sprinkle of pistachio or walnuts
- Strong, thick Turkish coffee

Italian

It's no surprise that you'll find an Italian eatery everywhere in the world. They certainly know how to prepare and serve good food! Most of these restaurants are based on the cuisine of southern Italy, the cornerstone of the famed Mediterranean diet. Prawns, calamari, fish, ricotta, pasta, olive oil and tomatoes give you heaps of omega-3s, phytochemicals – like those greenish polyphenols from olive oil – vitamins and little in the way of saturated fat. There are strong, gutsy flavours from garlic, red wine and herbs like basil and thyme. Not forgetting rucola (rocket) and other green leaves in the warmer months.

This cuisine serves vegetables in ways that make you want to eat them.

This cuisine serves vegetables in ways that make you *want* to eat them. So make sure you order chargrilled baby eggplant with olive oil and shaved parmesan or a salad of tomatoes, basil and slabs of bocconcini. As mentioned, if you follow the Mediterranean diet, you are less likely to suffer from heart disease, high blood pressure and certain types of cancer. In short, you can expect to live longer!

Research backs up the benefits of eating a Mediterranean diet. For instance, when Greek people migrate to Australia, their rates of heart disease are low compared to Australians. But once that first generation of Greek-Australians grows up, their heart disease rates rise to approach that of Australians. The reason? Traditional plant dishes are replaced

with more kilojoule-dense foods and larger serves of meat, chicken, sweets, treats and fast foods.

The good health associated with Mediterranean diets cannot be attributed to a single food factor. Many foods play a role, as does having a relaxed lifestyle (one does suspect the post-lunch siesta helps), a mixing of three or more generations at the table and regular but low-level physical activity like gardening or walking.

The one big negative is its reliance on processed meats (whether cured, salted or smoked) such as salami, prosciutto and bresaola that form a key part of the cuisine. These tend to be high in salt and nitrites/nitrates that have been linked to cancer in later life. They were once a way of preserving meats for lean times during the year, but they are no longer necessary with today's refrigeration and freezing technologies.

Say No to:
- Huge bowls of linguine and other pasta with no protein but lots of oil or tomatoes
- Pasta with creamy or cheesey sauces like alfredo, carbonara or boscaiola
- Gnocchi, which is chock full of potato and is often served with creamy sauces

Vietnamese

One thing's for sure. If I'm wanting a meal in a hurry, instead of ordering pizza or burgers, it's Vietnamese I'd go for – one of the healthiest alternatives to fast food.

It's light, fragrant and fresh with its leaning towards seafood and quick cooking times. It's a cuisine that has much to recommend it nutritionally. Naturally, many similarities exist with dishes from neighbouring Laos, Cambodia, Thailand and Burma, all of which share the same Indo-Chinese heritage.

Noodles and rice are the staple foods and are enhanced with the flavours of garlic, chilli, lime, Vietnamese mint, basil and coriander. Pork, eggs and fish are the main proteins. What sets Vietnamese cuisine apart is its subtle use of fresh herbs and spices – just imagine a lovely salad with bean shoots, coriander, mint leaves and holy basil topped with cold chicken or prawns, and you'll see what I mean.

A bowl of steaming noodle soup or *pho* – considered to be the national dish – makes a quick, simple and healthy winter lunch. The simmering broth holds fine rice noodles and usually some chicken or beef, topped with sprigs of coriander and chives. It achieves its flavour from nuoc mam – a salty fish sauce more pungent than other Asian fish sauce – and is served with side dishes of fresh Vietnamese mint, crisp bean shoots, finely sliced chilli and quartered limes.

Nutritionally, other good choices when you look over the menu at a Vietnamese restaurant are:
- Fish balls
- Hot sour soup
- Chicken vermicelli soup
- Prawn and mint salad

For mains, look for any of the stir-fries or mixed dishes that combine seafood, pork or chicken with vegetables.

The historical French influence still lingers in Vietnamese cuisine and turns up as crusty baguettes or *banh mi* rolls loaded with interesting fillings such as pickles and flavoursome herbs.

Say No to:
- Processed food as much as possible – Western-style foods are creeping into the traditional Vietnamese diet
- Anything deep fried (although there's not much, really)
- Highly sweet or salty sauces – don't ban them totally, just have minimal amounts

Vegetarian and vegan diets

Vegetarianism and veganism and general avoidance of certain meats have long been practised by many communities. Well-known vegetarians include Ellen DeGeneres, Paul McCartney, Mike Tyson, Natalie Portman, Daniel Johns (Silverchair guitarist) and Peter Siddle (cricketer). Vegetarianism has been built into the philosophy of several religious faiths like Seventh Day Adventists, Buddhists, Trappist Catholic Monks and Hare Krishnas.

Today, many people are choosing a meat-free lifestyle for reasons such as a concern for the welfare of the world, the needless slaughter of animals (animal rights) or because of an allergy to dairy or eggs. While only 2–3 per cent of the population are completely vegetarian, many more are now eating meatless meals – just witness the huge rise in Meat-free Monday and Veganuary – and restaurants now offer a wider range of meat-free choices such as grilled mushrooms or eggplant Parmigiana, which is great to see.

Health benefits of going vego

Once viewed as 'fringe' or 'hippie', vegetarianism is now accepted as having proven health benefits. Research has shown that compared to the general omnivore population, vegetarians on average:
- Are less likely to suffer heart disease
- Are less likely to suffer cancer, notably of the bowel, breast and lung
- Have lower blood pressure
- Have a healthy body weight
- Have a lower risk of type 2 diabetes

This positive health profile is attributed to four dietary factors:
- Less saturated fat
- Less nitrates from processed meats (bacon, sausages, salamis)
- More fibre
- More phytochemicals from nuts, grains, pulses, fruits and vegetables

In addition, vegetarians in general tend to smoke less, drink less alcohol, have little or no caffeine and practice stress-lowering techniques like meditation, all of which help to keep them in top health.

However, people often declare they are vegetarian or vegan, but in fact they are 'flexitarian' – eating a little meat from time to time when it's on offer or when they visit their grandma. It seems to me that this flexible approach is the best type of diet – lots of vegetables and salads but a little meat from time to time.

Types of vegetarian diets

Vegans avoid all foods of animal origin. They live on products from the plant kingdom and so rely on grains, vegetables, pulses, nuts and fruits. They also avoid leather, wool, honey, cosmetics, soap and shampoo derived from animal ingredients or tested on animals.

Lacto-vegetarians eat dairy foods as well as plant foods.

Lacto-ovo vegetarians eat dairy foods and eggs as well as plant foods. This type of vegetarianism is recommended for children, pregnant or breastfeeding women and anyone who is embarking on a vegetarian way of eating for the first time. Nutritionally, it is similar to a meat-based diet and can meet the body's requirements for vitamins and minerals.

Flexitarians eat dairy foods and eggs plus the occasional meal with meat, fish or chicken if they're out or don't want to say No (say at Grandma's). This style of eating is recommended.

Fruitarians eat only fruit and nuts. This diet is considered too limited and may lead to nutrient deficiencies.

Vegetarian pitfalls – the five nutrients likely to be in short supply

1. Vitamin B12
Strict vegan diets lack vitamin B12, which is virtutally only found in animal foods. Although needed in minute quantities, vitamin B12 is essential for healthy red blood cells, DNA genetic material and nerve tissues. A lack of it can bring on pernicious anaemia and degeneration of the nervous system. However, because vitamin B12 is stored in the liver, it takes three to five years for a healthy vegetarian to develop any deficiency.

While rare, B12 deficiency has been reported in elderly vegetarians and in babies of vegan mothers, where it has caused impaired mental functioning. The demands of pregnancy and breastfeeding soon deplete the mother's B12 stores and leave her milk without sufficient B12. Pregnant and breastfeeding vegetarian women should therefore make sure that any plant mylks they buy are fortified with B12 or else take a B12 supplement (2 micrograms a day is recommended; supplements contain 2–100 micrograms).

Vegetarian B12 *sources*: yoghurt, milk, cheese, eggs and fortified plant mylks.

Mushrooms have been on and off as a source of vitamin B12 for years, but the latest analyses show there is B12 present in mushrooms, so add a few to your daily diet.

In contrast, seaweed and fermented foods like tempeh were once suggested as sources of B12, but are now not considered reliable sources. Tests reveal that any B12 they contain is in the form of inactive B12 analogues (look-alikes). See more on page 65.

2. Iron
Anaemia caused by iron deficiency is one of the most common nutrition problems for vegetarians, especially women. Lack of iron can also prevent children achieving their full intellectual potential. Due to the presence of phytates and oxalates in plant foods, less than 5 per cent of the iron in plant foods is absorbed by our bodies, compared to 20 per cent or more of the iron found in red meat. Also plant iron occurs in an inorganic form as non-haem iron compared to meat's haem (easy to absorb) iron.

> ## Lack of iron can prevent children achieving their full intellectual potential.

Vegetarian iron sources: iron-fortified breakfast cereals, dark green vegetables (spinach, silverbeet, broccoli), beans, lentils, meat substitutes like tofu, quorn or soy steaks, dried fruit and cocoa powder.

Vegetarian meals are typically high in vitamin C (capsicum, tomatoes, orange or lemon juice), which greatly boosts the absorption of non-haem iron. See more on page 66.

3. Calcium
Calcium is critical for children and pregnant women; a deficiency causes stunted growth and malformed bones and teeth. Vegetarians who consume milk, yoghurt or cheese are fine, but many avoid these dairy products and need non-dairy calcium.

Vegetarian calcium sources: plant mylks fortified with calcium (look for about 120 milligrams per 100 millilitres), green leafy vegetables with low phytates (kale, Asian greens), tahini (sesame seed paste), almonds, Brazil nuts, hazelnuts, tofu, dried figs.

4. Zinc
Zinc is vital for the function of many enzymes in the body and for a strong immune system. The richest sources are animal foods such as meat, fish, oysters and chicken. Zinc from these foods is absorbed better than zinc from plant foods.

Vegetarian zinc sources: wholemeal and grain breads, bran and wholegrain breakfast cereals, legumes, nuts.

Baseline vegetarian diet

What you should eat

You need the following minimum quantities each day to ensure a nutritionally balanced vegetarian diet.

Grains

6 serves of whole grains – brown rice, quinoa, millet, barley, farro, freekeh, pasta, burghul, bread, noodles, breakfast cereal, oats (1 serve = ½ cup cooked grain or 2 slices of bread)

Vegetables, salads and sprouts

5 serves of vegetables, salads and sprouts, some raw and some cooked (1 serve = ½ cup cooked vegetables [around 75 grams] or 1 cup salad leaves)

Fruit and juices

2 serves

Protein sources

- 2 serves of cooked or canned legumes (1 serve = 1 cup [150 grams] cooked beans, peas and lentils or 170 grams tofu or tempeh)
- *Or* 2 serves of nuts or nutmeat (1 serve = ¼ cup or a small handful [30 grams] of almonds, walnuts, pecans, macadamias, hazelnuts, peanuts, etc.)
- *Or* 2 eggs
- *Or* 40 grams cheese
- *Or* 1 tub (200 grams) of yoghurt
- *Or* any combination of the above

Calcium sources

200 millilitres milk for adults; 500 millilitres for children and pregnant and breastfeeding women. If you avoid dairy products, choose calcium-fortified plant mylks (almond, oat, pea, hemp) or soy yoghurt.

In place of 1 cup (250 millilitres) milk, you could choose 2 slices (40 grams) of cheese or ½ cup (120 grams) ricotta or cottage cheese or 1 cup (250 millilitres) buttermilk or kefir or 1 tub (200 grams) of yoghurt

Good fats

1 tablespoon (20 grams) oil, tahini, peanut butter, mayonnaise, salad dressing, seeds (sunflower, pumpkin, sesame, etc.), avocado, wheatgerm or olives. Coconut fat is not included here because it provides little of these good fats.

5. Omega-3 fats

Vegans consuming no animal foods at all may miss out on the valuable omega-3 fatty acids from oily fish and grass-fed meats.

Vegetarian omega-3 sources: linseeds (flaxseeds), linseed oil, hemp seeds, hemp oil, omega-3 enriched products (eggs, bread), walnuts, pecans, soybeans, dark-green leafy vegetables and rocket.

However, to be used in the body, these must be converted to the long-chain form, a process that's not efficient, with around 10 per cent conversion. See more on pages 70–3.

Vegetarian eating for children

Nutritionists recommend that children in vegetarian families eat eggs and dairy products to ensure readily available sources of protein, as well as vitamin B12, calcium, iron and zinc. For the first six months of life, breast milk can provide all the nutrients a baby needs, provided the mother is well nourished. The infant can then be weaned onto yoghurt, baby cereals, mashed avocado, soft tofu, pureed vegetables, fruit juices and soft-cooked eggs.

Concentrated foods like cheese, avocado, eggs, honey, dried fruit or oil are handy for adding kilojoules without bulk.

Difficulty arises when a toddler starts eating general family food with its bulky vegetables, filling beans and whole grains (remember that these foods have plenty of fibre, which may be good for an adult, but not for a rapidly growing child who needs lots of kilojoules but has a small stomach with limited capacity). If the child is unable to consume sufficient food (because it is too full from all the fibre-rich foods), then its energy, vitamin and mineral requirements won't be met.

Small meals with snacks in between is the key. Concentrated foods like cheese, avocado, eggs, honey, dried fruit or oil are handy for adding kilojoules without bulk. Nuts and seeds should be chopped or ground to break up their fibrous hulls and improve digestion. Milk or plant mylk should be full-fat, not low-fat.

Want to eat vegetarian but don't know where to start?

Quick and easy vegetarian meals to get you started

Try these meal ideas once a week, maybe for Meatless Mondays or until you build up a repertoire of three or four dishes:

Chickpeas
- Add cooked or canned (and drained) chickpeas into vegetable curries and soups.
- Make an easy summer main meal salad by mixing chickpeas with quartered artichoke hearts, mixed lettuce leaves, sliced cucumber and oven-roasted baby tomatoes. Drizzle over a vinaigrette.
- Serve peas over cooked penne or with grain or rye bread or toast.

Kidney beans
- Make a spicy bean hotpot by simmering soaked kidney beans with garlic, onion, chilli, stock and canned tomatoes until cooked. Serve over macaroni or rice or quinoa.

Lentil loaf

· Combine cooked brown rice with cooked soft red lentils and grated onion, grated carrot, mixed herbs and an egg to bind. Pack into a loaf tin and bake until golden. Serve with cooked green vegetables or a large tossed salad.

Bean soup

· Mix diced onion, potato, turnip, carrot and celery stalks in a large pot. Throw in a few celery leaves and a bay leaf. Cover with water and simmer. Add cooked beans (soy, kidney, navy, borlotti) with herbs and tomato.

How not to go vegetarian

Simply eliminating the meat component of a traditional meal leaves just the vegetables, which alone do not make a balanced meal. You need to replace the meat with a cup of beans or sliced tofu or a lentil loaf. In protein value, ½ cup (75 grams) of cooked legumes gives you 6 grams of protein, which is equal to the protein found in 1 egg or around 30 grams of meat.

> You need to replace the meat with a cup of beans or sliced tofu or a lentil loaf.

An oil trap

Most vegetarian diets are low in fat compared to meat-based diets. It's one of their great nutritional advantages. But don't fall into the trap of eating a high-fat vegetarian diet. This can easily happen if you experiment with recipes from some of the popular vegetarian cookbooks.

Deep-frying in oil, topping bean casseroles with a rich cheese sauce, using shortcrust pastry, baking hearty slices and cakes (even if wholemeal) all spell lots of oil – and can be heavy on the fat. Consider the fat in an average serve of four popular vegetarian dishes:

Food	fat in average serve (grams)
Vegetarian lasagne	35
Cheese and vegetable flan	40
Spinach and feta cheese filo triangles	38
Vegetable laksa with fried tofu cube	36

A healthy intake of fat is 60–100 grams a day

'PAY THE FARMER OR PAY THE HOSPITAL.'

BIRKE BAEHR, AGED 16, AN ADVOCATE FOR
ORGANIC AND SUSTAINABLE FOOD IN
NORTH CAROLINA, USA

5 Food, health and ethics

What we buy and eat each day isn't just about nutrition: it's about avoiding waste, eating seasonally and locally; maybe eating organically or foraging for your own; and keeping your food safe.

Food waste and what you can do

Food waste is a huge problem. We throw out up to 20 per cent of all the food we buy, which is such a shame considering all the energy it takes to grow, harvest, package, transport, store and cook it all. Not to mention the fact that we're wasting our own hard-earned money every time we throw food out. Everyone, from chefs to supermarkets, is trying to minimise what we throw out.

I have also changed the way I cook in order to minimise waste. I now aim to use up every last scrap and get creative with leftovers, including cooked but uneaten grains, too many lemons from the lemon tree, and stale bread. From compost bins to recipes that use up what's in the veg drawer, I like to recycle and make anew.

Food is valuable – let's not throw it away

Conservative estimates of food waste per household is worth more than $1000 per year, says FoodWise, a national campaign from DoSomething to reduce the environmental impact of Australia's food consumption. But it's not only a waste of money – as landfill food waste generates methane, a potent

Conservative estimates of food waste per household is worth more than $1000 per year

greenhouse gas. The Australia Institute claims that each tonne of food waste also releases the equivalent of almost a tonne of carbon dioxide, not to mention the fact that it requires great tracts of precious land to bury it in.

Ways to cut food waste

Creative use of leftovers and composting – things that were second nature to previous generations – are the way to go. All it takes is to buy foods that are in season, store them correctly, recycle any packaging and compost food waste. Here's what we need to do:

· Plan meals in advance – check what you already have, buy only what you need and chill or freeze leftovers for another day.
· Compost your food scraps or use a worm farm. Compact small systems for apartments are widely available.
· Home-grown vegetables and herbs need no packaging, are fun to grow and good to eat. Grow herbs in pots on a balcony, or start a vegetable patch in the back garden.
· Join a community garden. Contact your local council if more community gardens are needed in your area. Schools can get involved via Stephanie Alexander's Kitchen Garden project.
· Select foods with minimal packaging. Buy foods such as rice, pasta, legumes, oats and nuts in bulk and save money too.
· Get into recycling – have separate kitchen bins for bottles/cans, paper/cardboard and green waste depending on what your local council collects. Check packaging for the recycling symbol and code numbers.
· Buy a reusable drink bottle to carry water with you, and a reusable cup for those takeaway coffees.
· Every night when you peel or chop veggies, wash the veggies before you peel them and then pop the trimmings into a freezer bag. Then on the weekend, thaw and use them to make a pot of stock.
· Buy what you can from farmers' markets and local growers, taking care that it is genuinely local produce. It connects you with the people that live

around you and supports the local farmers that grow our food.

Rescue the food

Edible, unwanted food that was destined for landfill, including restaurant leftovers and factory seconds, is often 'rescued' by organisations such as Foodbank, OzHarvest and SecondBite that feed people who don't have enough to eat. These and other food rescuers act as a conduit between manufacturers and retailers to supply unused food to those in need.

Eating seasonally and locally

Eating food that's in season is not just a trendy new food movement; it makes sense from both a taste and nutrition point of view. Food at its peak will have the maximum nutritional value and be at its lowest price. It's time to say 'No!' to cherries in winter or oranges in the middle of summer.

When you buy what's in season, you buy food that:
· Is at the peak of its supply so it's fresher
· Costs less for farmers to harvest and to get to your supermarket or greengrocer
· Is sold before it spoils, and not refrigerated or put into cold storage

Minimise the food miles by eating locally

It's always good to seek out local produce. Local produce travels less and needs less refrigeration, which means less fossil fuels are used and less greenhouse gases are produced. Buying food grown or caught within a radius of 160 kilometres can allow fresh foods to be bought without packaging and gives small producers a better chance to compete. Plus, it'll taste better: ideally we all want fresh produce that is picked for taste, not transport.

However, eating locally doesn't always result in the cheapest food or the least environmental impact – it's a complex issue with many factors. For example, coffee beans can be grown in a more environmentally friendly manner in Kenya than in most other countries due to its soil, natural sunlight and less fuel-intensive inputs. Dairy produced in Australia and delivered to the UK market generates fewer carbon emissions than locally produced British dairy thanks to more sunlight, better rainfall and open farmlands in Australia. The issue is not just distance, but the total use of energy from paddock to plate, including transport.

We have to also allow for transport costs if we wish to consume foods we are unable to produce, such as

What's in season

You can find out easily what's around in spring, summer, autumn and winter from websites, Instagram, apps and your local markets. Here's an example of what's around in February in Australia, which is the end of summer.

Fruits

Berries (blueberries, raspberries, strawberries)	Nectarines
	Passionfruit
	Pears (Howell, William)
Figs	Pineapples
Grapes	Plums
Lychees	Prickly pears
Mangosteens	Rambutans

Vegetables

Beans (butter, flat, green, snake)	Okra
	Radish
Capsicum (bell pepper)	Squash
	Sugar-snap peas (mangetout)
Chillies	
Chokos	Sweet corn
Cucumbers	Tomatoes
Eggplant	Zucchini

How to tell what's in season

Take a quick glance around the fruit and vegetable section of your supermarket.
• If you notice there's an abundance of one specific group, say mandarins or cauliflowers, or if they are merchandised in bulk bins near the store entrance, that's the best sign.
• If they're on sale or only a couple of dollars per kilo, that's another good indicator.

Source: Sydney Markets website at
https://www.sydneymarkets.com.au

Fairtrade for small farms

Fairtrade is an alternative marketing system designed to give disadvantaged, small-scale farmers a guaranteed price for their products as well as helping to empower them and facilitate decent working conditions. It enables growers and producers in the developing world to operate successfully in the global economy. Coffee is the movement's flagship product, followed by cocoa and tea. In recent years, foods like olive oil, hazelnuts, quinoa and Brazil nuts have entered the Fairtrade market. These foods can sometimes, but not always, cost more than conventional products, but you know that no one is being exploited. Fairtrade regulates the use of its logo, and there are now more than 2500 Fairtrade-certified products. It's not often possible to buy local produce that is Fairtrade but if you're going to buy imported foods, then Fairtrade is the best compromise.

FAIRTRADE
AUSTRALIA
NEW ZEALAND

Rainforest Alliance (merged with UTZ)

Rainforest Alliance focuses on sustainability and how farms are managed. Their standards cover the full range of worker protection: the right to a safe, clean working environment; the right to be paid at least the national minimum wage; dignified housing (including potable water); access to medical care for workers and their families; and access to free education for children. Their aim is to make sure all agricultural workers are well treated. Don't confuse it with organic – it's quite different from organic standards.

Organic certification and practices

No longer confined to health food stores, organic food is growing in popularity and being stocked by local supermarkets. Retail sales of organic produce in Australia are estimated to have increased from $28 million in 1990 to $2.2 billion in 2018–2019 and are growing at the rate of 25 per cent each year. In the UK and Europe, the organic movement is huge: the UK market alone is valued at over £2 billion due to past food scares such as mad cow disease and concern over genetically modified (GM) products.

Organic produce is not limited to fruit and vegetables. Organic meat, chicken, eggs and dairy products come from animals that have not been given antibiotics or growth hormones and graze on land

coffee, tea, cocoa and many spices. Freight by air is costly in terms of carbon emissions per tonne, but sea transport is relatively efficient. The electricity required for refrigeration adds to this impact, but then the ability of refrigeration to prevent food wastage could have a more positive effect on the environment overall. And it seems using your car to do the grocery shopping is more costly than all the transport used within the distribution system to get the produce to the point of sale.

that is free of synthetic agricultural chemicals such as herbicides. Even baby food, chocolate, beauty products, shampoo and wines are now on the shelves in organic form.

Organic farming is not simply farming without chemical fertilisers and insect spraying. It's the whole way a farm is managed so it's sustainable and in harmony with its environment. It aims to:

· Improve the fertility and level of organic matter in the soil (the soil is everything!)
· Prevent soil erosion
· Allow crops to grow at a natural pace, not force them with fertilisers
· Use natural farming cycles
· Conserve energy and water
· Provide biodiversity for the farm and its surrounds

A certified organic product in Australia is therefore guaranteed to be free-range, non-GMO, pasture-fed, water efficient and biodiversity friendly, as well as being free from synthetic pesticides, herbicides, hormones and antibiotics.

This means no caged chickens and no sow stalls. Animals must be given a quality of life that allows them to perform natural social and physical functions. Live export is also prohibited under organically certified operations.

How do you know it's organic?

Don't be taken in by 'greenwashing', where companies try to trick you with copycat logos or similar wording such as 'organic certified', not 'certified organic'.

Don't just buy anything labelled 'biodynamic' or 'organic' or 'free-range'. Look for the logo of one of the organic or biodynamic organisations that says 'certified organic', such as those below. This acts as a guarantee that the producer's farms or processors are inspected at least once a year, with random audits also made.

In Australia, these organic or biodynamic organisations are:

· Aus-Qual
· Australian Certified Organic (ACO)
· Bio-Dynamic Research Institute (BDRI or Demeter)
· National Association of Sustainable Agriculture Australia (NASAA)
· Organic Food Chain (OFC)

In the USA, look for the National Organic Program (NOP), regulated by the US Department of Agriculture.

In Australia, certified organic food and drink must contain a minimum of 95 per cent certified organic ingredients.

Qualifications for organics

In Australia, there are two levels of certification:

Fully organic

This is the highest grade and applies to foods produced on land that has been farmed using organic practices for at least three years. No artificial fertilisers or chemicals such as pesticides or fumigants are used. Organic methods like crop rotation, the use of compost or animal manure for fertiliser, the growing of nitrogen-carrying legumes and the addition of mineral-bearing rocks are relied on to maintain the soil. Insects, weeds and other pests are controlled by biological methods.

In conversion

This applies to farms under conversion where organic methods are practised and can be verified for the past year, but not all requirements have been met. For example, some synthetic products may have been used on the land in the past three years.

Is it more nutritious?

Vitamin and mineral levels in organic produce are similar to standard produce. So while organic produce may be free of or lower in pesticides, it is not necessarily higher in nutrients. Many people believe that organic foods have a better taste and flavour, even though they don't always look as attractive and blemish-free as conventionally produced foods.

The National Residue Survey, run by the Australian government's Department of Agriculture, of the pesticide residue of ordinary local produce consistently shows that the vast majority of non-organic foods have no detectable chemical residue, and the few samples that do have a trace of residue are well within safety limits. However, buying organic is definitely a vote for a better type of agriculture.

You don't have to buy organic to have a nutritious diet. Because Australian standard produce is already quite low in residues, you'll be eating well if you buy regular fruit and vegetables. Just try to eat a wide variety of different types, which will minimise the likelihood of residues – and don't forget that simply washing or peeling produce will also reduce residues.

Pesticides and food irradiation

Pesticide residues in fruit and vegetables

In order to grow fruit efficiently in serious quantities, farmers need to control pests, diseases and weeds that would otherwise ruin their crop. The timely and controlled use of pesticides is one way that helps them provide us with good food week after week.

In agriculture, the term 'residues' is generally used to describe the small amounts of agricultural fertilisers and pesticides and veterinary medicines, or their breakdown products, that remain in or on an agricultural product.

Each year, the foods tested are:
- Meat (such as cattle, pigs, sheep, goats, poultry, kangaroo)
- Honey
- Fish, both aquaculture and wild caught
- Grains (such as wheat, barley, oat, maize, sorghum, triticale)
- Pulses (such as chickpea, cow pea, pigeon pea, field pea, vetch)
- Oilseeds (such as canola or sunflower)
- Horticulture (such as apples, pears, citrus, almonds and macadamias)

Sources of residue include:
- Antibiotics used to control bacterial diseases in animals
- Anthelmintics used to control internal parasites in animals
- Fungicides used to control diseases in plants and plant products
- Insecticides used to control insect pests in crops, protect stored grain and control external parasites on animals
- Herbicides used to control weeds in crops
- Fumigants used to protect grain and sterilise soil, sheds and bee hives

In the broader context, residue can be defined as a 'contaminant' and can also be:
- Heavy metal (e.g. mercury, cadmium, lead)
- Naturally occurring mycotoxin (toxin produced by certain fungi)
- Micro-organisms

All of these may be present in food, either through natural circumstances or as a consequence of agricultural activities.

As already indicated, the National Residue Survey, which the Department of Agriculture has carried out every year since 1992 in Australia, shows that almost all of the produce we eat is 'clean'. This survey is an essential part of Australia's system for monitoring the levels of pesticides and veterinary medicine residues in our food supply. In 2016–2017, the overall compliance rate with Australian standards was excellent at 99.2 per cent.

For example, during 2016–2017, over 9000 samples of different types of fresh fruit and vegetables were tested and analysed for a range of pesticide residues and contaminants. Pesticide residues were either absent or within the maximum limit for 99 per cent of the samples. This is really good agricultural practice at work. At 87 per cent, almonds were the worst offender.

For animal products, over 9600 samples were collected and analysed. Again, there was a high level of compliance – over 99 per cent. Random monitoring results for 2016–2017 in poultry showed 100 per cent compliance.

Residue and the Dirty Dozen

In the absence of Australian figures, I've gone to US publications and unearthed this popular one called the Dirty Dozen.

For its 2018 list of the 'Dirty Dozen', the US Environmental Working Group singled out produce with the highest loads of pesticide residues. Each of these foods tested positive for a number of different pesticide residues and contained higher concentrations of pesticides than other produce.

In descending order, this list includes strawberries, spinach, nectarines, apples, grapes, peaches, cherries, pears, tomatoes, celery, potatoes and capsicums.

In contrast, there are 15 types of produce that are least likely to contain pesticide residues: avocado, sweet corn, pineapple, cabbage, onions, frozen sweet pea, papaya, asparagus, mango, eggplant, honeydew, kiwifruit, rockmelon, cauliflower and broccoli.

Irradiation

Irradiation uses ionising energy to help preserve fruit and vegetables by killing pests and bacteria and slowing down the ageing process. Food is exposed to gamma rays from a radioactive source such as Cobalt-60 inside a protected chamber. The gamma rays pass straight through food (just like X-rays), destroying some or all of the organisms that cause it to spoil.

Food irradiation, sometimes called 'cold pasteurisation', has been studied for more than 50 years. NASA first started using irradiation to sterilise meat for astronauts to eat in space way back in the 1970s, and the process is still used by NASA today.

Irradiation is approved for use in over 40

countries to:
- Stop sprouting of potatoes, onion and garlic
- Delay the ripening of tropical fruit
- Kill insects in wheat, flour and fruit
- Eliminate harmful bacteria in food (similar to pasteurisation of milk)
- Reduce the spoilage of highly perishable fish and shellfish
- Replace fumigation with harmful chemicals like ethylene oxide, propylene oxide, phosphine and methyl bromide

Irradiation in Australia

Irradiation was approved in Australia and New Zealand in 1999. Despite its myriad applications, irradiation is still a contentious issue. The number of irradiated foods on our shelves is extremely low, as is the case overseas. In Australia and New Zealand, herbs and spices, herbal infusions, and some fruits and vegetables – including apples, blueberries, cherries, lychee, mangoes, tomatoes and zucchinis – can be irradiated but rarely are.

Is it safe?

Expert committees within the United Nations, USA, UK and Australia have established a safe maximum

Irradiation pros and cons

Irradiation benefits
- Replacement of potentially harmful chemical pesticides; beneficial for exports to countries where fumigants are not permitted
- Less wastage and longer life for some fresh produce
- Delay of sprouting and ripening
- Reduction of dangerous bacteria in poultry and seafood

Irradiation risks
- Possible as yet unknown dangers
- Some loss of nutritional value (as with other forms of processing)
- Taste and texture can be affected
- Safety hazards of the radiation source, e.g. during its transportation
- Problems disposing of the spent cobalt source
- Safety of workers in irradiation plant
- Strains of bacteria may develop resistance to irradiation (like insects do to pesticides)

Hormones and GM foods

Some of the panic around hormones was fed by the widely held belief that girls were maturing earlier due to the added hormones in chicken. Shoppers now realise that the practice of feeding hormones to chickens was banned in Australia in the 1960s.

The National Residue Survey backs this up. Their annual tests indicate that to date no residues have ever been detected in chicken. For instance, the random monitoring program results for 2016–2017 for poultry showed 100 per cent compliance – so any chicken you buy will therefore be free from these hormones.

Hormones are often confused with antimicrobials, which are given to animals to enhance digestion and kill off any 'bad' bacteria that would otherwise cause disease. All of these antimicrobials are assessed and approved before use, and only those that are not absorbed from the gut are allowed to be used. So, you can buy your chicken with confidence.

However, you may have noticed that the major supermarket chains in Australia are now promoting chicken and beef that is 'hormone free, antibiotic free and free range or grass-fed'. It seems there is now a groundswell of public opinion that favours food that hasn't been 'enhanced' in some artificial way.

GM crops such as cotton and canola

Genetically modified (GM) foods have been altered using a process that involves taking genes from the cells of one plant, animal or microbe and inserting them into another organism to give it a desired characteristic or function. This process has been used in the pharmaceutical industry to produce synthetic insulin and commercial quantities of other drugs. In agriculture, it has been used to produce resistance to insect attack in corn, potato and cotton, and herbicide resistance in soybeans, corn, cotton and canola.

Genetic modifications to food allow producers to use plant strains with resistance to insects and herbicides, so farmers don't have to spray as much to kill weeds or slow insect attack, which results in fewer chemicals that could otherwise end up in our food.

GM yeasts and bacteria in the cheese and wine industries have been used for some years, and, more recently, GM cottonseed, safflower, soybeans, canola, corn, potatoes and sugar beet have also been approved in Australia and New Zealand. Currently no GM fresh fruit, non-starchy vegetables or meat are permitted, though meat from livestock fed GM stock food is not regarded as GM meat.

dose of irradiation, a level at which it presents no toxicological hazard and introduces no special nutritional or microbiological problems.

Irradiation can affect levels of vitamins B1, B6, C, E, folate and fatty acids, while other vitamins, proteins, carbohydrates and minerals suffer little damage. However, remember that all processing will reduce these sensitive vitamins to some degree – drying fruit causes a drop in vitamin C, while pasteurisation of milk reduces a fraction of milk's B vitamins.

How can you tell if a food is irradiated?

All irradiated foods must be labelled as 'Irradiated' or 'Treated with ionising radiation' so consumers are able to choose whether or not to buy them.

Edible weeds (wild food) and foraging

Humans have always foraged for foods but our current generation has lost the skill of finding those wild and unwanted things. Our forebears in the 1930s and 1940s had such a skill and foraged for mulberries, blackberries, nasturtium leaves, purslane, wild fennel, wild figs, watercress, samphire, wood sorrel and stinging nettle. With increasing urbanisation and our reliance on supermarkets, this knowledge has all but disappeared. Fortunately, now it's undergoing a revival and you can learn more here.

Foraging is a way of life

Many cultures around the globe practise foraging for both food and medicine. Here are some examples:

- Collecting wild mushrooms in the forest that pop up after rain. (Note: don't attempt this yourself unless you are absolutely sure you're picking the right mushrooms as there are deaths every year from people eating the wrong ones!)
- Women in villages in Greece picking 'horta' or wild greens each spring.
- Picking fresh fronds of wild fennel (*Foeniculum vulgare*), with its liquorice overtones, found growing around old railway tracks or vacant blocks.
- Common mallow was once a 'cure all' of medieval herbal medicine. It was used to treat many conditions from stomach ache to problems during childbirth. In Britain and Ireland, the plant has been used as a laxative, to cleanse the liver, to cure blood poisoning, and to treat urinary problems, rheumatism, heartburn, coughs and cuts.

5 popular wild greens

Dandelion

It's a handy skill to be able to differentiate dandelion (*Taraxacum officinale*) from its look-alikes and pick the fresh young leaves for a salad. Dandelion is the 'king of detox weeds' and a well-documented detoxification herb, with a long history of use by many different cultures.

Pigface

Pigface (*Carpobrotus*) is a juicy succulent with a pretty pink flower that is a common groundcover. Introduced as an ornamental plant for erosion control, it has now taken over sandy dunes; it is highly drought, wind

and salt-spray resistant. Every part of this plant is edible, eaten raw or cooked. Even its water! Squeeze the bottom of the leaves to collect the juice, seeds and the fruit. The flesh tends to have a slightly gelatinous texture similar to that of a kiwifruit or strawberry. It is also great in a chutney or pickle.

Warrigal greens

Warrigal greens (*Tetragonia tetragonoides*) would have saved the early British settlers from scurvy but they didn't know about it or refused to eat it. It makes a nice green veg but has not much taste. It's best to pick the younger leaves to use as a substitute for English spinach.

Farmer's friend

The young yellowish flower head of farmer's friend (*Bidens pilosa*) is edible and has a pleasant tang to it. I'd love it if we all ate it before it matured into those awful stick-onto-everything long brown seeds – then we'd be ridding the outdoors of something definitely wild and unwanted.

African olive tree

You can often spy this tall olive tree (*Olea europaea* sub spp. *cuspidata*) somehow managing to grow in the crevice of a stony outcrop. With its longish silvery leaves, it looks strong and attractive. It bears a black olive fruit that has a large pip but not much flesh. It is rather bitter in taste too, as are regular fresh olives.

Other wild foods include:
- Common purslane (*Portulaca oleracea*)
- Chickweed (*Stellaria media*)
- Wild fennel (*Foeniculum vulgare*)
- Wood sorrel (oxalis) (Note: varieties of fennel, sorrel and purslane have high concentrations of oxalic acid, which has been linked to kidney stones and is poisonous in large amounts.)
- Nettle (*Urtica urens*)
- Mallow (*Malva*)
- Wild brassica (*Brassica*)

Golden rules of foraging

Diego Bonetto, a professional forager with more than 20 years' experience, has three golden rules for when you're out foraging:

1. Know your local area, so you know what grows where each year (and whether they've been sprayed or if it's likely that a dog has wee'd on them).
2. Be sure you know what you're picking. If you're unsure, don't eat it.
3. Don't harvest the whole lot. Leave some for the next season or for someone else.

Source: Diego Bonetto from https://www.diegobonetto.com/blog/why-foraging

With their fresh and free flavour, edible weeds can make a delicious addition to your diet. They are definitely not 'unwanted'. Many edible weeds are actually higher in important vitamins (e.g. beta-carotene), minerals (potassium) and phytonutrients (polyphenols) than cultivated vegetables, which have been bred for less bitterness, greater yield, ease of transport and bigger leaves – and not nutrition.

Food scares

Listeria

Listeria is an illness usually caused by eating foods contaminated by the bacteria *Listeria monocytogenes*. For healthy people, an infection of Listeria (also known as listeriosis) usually causes only mild illness. However, during pregnancy, it can lead to serious illness or even miscarriage. And in newborns it's a deadly illness. It's also serious for people over 70 or those with suppressed immune systems who cannot fight off infections.

Listeria can be picked up by eating contaminated food. So during pregnancy, it's crucial to avoid eating any suspect food. Listeria bacteria are found widely in nature but they can be in higher concentrations in things such as pre-prepared foods, raw foods or cooked foods that have been kept for some time after they have cooled down. Hence all the warnings that pregnant women face.

How to avoid Listeria

You can take precautions to avoid Listeria by:
- Eating only freshly prepared and well-washed food
- Following good food hygiene such as washing and drying hands
- Reheating foods to 'steaming' hot
- Refrigerating leftovers immediately and not keeping them any longer than a day
- Buying from places that look clean, have a high turnover and/or make foods to order (i.e. not selling sandwiches that have been made up hours before)

High-risk foods
- Soft cheeses (brie, camembert, ricotta and feta) – hard cheese, cream cheese and cottage cheese are safe if eaten when fresh
- Pâté and cold deli meats such as ham and salami
- Takeaway cooked chicken, particularly cold chicken used in sandwiches
- Raw seafood such as oysters and sashimi
- Smoked seafood (canned is safe)
- Ready-made sandwiches
- Ready-made salads
- Soft-serve ice cream and unpasteurised dairy products
- Fruits and vegetables that are pre-packaged or served from smorgasbords or salad bars

Raw milk

Raw unpasteurised milk is sometimes sold at health food shops 'for cosmetic use' and is sought after by alternative health groups for its 'friendly bacteria' and natural enzymes. You need to weigh up the benefits of raw milk against the risk of disease. In Australia, by law, all milk sold for consumption must be pasteurised. Pasteurisation involves a brief heat treatment that deactivates disease-producing bacteria that could cause tuberculosis (TB) or brucellosis, a related disease. However, it may also deactivate some of the bioactive substances in fresh milk that have health benefits, and it may slightly reduce levels of vitamins.

Weigh this up against the fact that drinking raw milk is a well-documented risk factor for gastrointestinal diseases, because it can contain pathogens such as campylobacter, cryptosporidium, *E. coli* and Listeria.

In Victoria, Australia, the death of a three-year-old boy in 2014 from organ failure caused by drinking raw milk highlights the potential risk around raw milk. Four other children also became seriously ill from drinking the same brand of milk. Three of them developed haemolytic uraemic syndrome, which can lead to kidney failure. The other developed cryptosporidiosis, a parasitic infection associated with gastroenteritis. Milk can become contaminated as soon as it touches the teats of a cow, which are located close to the animal's bowel and are often in contact with faeces.

Mercury in fish

Mercury is used in thermometers, batteries, blood-pressure devices and some dental fillings, but it's the mercury that ends up in fish – one of our healthiest foods – that is the major source of mercury in people's bodies (see also page 69).

Its toxic form, methyl mercury, has been in the news after surveys from the USA reported that approximately 8 per cent of women had blood levels of mercury over the USA's safe reference level. What's worse, women who regularly ate lots of fish had the highest blood levels.

Food authorities have responded by reviewing their guidelines on fish consumption, and they have stressed that there has never been a documented case of mercury poisoning from fish in Australia. Australians are comparatively low consumers of fish, eating on average only one fish or seafood meal a week. Plus the majority of fish has such low levels

There is one group who need to limit fish, but not avoid it completely – women who are pregnant, planning to become pregnant or breastfeeding.

of mercury that it's undetectable. In the Seychelles, where 12 times more fish is eaten than in the USA, there have been no adverse reports.

There is one group who need to *limit* fish, but not avoid it completely – women who are pregnant, planning to become pregnant or breastfeeding. See page 69 for more details.

Aflatoxin

Aflatoxin is a poisonous compound produced by moulds growing on peanuts, wheat, corn and peas when grown or harvested in damp conditions. Aflatoxin can cause liver cancer in animals and has been correlated with liver cancer in humans in Africa and South-East Asia, where exposure to high levels of aflatoxin occurs.

Much has been done to minimise aflatoxin contamination in peanuts. Maximum allowable levels (under 0.015 milligrams per kilogram) are adhered to – affected foods have been withdrawn from sale in instances of contamination.

6   Body matters

Here we dive into diets. Which, if any, would work for you? Why not try exercising and eating right instead; or think about shame-free body zones and intuitive eating?

The healthiest way to lose weight

Ever wondered why there's a fabulous 'new' diet each month that's guaranteed to get rid of unwanted flab? It's because, in the long haul, diets simply don't work. Sure, you can certainly reduce weight on a diet, motivated by the temptation to 'drop a size over the weekend', but once the diet is finished, you go back to your previous eating habits. Because you've been deprived and real food looks so good, you might lash out and overeat. Your weight then zooms back to where it was originally, until you embark on another diet and start the downward cycle again.

This 'yo-yo' style of weight control is considered even unhealthier than the excess weight in the first place. Diets don't re-educate your eating habits, so you revert to your former way of eating once the diet is over. Diets leave you irritable, hungry, sleepless and lacking energy. They are not nutritionally balanced, so can make you constipated and prone to infections. Forget diets – stick to healthy eating instead, with the occasional treat to keep you satisfied.

There are no magic foods, supplements, shakes or diets that will dissolve unwanted fat – not grapefruit, kelp or apple cider vinegar, nor stevia, extra protein or raspberry ketones. Nor can you simply swallow a pill to 'boost your body's metabolism'. I wish I could simply wave a magic wand and make excess weight disappear – but I can't. For those looking to lose weight, nutritionists recommend a steady weight loss of 1 kilogram per week (of body fat, not fluid). It won't be dramatic, but hopefully it will be permanent. Excess weight takes months or even years to accumulate – it is not going to disappear overnight.

8 most common weight-loss traps

Trying to slim down? Watch out for these eight traps that will derail your efforts.

1. Wanting to lose weight too fast
You can shed 2 or 3 kilos in a week on a detox or juice-only fast, but the weight will come straight back on once you resume your normal eating patterns. Slow and steady is what's recommended for permanent weight loss.

2. Eating big after the gym
Don't let yourself think you can tuck into a big feed just because you've done a workout. Your goal is to slightly under-eat so your body is forced to tap into its fat stores.

3. Going vegetarian to save kilojoules
Skipping meat will cut your kilojoule intake but it also cuts out vital nutrients like iron, zinc and vitamin B12, which many women in particular run short on. And it cuts out one of the most filling and satisfying foods for dieters. Don't skip meat just to lose weight.

4. Forgetting that kilojoules count
With all the hype about carbs and keto, it's easy to think that meat, fish, chicken or eggs can be consumed in any quantity without being converted into body fat. The bottom line is that kilojoules do count – if you eat more kilojoules than you burn off, you won't lose that excess fat. You want to create a deficit of energy so your body draws from its fat stores to make up the difference. Exercise and a balanced diet plan that suits you over the long term is the key.

5. Giving up after a binge
Everyone falls off the wagon at some stage! The trick is to pick yourself up and get back on track. A single pig-out isn't the problem. It's when you give up and start a week-long meal marathon that the weight piles

on. In fact, some diets deliberately allow you a small daily 'treat' to prevent that deprived feeling, which I do think is a top idea.

6. Skipping breakfast
Eating a nutritious breakfast 'kickstarts' your metabolism, so that you can burn off fat during the day and not start your day feeling tired or sluggish.

7. Trying *every* new diet you discover
Keto, Paleo, gluten-free, detox, liver cleansing, blood type, Weight Watchers – you've done them all. You lose some weight but it creeps back again. Why? Because you haven't changed your eating habits for the long term.

8. Giving up the carbs
Keto and high-protein diets may have you thinking carbs are automatically bad for you and responsible for obesity, and that you just have to avoid all bread, potatoes, pasta and rice. The reality is that carbs aren't the villain – junk foods are, and they are a combo of starch plus fats plus sugar. Think of doughnuts, iced confections, crisps, desserts and muffins. Choose the healthier wholegrain or high-fibre carbs such as brown rice or grainy bread, but eat smaller portions of them. See the section on carbs on page 8.

New Year's resolutions and why they don't last

We've all done it – sworn that we'll turn over a new leaf and decide to lose those last stubborn kilos, exercise each and every day, quit smoking, give up alcohol and become healthier. Come January, it's a familiar mantra yet it often lasts only a week. And after that, it's all gone – until next year.

Exercise gets dropped first. Why? Because we have to find the time to fit in exercise and that's not always easy. Food is easier, as we all have to eat something – but you need to decide whether it's a tuna salad or fish and chips that you'll be eating.

To work, resolutions need to be positive rather than negative, as well as realistic and specific, and done in baby steps. For example, a goal of 'I'm not going to gain any more weight' just won't work! Framing it more positively is better, e.g. 'I'm going to be a healthy weight'. Better still is a more specific set of baby steps, like 'I'm going to eat healthy foods'; 'I will

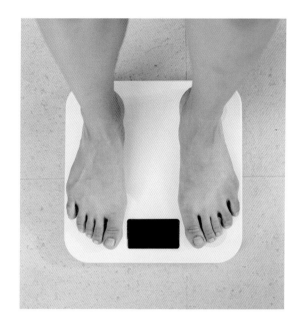

eat mindfully'; 'I will watch my portion size'. Get the picture? These are much more achievable resolutions. In the end, it's about eating better and getting more movement into your day.

Know your own weaknesses
Think over how much you eat or drink and what your 'biggies' are. If you like a large serve of meat or mash or dessert, these are the foods to halve – not the vegetables or salads. These are the most common weaknesses:
- Too much alcohol (which adds kilojoules)
- Too many chocolates, ice cream and other sweet treats after dinner
- Not enough movement or exercise
- Too many eating out occasions (which become opportunities to overeat)
- Too much snacking

Find your weaknesses and tackle them!

Weight loss fundamentals

Finding it hard to shed those extra kilos? Here are 10 tried-and-tested tips to help you to achieve your weight goal happily and healthily.

1. Downsize your portions
You don't need to eat everything on your plate or have second helpings. When you eat out, order two entrées instead of an entrée plus a main, or go for a main plus a salad.

6. Plan meals with nutrition in mind

To lose weight, you want to eat as much nutritious, tasty food for as few kilojoules as possible. This is called a nutrient-dense diet. No food has to be eliminated entirely, but minimal quantities of fats, refined carbohydrates such as white rice and sugar, and alcohol are a must.

7. Never skip meals

Missing meals almost guarantees you'll be hungrier and more likely to overeat later on. This is especially true at breakfast. Research shows breakfast 'switches on' your body's metabolism and prevents you from becoming ravenously hungry by 11 am and tucking into pastries or hot chips. If you can't face food first thing in the morning, make sure you have a sandwich or smoothie mid-morning.

8. Spread your food over the day

Five mini-meals a day or three main meals plus two snacks can help 'turn up' your body's metabolic rate, so you burn off fat faster. Regular meals – small and often – also stop extreme hunger and 'breakthrough' bingeing.

9. Don't eat big late at night

Evenings are inactive times for most people so whatever you eat is more likely to be converted to fat stores. This is one reason why some fasts work. Aim to eat your main meal at lunch or have an early dinner. Allow two hours before sleep.

10. Don't weigh yourself each day

Everyone's weight has daily fluctuations, which reflect fluid balance, bowel movements, monthly periods and recent food intake. Weighing once a week is enough. Or gauge your weight loss by how your clothes fit.

Diet – when you're on a roll

Eliminate the junk

Junk food or extras or treats are a big barrier to sustained weight loss. They are high in bad fats, added sugar and salt, with little fibre or filling power. It's time to ditch fries, pizza, fancy flavoured ice creams, fizzy drinks and heavy desserts like cheesecake and chocolate fudge mousse.

Save alcohol for the weekends

Wine, bubbly, cocktails and mixer drinks all take their toll on weight. They slip down effortlessly but quickly add on kilojoules. Yes, they add to the enjoyment of

2. Make your meals diet-friendly

Substitute diet foods or simply use less whenever it won't affect the food's final taste. Often you'll not notice it. Spread margarine thinly on sandwiches or toast; buy reduced-fat ice cream or gelato instead of full-fat ice cream; use reduced-fat milk; trim fat off meat and remove chicken skin; 'fry' in a non-stick pan brushed or sprayed with oil (cook over moderate not high heat); use less rice or barley and more vegetables.

3. Slow down

Eat slowly and chew each mouthful thoroughly. Stretch each meal out to last 20 minutes so that the brain's appetite-control centre registers you are full. Put your fork or spoon down between mouthfuls.

4. Keep food out of sight

It's easier to avoid overeating if you are not constantly facing temptation.

5. Listen to your body

Eat only when hungry. Stop eating when you're satisfied, not when you're full. Get used to leaving the table feeling comfortable but not 'stuffed full'. The clever Japanese have a word for this – it's called '*hara hachi bu*', which translates to only eating until you're 80 per cent full.

Kilojoules in your favourite drink

Drink	serve	kJ
Sparkling wine	150 ml glass	405
Wine, dry, white or red	150 ml glass	500
RTD Alcopop or Spirit Cooler (Breezer, Cruiser)	300 ml bottle	600
Sherry, dry	50 ml glass	235
Spirits	30 ml shot +	260
(brandy, gin, rum, vodka, whisky)	200 ml glass (with mixers)	560
Beer, full-strength 4–5%	375 ml can	574
Beer, mid-strength 3–4%	375 ml can	485
Cider, dry, 4–5%	200 ml glass	415
Port or fortified wine	60 ml glass	370

Source: Australian Food Composition Database Release 1.0 (2019), plus manufacturer's figures.

an event or get-together, but if you are serious about losing weight, stick to two standard drinks when out, then go on to mineral water or diet drinks. Better still, steer clear of alcohol entirely – it is sometimes the easiest approach. Juices or regular sweetened soft drinks are not an option.

Alcohol is a concentrated form of kilojoules – just one small glass of dry wine or a nip of spirits has 300 kilojoules (70 calories). Plus, many people eat more following a couple of drinks. Don't drink daily, but allow yourself a couple of drinks once or twice a week, say on the weekend.

Steer clear of takeaways

Avoid takeaways, as they are notoriously high in fat and are soft and easy to swallow. Plan ahead so you don't arrive home feeling tired and hungry – that's when you're an easy victim for home delivery. If you have a balanced meal ready, you'll find it easier to eat well. Cooking at home means you can keep food healthy. Spraying oil, using lean meat, being frugal with cream or sour cream, adding plenty of vegetables or salad, which fill you up, are all things fast food places never do.

Keep track of your thoughts and emotions

Make food your friend to make your life less stressful, not the other way around. Food should give you energy, helping you become the best you can. Think of food as fuel and don't get obsessed. Don't 'live to eat' and think of nothing else but your next meal. Don't be gluttonous.

Think longer than three days

Your excess weight won't disappear in three days (despite diet promises), but it will over three weeks. Aim for small, gradual losses, and you won't trigger your body's natural 'famine/starvation' response, which really serves to preserve your fat stores for lean times. This is why ultra-strict or crash diets often leave you fatter than before.

Keep a diary

Make a note of your food, drink and times you eat. Record the place where you eat (e.g. kitchen, cafe) and when you feel most hungry (use a scale from 0 to 10). Analyse your hunger ratings and discover when your hunger is strongest. For instance, I found out that my hunger hits the high scale when I first wake up and then around 11 am. Yet I can go all afternoon without any desire for food. Don't ignore 'unconscious eating' – for example, when cooking, clearing away leftovers or feeding children.

Keep busy

The busier you are, the less time you'll have to be tempted to overeat. Preferably keep away from the kitchen and do something that occupies your hands – sewing, gardening or cleaning, for example.

Manage cravings

When you feel a craving for a particular food, say to yourself, 'I can eat this food but I'll postpone it for 10 minutes.' When the 10 minutes is up, check how strong your craving is. You may have become involved in something else and no longer feel like eating. But if you're still dreaming of, say, chocolate, have one piece. But sit by yourself and place the chocolate on your tongue. Don't chew. Just suck it slowly for as long as you can. Enjoy it. That may be all you need to satisfy your desire.

Don't use food to cope

Don't use food to 'numb' out your feelings and comfort eat. A couple of biscuits or a chocolate bar will not help the situation. If you have learnt to use food as an emotional crutch or tension-buster, it can be unlearnt. Take up yoga or meditation to help yourself unwind without food. Don't let food take on greater meaning.

Don't shop when you are hungry

When you are hungry you put more into your trolley, especially treats that you wouldn't normally buy such as chocolate, chips or ice cream. By buying these foods, you're making it harder to resist them at home. And always shop from a list to ensure that you are making the best choices to help with your goals and stop impulse buys.

Exercise matters for weight loss

It's true – the more kilojoules you can burn off, the easier it is to both lose weight and to prevent becoming overweight. Remember how exercise was once believed to be of limited help for fat loss? It was thought that you needed to exercise strenuously just to burn off a few kilojoules (counters would rank eating one muffin as equal to 60 minutes of jogging). But regular exercise has numerous other benefits. It:

- Increases your resting metabolic rate for 24 hours afterwards, so your body 'revs' at a higher rate (resting metabolism accounts for some 70 per cent of total kilojoule expenditure)
- Has a regulating effect on your appetite
- Helps reduce blood pressure in mildly hypertensive people
- Reduces blood glucose levels and improves insulin resistance
- Helps lower blood cholesterol, including a proportion of LDL cholesterol
- Improves muscles strength and joint flexibility, which helps fight osteoarthritis
- Reduces the risk of bone fractures and osteoporosis in later life (if exercise is weight-bearing)
- Improves sleep patterns
- Can alleviate mild depression and stress

Keeping it off with movement

Here are eight ways to incorporate more activity into your day's routine so you don't store the extra kilojoules as fat (and so you don't have to restrict your eating):

1. Walk wherever you can instead of driving.
2. Climb up stairs instead of taking the escalator.
3. Park furthest away from the car park exit and enjoy the longer walk.
4. Stand up when typing, reading a screen or talking on the phone.
5. Hire an exercise bike and pedal while watching television or reading.
6. Attack the housework with vigour and energy.
7. When you go out, get up and dance.
8. Remember you can exercise in two or three short spells during the day – it doesn't have to be done in one block.

If you are unfit, check with your doctor before undertaking vigorous exercise.

To shed body fat successfully, you need to expend energy in a way that is 'aerobic'.

Rev your body at a higher rate

To shed body fat successfully, you need to expend energy in a way that is 'aerobic' – that is, any activity that increases the oxygen needs of the body, so exercising the heart and lungs. Exercise that uses the large muscles of the body (thighs and torso) over an extended period is a good form of aerobic conditioning. Think running (and any sport that relies on running like soccer or touch football), rowing or cycling.

Find an activity that is convenient, enjoyable and can fit into your weekly schedule. Walking, swimming, bicycling, skipping, jogging or aerobic classes are all good. Start at a low level and build up gradually as you develop stamina and condition. Some people find motivation easier if they join a club or gym; others prefer to set the alarm half an hour earlier, slotting their exercise in first thing in the morning; others like a home workout in front of the TV. Whichever way you choose, make sure you tailor it to suit you. Keep your exercise ambitions modest and realistic. Make it fun or choose a sport that you like, then you're more likely to do it.

It's not exercise; it's just activity

These days, nutritionists talk about being active, not exercising (which can sound too hard and too planned).

Stand up more

Prolonged sitting is slowly killing us. It increases the risk of cancer, cardiovascular disease, and glucose metabolism and blood fat problems, even in those of us who are otherwise fit and not overweight. There's a new saying, 'Sitting is the new smoking', to remind us of the evils of sitting for long periods.

Standing can often be a great energy boost. Standing while working seems to keep you more alert and encourages you to move more; many people have found that when they incorporate more standing into their lives their weight normalises without recourse to dieting. It also helps with back fatigue, which is important if you are seated for most of the day. If you have to talk on the phone, use that time as a mental reminder to stand up. You can easily still talk or write notes from a standing position.

Be a fidget

Non-Exercise Activity Thermogenesis (NEAT) or fidgeting, as it's commonly known, is thought to be even more powerful than moderate exercise in determining how fast you burn kilojoules. So don't just sit there – wiggle, wriggle, squirm and jiggle those feet as often as you like.

Ponder this: *Any* exercise is better than none at all.

Gadgets get physical

Today we have a myriad gadgets that eliminate the need to move – remotes or your voice can turn on the TV, the garage door, airconditioner, fans, window shutters, awnings, heaters, and even move the curtains on their track.

We have battery-powered lawnmowers, garden trimmers (whipper-snippers), chainsaws, blowers and hedgers that take much of the hard work of days gone by out of gardening. We drive our car to the local car wash rather than wash it ourselves by hand.

Technology has reduced the amount of 'moving' in our lives. It's great for creature comfort, but we have become couch potatoes! Then we wonder why there's an obesity problem. Change the way you view these 'chores' and you'll suddenly see them as 'opportunities' to exercise.

Staying slim for life and keeping it off

Here are my fave seven hacks to boost your metabolism, burn more energy and prevent you from gaining weight in the first place. I like to think of them as prevention strategies for the long haul. Prevention is better than cure!

1. Serve main meals on a small side plate

This simple trick will force you to serve less without effort and still feel as if you are eating enough. Remember to eat slowly, chew well and pause often so your stomach has time to signal your brain when it's 'had enough'. Sit down to eat and stretch out your meal to last 20 minutes.

2. Drink water

Drink a glass of water before you eat and continue drinking water throughout the meal. This has been proven to reduce the amount you consume by as much as 13 per cent. It's a dead-easy hack.

3. Fill up on salad before your main

Start a meal with the salad to satisfy your appetite and create bulk inside. You can order many interesting salad-based starters at restaurants.

4. Limit liquid kilojoules

The problem with liquids is that we don't eat less to account for their kilojoules so we unconsciously end up consuming more overall. From juice to beer, this applies to anything you drink, really. Chewing an intact whole structure somehow helps you feel fuller sooner – another sound reason to eat whole foods. What to do? Swap juices and fizzy drinks for water. I often say, 'Don't drink juice – eat the fruit whole and drink water.'

5. Rev up the spicy heat

Spicy foods, such as chilli, horseradish, ginger and cayenne pepper, can increase your metabolism by up to 50 per cent after eating. No other change is needed and you'll burn off more. So be liberal with the hot (sriracha/pepper/Tabasco/peri-peri) sauce, chop up hot red chillies to scatter over your food, indulge in a hot curry or serve a fiery salsa alongside your steak.

6. Less alcohol, not zero alcohol

Here's an easy way to cut back on alcohol without missing it – dilute it down. You can still enjoy a drink with friends but you'll be drinking a lot less. Obviously the less alcohol you drink, the easier your fat loss efforts will be. Alcohol is concentrated kilojoules and diverts the body from burning off the fat stores. For instance:

·   Dilute wine with ice or sparkling water; at 14 per cent alcohol, wine is too concentrated on its own
·   Order light beer instead of full-strength
·   Have a half-nip instead of a full one; top up with soda water or a diet drink
·   Steer clear of cocktails, which are hard to modify to be lighter
·   Swap to sugar-free diet drinks or sparkling mineral water

> Alcohol is concentrated kilojoules and diverts the body from burning off the fat stores.

7. Close the kitchen between meals

Have a rule that you're not allowed into the kitchen except at meal times. This is a handy trick to prevent mindless snacking between meals. Allow yourself water, tea and perhaps a piece of fruit or raw vegetables if you can't make it to the next meal.

Cutting carbs for weight loss

Carbs – cut down, don't cut out!

There's no need to cut out *all* carbs, despite the hype of the keto or Paleo diets. Carbs – the right types – are an important nutrient in a healthy, balanced diet. You need some, not lots. These five points offer a sound lower-carb approach:

1. Avoid the 'junk' carbs like soft drinks, lollies, chips, muffins and biscuits.
2. Swap your breakfast cereal for one made from oats (muesli or porridge), whole wheat (wheat flakes) or bran (All-Bran or bran flakes). A bowl at breakfast is convenient and will keep your bowels working and your microbiome healthy.
3. Opt for whole grains in the bread you regularly buy. If it's white, it's not as filling or nutritious as a grainy loaf or chewy wholemeal bread. Don't give up all bread. One or two slices a day of a decent slow-digesting bread will keep you full and stop you snacking between meals.
4. Check how much potato and rice you serve up for dinner. One medium potato or half a cup of rice will balance your meal without overloading you with carbs. Add plenty of non-starchy vegetables to bulk out the meal. Broccoli, zucchini, spinach, asparagus and green beans are filling and nutritious for very few kilojoules. Some vegetables contain higher carbohydrate values but are still nutritious. Just have a small serve of pumpkin, carrots, corn and peas.
5. Don't give up fruit: include two pieces a day. Skip juice, which has had its fibre removed and is easy to over-consume.

Lower-carb, not no-carbs

From bread to crackers, low-carb foods are all the go at the moment. Here are the ones that are worth it and the ones to say no to.

Lower-carb breads

Whether you're following a keto diet or just want to reduce your carbs, bread is the one food that most people find hard to live without. Bread has been under attack thanks to the grain-free diets beloved by 'Paleo Passionates' as well as the ever-increasing trend away from gluten, the main protein of basic wheat flour.

Most breads have around 40 per cent carb but you can buy lower-carb breads that come in at 30 per cent, which works out to be 75 per cent of the carb content in the original bread. Or, turning it around, as marketing-speak does, this means 25 per cent less carbs.

Why we're getting heavier

We live in an 'obesogenic world' where everything is contrived to make you put on weight. Don't fall into this trap. Notice what has changed around you over the past 20 years:

- We have more labour-saving gadgets like remotes and smart speakers
- We do less daily exercise
- We drive everywhere in the car
- We walk and cycle less and play outdoors less due to safety worries
- We spend our free time in front of screens – laptops, TVs, tablets, smartphones or games – so have a low energy expenditure (essentially we are sitting)
- We do less manual work
- We pay others to do the manual work our parents did, like mowing the lawn, weeding, pruning, cleaning, window washing
- There has been a decline in the cooking skills needed to create healthy meals
- Our portion sizes have got bigger
- We eat more junk, like muffins, chips and doughnuts
- There are more food outlets, coffee carts and vending machines to tempt us
- High-sugar, nutrient-poor drinks, fatty takeaways and easy home meal delivery services (such as Uber Eats) are aggressively marketed
- We don't get enough sleep so we seek to overcome fatigue and boost our mental alertness via food and drink of some kind. What's more, being tired means we lack the energy and motivation for physical activity.

Obesity is affecting more and more Australians. Latest figures say that 63 per cent of Aussie adults are overweight while 37 per cent are clinically obese (morbidly overweight). There are debates and arguments over the precise cause but I really believe you can't pick just one. They are many and varied and will differ for each person. And no, it's not just sugar.

Surprisingly you'll also find some low-carb loaves with less than 10 per cent carbs, but they are dark in colour and don't toast well.

How do they lower the carbs? It's simple: they use less flour and more seeds! They bake with things like almond meal, ground linseed (flaxseeds), sunflower seeds, soy protein, kibbled soy, lupin protein, pea protein and whey protein. And often the weight of a slice is smaller, so you're getting less bread.

Most of these breads end up being higher in protein, higher in fibre, with a lower GI, which will be of interest to people with diabetes. They have an appetising aroma and pleasant bite. They toast nicely and keep well in the plastic bag.

But remember: you can't eat twice as much. You can only eat 25 per cent more, which is another quarter of a slice more – hardly huge!

Brands: Bodhi's Hi Protein Low Carbs, Helga's Lower Carb Wholemeal & Seed, Aldi 85% Lower Carb, Herman Brot Low Carb Bread, Protein Bread

Lower-carb potatoes

You may spy a bag of these lower-carb golden-cream potatoes at your supermarket. At 9 per cent carbs, they have less carb than the average of 13 per cent carbs for other types of potatoes. They're even lower than the washed baby potatoes or mini round white potatoes that we once called 'chats'. But it's not a huge saving.

The lower-carb varieties usually come from a potato variety that evolved out of a natural cross-pollination without any genetic modification. They were first discovered when growers noticed that a couple of varieties had a naturally lower carb content combined with a higher moisture level. I have found they boil, mash and bake nicely – quite the all-rounder – which is good news.

Overall they are only 25 per cent lower in carbs (even though at times they may be lower than this but this is not claimed). Remember that they are not carb-free so you can't eat them as if there was nothing there. A serve of two potatoes gives you around 11 grams of starchy carbs and 260 kilojoules (62 calories) and needs to be counted.

Yes they cost more per kilo, but it's not a hefty increase. A 750 gram bag costs you $2.50, which is $3.33 per kilo.

Brand: Spud Lite

High-fibre pulse pasta

Pasta has re-invented itself after years of trying to get it right with wholemeal pasta, oat pasta or any sort of high-fibre pasta – often dark and inedible. Made from pulses and no durum wheat, pulse pasta is high in protein and fibre with reduced carbs. It has no added salt, is tasty and filling, with five Health Stars.

Brand: San Remo, Barilla

Konjac (shirataki) noodles

These noodles taste just like those bean-thread cellophane noodles that you buy in Asian grocery stores. Thin, clear, gel-like and completely tasteless! They need lots of flavour added from garlic, fresh mint or basil, chilli, meat or fish, and lime juice and other ingredients.

Anywhere you use cellophane noodles you can easily substitute konjac noodles. They're sensational in an Asian-style salad. They are fine added to a clear soup or to throw in a stir-fry at the end, but I doubt they'd hold up to a gutsy dish of meatballs.

If you crave noodles but need to lose weight, these are perfect for you. Just don't expect them to work in the same way as your usual spaghetti or linguine. Think of them more as a replacement for thin, translucent Asian noodles and you won't be disappointed.

Konjac noodles *are* everything they claim – they have no fat, no carbs, no protein, just fibre. And only a tiny 44 kilojoules (10 calories) per 100 grams. They're not made from a grain, so there's no gluten.

Thanks to konjac's composition, it has 4 per cent fibre, which is twice as much fibre as regular pasta and is on par with wholemeal pasta at 5 per cent. In contrast, boiled cellophane noodles supply around 20 per cent carbs, 365 kilojoules (87 calories) per 100 grams and little fibre.

Brands: Chang's Super Lo-Cal Wok-Ready Noodles, Slim Pasta, D'Lite, Food Slendier

Diet trends

I have put myself on some of these diet plans for a week to see how bearable they are and whether I could lose weight on them. Here's what I found:

The Paleo diet

'Paleo' is short for the Paleolithic era, which is the time from two million years ago up until approximately 10,000 years ago, when agriculture and village life began. Also known as the caveman diet, hunter-gatherer diet or the primal diet, it's a diet with a huge following, many of whom were introduced to it via a gym program called CrossFit.

What's removed

All those foods that came into our food supply in a big way after the Agricultural Revolution:
- Grains (e.g. wheat, barley, rye, oats)
- Legumes (e.g. chickpeas, lentils, peanuts)
- Dairy
- Refined sugar (although honey is okay)
- Refined oils
- Potatoes (I'm not sure why, as tomatoes and capsicum, from the same botanic family, are allowed)
- Added salt

What you can eat

Guiding rule: 'Anything that you can catch, fish, pull out of the ground or pick off a tree':
- Meats, grass-fed and fresh, including their internal organs (e.g. liver, kidney, brains, stomach as well as eyes, ears and tails)
- Eggs
- Fish, seafood
- Nuts, seeds
- Vegetables, salads
- Fresh fruit
- Healthy oils that could have been obtained without the use of solvents (e.g. extra-virgin olive oil, extra-virgin coconut oil, macadamia, walnut, flaxseed)

This diet is high in protein, thanks to its high intake of meat, chicken, fish and eggs, and it's much lower in carbohydrates than the average modern diet as it cuts out grains, legumes and sugar, which are the main sources of carbs these days. You're getting your few carbs from starchy root vegetables (sweet potato, other tubers, beetroot) and fresh fruit.

It's high in fibre from all the vegetables and fruit and supplies a higher intake of vitamins, minerals and phytochemicals – there are more phytochemicals in vegetables and fruit, and these are better studied than those in whole grains. You eat plenty of fat, but it's not the bad fats in processed foods or overdoing it with omega-6 from seed oils (you can have too much of a good thing).

According to Dr Loren Cordain, the founder of the Paleo movement and a researcher at Colorado University, it's the discordance between the modern-day diet and our ancestral way of eating that is the underlying cause of ill health and modern illnesses such as type 2 diabetes, heart disease, auto-immune diseases, dementia and certain cancers.

Dr Cordain has the '85:15 Rule', which allows you three non-Paleo meals a week. The essence of a Paleo diet is to 'eat minimally processed foods in the forms that our ancestors would have had sufficient access to', says Dr Cordain.

> You eat plenty of fat, but it's not the bad fats in processed foods.

What you'll eat on the Paleo diet

Breakfast
- 2–3 eggs, poached or pan-fried in oil
- Wilted spinach
- Grilled tomato halves
- Mushrooms

Lunch
- 100 gram can of tuna or salmon or 100 grams cooked chicken
- 1 hard-boiled egg
- Large mixed salad including cucumber, tomato and avocado with a dressing of extra-virgin olive oil and lemon juice

Dinner
- Barbecued steak or fish fillet, about 200 grams raw weight
- Baked kumara chunks or cauliflower mash
- Big serve of stir-fried or steamed vegetables like beans, carrots, broccoli, asparagus, broccolini

Snacks
All meals are taken with a glass of water with a squeeze of lemon.
- Large handful of unsalted roasted macadamias or other nuts

- 1 peach, banana or other fresh fruit
- 1 avocado
- Hard-boiled egg
- Leftover cold meats or chicken

Key food
- Meat

Energy deficit created by:
- Little or no carbs, no alcohol, no junk food

Keto

'Keto' is short for 'ketogenic' and means you're on a diet that forces your body's metabolism to burn stored fat for fuel in place of glucose. And so in theory you shed the weight. In the process, your body produces ketones, the end-products of fat breakdown, which can be used as a temporary fuel by the brain and blood cells.

Originally a ketogenic diet was prescribed to control seizures in children with epilepsy where all other methods and medications had failed. There have been studies that suggest that there may also be some benefits for people with Parkinson's or Alzheimer's diseases.

The downsides

Nutritionally, you're starving your gut bacteria of the resistant starch and other fibres they need. And a healthy gut biome is important for your overall good health.

You'll get unpleasant, if minor, side effects such as tiredness, lethargy, bad breath, constipation and hunger, especially in the first week.

This way of eating is not recommended long term and is not recommended for anyone with diabetes or with existing kidney or liver problems. Studies comparing low-carb with low-fat diets show they both produce the same amount of weight loss over a 12-month period.

What's removed
- All carbs and anything that could break down to glucose, fructose, lactose or similar sugars; this means no bread, rice, potatoes, pasta or cereals – you're aiming to keep your total carbs under 50 grams a day
- No fruit or juice
- No sugar or sugar-containing foods
- No milk or yoghurt (but cheese, cream and butter is okay)
- No junk food that contains carbs (pizza, chips, fries, nuggets)

What you can eat
- Butter, full-fat cream and soft cheeses, ghee
- Fatty meats like fatty pork shoulder, pork belly
- Bacon, salami, sausages, smallgoods
- Chicken with the skin on
- Eggs
- Non-starchy vegetables
- Nuts, seeds
- Oils – olive oil, coconut oil

What you'll eat on the keto diet

Breakfast
- Eggs cooked in butter or ghee and bacon (but no toast)
- Bulletproof coffee (shot of coffee topped up with coconut milk and/or butter)

Lunch
- Cold chicken, tuna or hard-boiled eggs
- Large salad (no bread or roll)

Dinner
- Grilled steak or slices of roast (no roast potato)
- Green vegetables such as green beans and broccoli
- Non-starchy vegetables

Snacks
- Avocado
- Nuts
- Hard-boiled eggs
- Coconut fat by the spoon

Key food
- Bulletproof coffee

Energy deficit created by:
- No carbs, no junk food, no alcohol

Don't forget: not all carbs are 'bad'. There are good carbs – wholegrain foods, legumes, apples, sweet potatoes and other fibre-rich foods – then there are bad carbs, which one should eat sparingly if at all: lollies, alcohol, sugar, processed foods such as cakes, white rice and noodles, etc.

No-sugar diets

No-sugar diets allow nothing sweet. No honey, agave or maple syrup. Nor anything sweetened with intense sweeteners like stevia or aspartame. This is designed intentionally to 're-calibrate your sweet tooth' to a new

set point for the first six weeks. By then, hopefully, you will find normal food tastes way too sweet and unpleasant and this makes cutting back effortless. If you like dessert or baking or always like to finish off a meal with something sweet, then this diet is *not* for you as it would be too restrictive, though the founders would argue that you are exactly the sort of person who should be on the diet.

After six weeks, you can gradually introduce one or two pieces of fruit a day or select foods with no more than 3 to 6 grams of sugars per 100 grams, which doesn't allow you much, really: lime sports water or coconut water has around 4 or 5 grams per 100 millilitres. Don't figure on a vanilla yoghurt (10 grams) or a flavoured lemon mineral water (8 grams) – they're too high in sugars.

What's removed

- Sugar and any food containing sugar, such as biscuits, bars, slices, soft drink, lollies, chocolate, desserts
- Foods sweetened with sugar such as flavoured yoghurts, canned fruit, breakfast cereals
- Foods preserved with sugar such as jams, sauces
- Juice
- Dried fruits like sultanas and raisins
- Prunes
- Diet drinks and diet desserts sweetened with aspartame, stevia or acesulfame K.

What you can eat

You'll be tucking into solid meals of vegetables, nuts, meats, fish, eggs, cheese, whole grains and avocado. There is no packet food nor any processed foods, which eliminates a whole category of what I call 'cheap junk food', which is high in sugar, fat and salt and is the real problem with obesity.

How no-sugar differs from Paleo and keto

No-sugar diets are different to Paleo and keto diets in that they:
- Allow grains, toast, granola
- Allow dairy, such as yoghurt and cheeses
- Allow legumes but in the form of sprouted legumes (ones you soak first, allow to germinate and then heat to dry them off in the oven)
- Are big on nut butters, almond milk
- Let you sweeten with rice malt syrup, glucose and stevia (after the first weeks)
- Are big on coconut fat for everything from greasing baking trays to chocolate nut butter cups

Cutting out sugar removes a whole category of junk food. Think about it for a moment. It's not just the sugar you put in your tea or coffee that's going. It's the doughnut, muffin, choc chip cookie, lollies, chocolate bar, thickshake or ice cream that's suddenly not permitted, whether low-fat or not. Yes, you're removing sugar, but along with it you're removing a heck of a lot of fat and refined starch along with undesirable colours and preservatives. Not forgetting soft drinks, cordial, sports drinks, iced teas and various smoothies as well as sweet alcoholic drinks or cocktails with their juices and syrups.

Yet you can still eat junk while avoiding sugar entirely, by eating potato crisps, corn chips and similar salty snacks (the plain types, not the flavoured ones that often have sugar). Ditto for the vast cheese platters that I see being wolfed down with drinks.

After I tried it for a week, I didn't crave any chocolate or sugar-sweetened foods and found I actually developed a more savoury palate, which was due to having protein-rich meals of meat, fish, chicken with three vegetables and small grains – hearty and filling so I didn't get hungry after dinner.

I was allowed a glass of wine on three days a week on I Quit Sugar (IQS). Alcohol is a huge problem for many dieters and is responsible for much of the excess intake at the moment, not to mention the greasy wedges swallowed when having one too many drinks. The less you have, the easier the weight loss will be.

My verdict? It is a healthy way of eating, as you remove an ingredient that offers no nutrition and it eliminates most of the junk food in modern diets. But it's easy to become obsessive about the smallish amounts of sugar in dairy foods and muesli. If I were to adopt it long term, I'd tweak it a bit by adding in fresh fruit, muesli and prunes after dinner.

On the plus side, it's a good starting point for those who can't exercise much or who want to de-junk their diet – it eliminates a lot of the junk food, which is a step in the right direction.

What you'll eat on a sugar-free diet

Breakfast
- Eggs, poached or fried, on grainy toast (no butter)
- Roasted tomatoes
- Wilted spinach
- Mushrooms
- Tea (no sugar)

Lunch
- Large mixed salad
- Chicken or hard-boiled eggs or canned tuna

Dinner
- Grilled meat/chicken/fish with pesto on top
- Brown rice/quinoa/pasta/potato with skin
- Broccoli, zucchini, carrots, asparagus or other

non-starchy vegetables (large serve to fill you up)
- If hungry later, cheese but no dessert

Snacks
- Hard-boiled egg
- Tub of natural yoghurt
- Handful of mixed nuts
- 100 per cent peanut butter on crackers
- Avocado mashed with lime juice served with vegetable sticks
- Handful of shaved chicken or turkey

Key food
- Rice malt syrup or similar non-sugar sweetener

Energy deficit created by:
- No junk, little or no alcohol, no sugar (carbs)

Raw diet

Raw food includes any unheated food or food cooked at less than 40°C (104°F). The concept behind this idea is that heating food destroys its nutrients and natural enzymes, which is bad because enzymes boost digestion and fight chronic disease. A raw diet may or may not be vegan – there are degrees of 'raw-ness'.

Some rawists eat raw meat (think carpaccio) and raw fish (think sashimi or ceviche) or raw eggs, and some eat unpasteurised dairy (such as raw milk and raw milk yoghurt) – but not in Australia, as unpasteurised milk is not allowed by law.

What's removed
- Anything cooked or heated

What you can eat
- Raw fresh fruit, vegetables, salads
- Sun-dried fruits and vegetables, including dates, that have been dried at low temperatures
- Nuts, seeds
- Sprouted grains and legumes
- Fermented foods such as miso, kimchi, sauerkraut, kefir, kombucha
- Cold-pressed virgin oils such as extra-virgin olive oil, raw coconut oil

If you get tired of raw vegetables, fruit and nuts, there are lots of interesting raw recipes for things such as:
- Zucchini spaghetti (zoodles)
- Cashew cream (vegetarian cream cheese)
- Raw cacao balls (bliss bombs)
- Avocado banana mousse

Is cooking food all that bad?

No. Cooking does reduce levels of heat-sensitive vitamins such as folate and vitamins C and B1. But it also increases digestibility and makes other nutrients more bio-available, such as the lycopene in tomatoes.

In his book *Catching Fire: How Cooking Made Us Human*, Richard Wagman argues that the ability to control fire and cook our food was one of the reasons that the human race evolved as the dominant species on the planet. This is worth pondering.

Cooking also protects you from food poisoning as it kills nasty bacteria. If the food is fresh and you trust

Cooking also protects you from food poisoning.

the source, go ahead and eat it raw. But if not (and this can apply to food sold in remote areas), say no and choose something that's been cooked and is safe.

A 100 per cent raw diet is hard work and not family friendly, as one can't eat with others nor share a meal. When I tried it, I was hungry most days as the fruit and vegetables on their own didn't stick with me for long and I couldn't buy sashimi *every* night of the week. It's best if you can eat at a raw restaurant or start whipping up dishes like cashew cheese, zucchini ribbon salad and avo banana choc mousse, which look more 'normal'. Because of this, many people eat raw during the day but then sit down to a cooked dinner at night. This is called 'Raw Till 4' and is a good compromise.

Is it healthy?

- Partially. Aim for 50 per cent raw. Like everything, it's a balance.
- There is no proof that an all-raw diet prevents disease or fights ill health.
- It certainly boosts your fibre, vitamins and minerals.

What you'll eat on a raw diet

Breakfast
- Blender smoothie with kale, coconut water, banana and berries

Lunch
- Large mixed salad

Dinner
- Zucchini spaghetti

Snacks
- Half an avocado
- Banana
- Any fresh fruit
- Fruit salad
- Handful of mixed raw nuts
- Raw cacao ball
- Avocado banana mousse

Key food
- Salad or spiralised zucchini

Energy deficit created by:
- No processed food, no junk food, not much meat or fish

Gluten-free

Don't believe the tales that, without gluten, your digestion will improve so you'll absorb fewer kilojoules. The gluten-free diet is often used for weight loss, which is why it is listed here. It really shouldn't be. There is no proof that gluten does anything to encourage weight gain. Nor does it interfere with absorption unless you have coeliac disease, dermatitis herpetiformis or non-coeliac gluten sensitivity.

What is gluten?

Gluten is part of a protein found in wheat, rye, oats, barley and triticale (a cereal which is a cross between wheat and rye). When mixed with water, gluten forms an elastic-like substance, which expands when dough rises. It gives structure to bread and cakes and enables pastry and biscuits to 'hold together'. Without gluten, most baked goods do not rise as well and so are flatter and less aerated.

What's removed
- All regular bread, pasta, noodles, breakfast cereals
- Any prepared food made from wheat flour such as muffins, slices and desserts
- Any commercial food containing wheat-based thickeners (check the label – most are now made from tapioca or potato starch)
- Malt powder, barley malt syrup, malted milk drinks
- Any food made from barley flour, rye flour, triticale flour
- Rolled oats, oat bran, oat cereals (while oats themselves are technically gluten free, they are not permitted to be classed as such in Australia and many other countries, as they're generally grown in fields near wheat and transported and stored in

silos alongside wheat, so the cross contamination with wheat means commercial oats contain some gluten; plus, some people with coeliac disease react to the proteins in oats
- Wheatgerm, burghul (bulgur wheat), couscous
- Barley bran, quick-cook barley, pearl barley
- Biscuits and baby rusks
- Sausages, salami and other smallgoods
- Stuffing in poultry
- Meat or fish coated in breadcrumbs or batter (crumbed cutlets, schnitzel, fried fish fillets, fish fingers)
- Soy sauce
- Gravies and meat extracts (with wheat)
- Most beers, malt whisky

What you can eat

You can enjoy a naturally gluten-free way of eating, without all the worry of buying gluten-free breads. Just cook from scratch and base your diet on:
- Fresh meat
- Fresh fish
- Fresh chicken
- Eggs
- Vegetables
- Fruits
- Plain milk, cheeses
- Plain yoghurt, fruit yoghurt (check the label)
- Nuts and seeds

- Potato, sweet potato
- Rice, millet, buckwheat, amaranth and other non-gluten grains
- Pure spices and herbs

What about gluten-free foods?

Despite their 'health halo', gluten-free foods are not healthier alternatives and they often have 'extras' added to their formulation to make up for the gluten that's been removed. They're often rapidly digested, low in fibre and B vitamins, and highly processed. So if you don't need to eat gluten-free, then don't part with your money.

Many celebrities and sports stars swear by a gluten-free diet prior to an event, but remember that gluten-free foods have around the same kilojoules, fat and carbs as regular products. Unlike diet foods, they don't save you anything.

Gluten-free breads and mixes are made using speciality ingredients like fibres such as carboxymethyl cellulose or methyl cellulose, along with stabilising gums such as xanthan or guar, which stop that cakey-ness and minimise the crumbliness.

What you'll eat on a gluten-free diet

Breakfast
- Egg, grilled or poached
- Tomatoes or mushrooms
- Tea, coffee or milk

Lunch
- Stir-fried chicken or pork and vegetables
- Steamed rice
- Tub of fruit salad
- Fruit juice, milk or soy drink (not malted)

Dinner
- Meat, chicken or vegetarian bean curry
- Potato or rice
- Vegetables or salad with oil–vinegar dressing
- Stewed apple with low-fat ice cream (check ingredients)
- Tea, coffee or low-fat milk

Snacks
- Keep a stock of gluten-free breads, muffins and cakes in your fridge or freezer

Energy deficit created by:
- No grains including no breads, cereals, pasta, cakes, muffins and biscuits

'Clean eating' for weight loss

'Clean eating' or 'eating clean' is a marketing term and it means different things to different people – for some, it means 'free from potentially harmful substances and additives', for others, it means 'less processed and more natural', and for others again, it means 'organically grown and good for the environment'. It has no basis in dietary guidelines, food regulations or science, as it's merely a marketing concept.

In essence, clean eating is about eating whole foods or 'real' foods – those that are minimally processed, unrefined and handled ethically, making them as close to their natural form as possible. Think fresh vegetables, fruits, nuts and seeds, fresh fish, whole milk – and any fresh food that is in season.

The eat-clean philosophy says that nutrition is far more important than exercise or genetics in shaping our bodies (something researchers don't agree with).

A clean eating diet is more or less a proxy for the important issues people care about – what's in food, what impact the food has on their health, and how might it affect the environment. It is usually linked to the belief that it's a healthier way of eating – despite the science not always supporting this notion.

And apart from weight loss, you get other supposed benefits: you may feel healthier and have more energy, your eyes may be brighter and more alert, your skin may improve, your teeth and gums may look healthier.

What's removed
- Over-processed foods, especially those based on white flour, salt and sugar
- Artificial sweeteners
- Sugary beverages such as fizzy soft drink and juice
- Alcohol
- Foods with chemical additives like colours, preservatives and flavourings
- Artificial foods such as processed cheese slices, bacon or fake crab
- Energy-dense foods with little nutritional value such as chocolates, chips or sweet biscuits

What you can eat
- Six small meals a day
- Breakfast every day within an hour of getting up

- Lean protein and starchy carbohydrates at every meal
- Two or three servings of healthy fats every day
- Fibre, vitamins, nutrients and enzymes from fresh fruits and vegetables
- Drink 2 to 3 litres of water (8 to 12 cups) every day

What you'll eat on the clean-eating diet

Breakfast
- Fresh berries
- Tub of whole yoghurt
- Water with a squeeze of lemon

Lunch
- Large tossed salad topped with cottage cheese

Dinner
- Fillet of fresh fish, grilled or baked
- Cooked green and orange vegetables such as broccoli, green beans, carrots and pumpkin

Snacks
- Fruit
- Handful of almonds or walnuts

Key food
- Freshly squeezed juice with vegetables

Energy deficit created by:
- No processed food or junk, no alcohol, cutting back on what you eat – control your portions

Intermittent fasting

Fasts have been around for thousands of years. Many religions, from Catholicism to Judaism to Islam, have some type of fasting or self-denial as a normal part of their worship. What it teaches you is that you won't die from a day with no food and that fasting is one way to tame the body and help the mind to focus on the spiritual aspects of life. Obviously there are groups who are exempt from fasting such as the elderly, those who are ill, travelling, pregnant, breastfeeding or menstruating.

Fasting diets

Intermittent fasting (IF for short) is a popular diet trend that seems simple enough: cycle between periods of semi-fasting and normal eating, and you'll gain the benefit of easy weight loss as well as health gains such as improved cholesterol and blood glucose levels; reduced levels of insulin-like growth factor 1 (with a consequent lessening of the risk of cancers and cell proliferation rates); and the switching on of 'repair' genes. It also lacks a set 'diet formula', which is something I like. Here are the three main types of IF and their practicality and supporting evidence.

Alternate Day Fasting (ADF)
ADF involves a 'feed day', where food and fluids are consumed at normal levels, alternated with a 'fast day', when only 25 per cent of an individual's requirement is consumed over a 24-hour period.

5:2
On two non-consecutive days each week, you eat little, cutting your intake to only a quarter of your usual intake, which is roughly 2000 kilojoules (500 calories) for women and 2400 kilojoules (600 calories) for men. To get past the hunger pangs, you can fill up on mineral water, tea, black coffee or raw vegetables.

However, on the non-fast days you are able to to dine out, enjoy the odd piece of cake, or eat junk food, something that's banned on regular diets. You can just live normally, which does have huge appeal. Best part – the diet doesn't last forever!

16:8
16:8 intermittent fasting involves fasting for 16 hours (including the 8 hours when you're asleep) and eating only during an 8-hour window. For instance, you eat only between the hours of 10 am and 6 pm, or noon and 8 pm. It may support weight loss and improve blood sugar, brain function and longevity. During your eating period, you should eat a quality diet and drink calorie-free beverages like water, unsweetened teas and coffee, or diet drinks.

Who would fasting diets suit?
- Anyone like me who hates formal diets with their prescribed meal plans.
- Busy people who want to slip in a 'light' day.
- Foodies and chefs who need to cut back so they can eat big on other days.

Remember that IF could result in 'rebound' overconsumption on unrestricted days, so these diets aren't for those who want rigid control. But at least you'll realise there are options for weight loss that do *not* involve calorie counting or eliminating certain foods.

Mindful eating

Distracted by watching a movie or reading our smartphone, we can mindlessly move our hand from bowl to mouth, not paying attention to the signals of fullness coming from our stomachs. Or not feeling them, as we're eating low-fibre snacks that taste so good and slip down so effortlessly. We keep on eating, unaware of the huge amounts we're putting away. In my opinion, such mindless eating is an oft-overlooked cause of obesity.

The modern food supply encourages us to graze via fast-food drive-ins, vending machines full of junk food, pop-up coffee carts and confectionery counters at every retail outlet. What's more, our modern world actually encourages us to eat while doing other tasks. 'Multi-tasking' has long been a business buzzword, but is often just a euphemism for eating while doing other things. Whether it's popcorn at the cinema, desktop dining while you work, dashboard dining as you drive or dinner in front of the TV, it all leads us to eat more than we need.

Eating with awareness

To help yourself to learn to eat with awareness, try these six simple steps to practise eating mindfully and prevent mindless consumption. Your goal is to be conscious of how you're eating and what your stomach registers. When you're in touch with what is going on inside, you'll know the exact moment you

Why you need to chew

Chewing your food does two things – it automatically slows down your rate of eating, so it helps you stop when you feel you're full. And it means less digestive distress, such as less gas, bloating and bowel irregularities.

Who else loved chewing? Horace Fletcher (1849–1919) did! He was an American health-food faddist of the Victorian era, who used to make his patients chew their food 32 times before they swallowed. He was given the nickname 'The Great Masticator' and was famous for saying 'Nature will castigate those who don't masticate.'

Fletcher argued that his mastication method would increase the amount of strength a person could have while actually decreasing the amount of food that they consumed. His chewing technique became known as 'Fletcherizing' and he claimed it would turn 'a pitiable glutton into an intelligent epicurean'. He also advised against eating before being 'Good and Hungry', or while angry or sad – strong emotions that can interfere with digestion and leave you with digestive upsets.

are physically satisfied rather than over-full or stuffed. It's the best technique for weight control I've seen and works regardless of what sort of diet you're on.

Obviously you can't eat like this for every meal,

every day, but it's very useful to practise on a quiet weekend or when you're on your own. The point is not to suggest all your meals be consumed as meticulously as this. Rather, by following these steps, you may discover things about your own eating habits. I follow these steps and highly recommend this way of eating!

1. Sit down to eat, even if it's only for a snack. Let the food be the sole centre of your attention. Turn the TV or laptop off and don't read.
2. Take two deep breaths before you eat. Pause to reflect on what you're about to eat, being respectful of the dish in front of you and thankful for the food (a little like the old-time tradition of saying grace before eating). This is the best step of these six to practise when eating out or with others.
3. Chew each mouthful thoughtfully, paying attention to the flavours. Put your knife and fork down between bites.
4. Eat slowly. If you know you're a fast eater, try eating with chopsticks or with your non-dominant hand to slow things down.
5. Plate up a standard portion of food.
6. Chew well, appreciate the textures and flavours. Stretch the meal out so it lasts 20 minutes.

Yoga helps
Yoga helps increase the effectiveness of mindfulness in a standard weight-loss program.

Research has found a strong association between yoga practice and mindful eating, but found no association between other types of physical activity, such as walking or running, and mindful eating.

It showed that regular yoga practice helped prevent middle-age spread in normal-weight people and appeared to promote weight loss in those who were overweight.

Shame-free body zones

Tired of always being on a diet? Or of being told that you are 'too fat'? Or of do-gooders asking if you should eat that cake or ice cream or doughnut?

Now it's time to embrace and share your 'flaws' instead of always striving to be perfect (which is never achievable anyway). Today there's a new message of love and body acceptance as an alternative to the stern fad diets of yesteryear.

If you have been yo-yo dieting and spending way too much time thinking about food, this non-diet approach can help you. It aims to help people stop dieting and, instead, enjoy all food and establish a healthy relationship with food and their bodies.

Rate your feeling of hunger from 10 to 0

Listen to your stomach – it is only the size of a clenched fist. It expands as you eat. If you eat slowly and chew well, your stomach will tell you when it's full. Here's how to rate your hunger and fullness and learn when to stop. Give your feelings a number from 10 to 0.

10. I'm ready to burst!
9. I'm absolutely full!
8. I feel like an overstuffed cushion!
7. I'm uncomfortably full.
6. Aaaah. I shouldn't have eaten that last mouthful.
5. I enjoyed that. I feel quite satisfied.
4. What's to eat? I'm peckish.
3. I'm running on empty.
2. Hey there! I'm starving!
1. I'm soooo ravenous.
0. If you don't feed me soon, I'll be too weak to chew!

Health At Every Size
Health At Every Size (HAES) says that traditional interventions such as dieting focus on weight loss as the end goal but do not reliably produce positive health outcomes. Health is a result of behaviours that are independent of body weight, and favouring being thin discriminates against the overweight and the obese.

The HAES concept, while handy for those with diet–binge mentalities, may not be helpful for everyone. How can a person who weighs 150 kilos (330 pounds) be healthy? This philosophy may encourage people to ignore their increasing weight.

The philosophy certainly has it right in the sense that a wide variety of body sizes can still be healthy and that exercise offers so many health benefits, from lowering blood pressure to coping with stress, regardless of whether it has any effect on weight. Regardless, it makes you feel good. Any movement that promotes health is a good thing.

Helping overweight kids

With over 25 per cent of children now overweight, here are 14 top hacks that parents and carers can utilise to help their children eat healthily.

1. Clean up your act
Set a good example – eat well yourself. Research shows that the eating habits of parents are closely related to the weight of their children.

2. Rewards
Don't use food as a reward for good behaviour. There are heaps of non-food things such as books, pens, stickers, clothing or an outing.

3. Meal sizes
Young kids need to eat small serves, and frequently, but that doesn't mean they should graze all day long. Keep meals regular with a small snack in between.

4. Drink more water
Make water the default drink with meals and inbetween. Cordial, fruit juice and soft drink are high in sugar.

5. Respect your child's appetite
Allow them to determine how much they need to eat. By asking them to eat more, they lose the ability to know how much is enough.

6. Limit junk food
Keep it for special occasions or outings.

7. Turn off the TV
The evidence is overwhelming – too much TV helps make our kids unfit! Experts recommend TV viewing should be limited to a maximum of one hour a day. This includes all other screens too.

8. Monitor school food
Find out what foods are available at the school canteen. If there aren't many healthy alternatives, limit meals purchased at school to once a week.

9. Think long term
Don't expect rapid weight loss. It often takes a year for your child's weight to go down as they grow taller.

10. Snack right
Much of the reason for kids' weight problems is that 'snack foods' are not suitable snacks – they're loaded with fat, sugar or salt. Instead, get your kids onto simpler things like dip and carrots, half an avocado, a handful or two of whole nuts (for toddlers over three), a piece of fresh fruit, a hard-boiled egg, toasted fruit loaf, half an English muffin toasted, a crumpet toasted, a mug of vegetable soup, or peanut butter on celery sticks, crackers or rice cakes.

11. Get active
Head outdoors to play footy, go cycling or visit the park – anything to get your kids moving. Have fun!

12. Stick to real foods
Serve up foods that need chewing, are whole foods and are *not* easy to swallow – meats, vegetables, whole grains, fruit, nuts and eggs.

13. Tread carefully
Never make derogatory comments about your child's shape or weight, as this will affect their confidence and self-image. Focus on habits and fitness and things they do regularly.

14. Be positive
There are lots of yummy foods that your child can eat, such as fruit, breads, cereals, yoghurt, meat and eggs. Don't dwell on what they can't eat.

Ways to end food shame

- Don't call individual foods 'good' or 'bad' – labels that don't quite fit, because what really matters is our eating patterns and cultivating a joyful relationship to food. Sometimes it depends on the context too.
- Don't make any critical or potentially humiliating comment about another person's body size or weight.
- Be aware of the unhealthy messaging from the fitness and diet industries. They hope to profit off people (overwhelmingly women) spending their hard-earned money trying to make themselves smaller.
- Be body positive with others, especially your children. Remember, you want the acceptance of all bodies and shapes, regardless of size.
- Eat to nourish your body, not to lose weight and satisfy beauty standards.

Detoxing

First off, let me say that there's really no proof that a detox diet cleans out the body, or that the average person needs to detox at all. The liver and kidneys are highly efficient organs that have evolved to break down and remove toxins from the bloodstream on their own, without the need for a detox. That said, given our over-consumption of processed foods and alcohol, a few days with little food can do us all good – but that's not a formal detox.

You might feel better after detoxing because you've cut out 'junk' and boosted your intake of phytochemicals, fibre and vitamins, but you can achieve this every day by eating a healthy, balanced diet, and not putting yourself through a horrible semi-fast.

A detox is touted to improve a whole range of common conditions such as indigestion, heartburn, poor immunity, fatigue, headaches, allergies, muscle aches, acne, dry skin and eye puffiness. The claims that suck most women in are promises of weight loss, radiant skin and clear eyes.

Detox diets are commonly promoted to 'kickstart' a long-term diet, but they don't re-educate your eating patterns. Once people finish detoxing, most happily go back to their former (unhealthy) way of eating and the weight comes back on.

Many detox diets are simply a healthy but minimalist eating plan.

Many detox diets are simply a healthy but minimalist eating plan, followed for two to 10 days, which for most of us is fine. Others require you to take a number of herbal extracts and supplements, such as digestive bitters, goldenseal and elecampane for the stomach; milk thistle and dandelion for the liver; acidophilus for the intestines; and mild laxatives such as senna, cascara, psyllium, slippery elm, resistant starch, aniseed, liquorice, uva ursi, Irish moss or agar for the colon. There are also many detox kits sold through pharmacies (at great expense) that you can buy before you embark on a torturous 14 days of 'cleansing'.

There's no doubt detoxing is popular. The key appeal is that it's a quick fix – you only have to endure it for a short, finite time. It's also simple: there's no counting kilojoules, and it eliminates all the 'baddies' like alcohol, caffeine, sugar, meat and highly processed foods.

Detoxing reminds me of penance. You 'atone' for your sins of excess, and feel saintly and virtuous. It is also in line with today's additive anxiety, which has seen shoppers shy away from preservatives and chemicals and seek out 'natural', 'biodynamic' and 'organic' foods. This is all supported by clever marketing featuring excited endorsements from movie stars, models and celebrities.

Lemon detox diet

The lemon detox attempts to ride the tail of lemon's long association with weight loss. For 10 days, you don't eat at all, but exist on a sweet lemonade-style drink made with lemon juice, cayenne pepper and a special syrup called the Madal Bal Natural Tree Syrup, an expensive, high-sugar product derived from palm and maple trees. You also get a herbal laxative tea to drink, which further increases weight loss. Even with the sugar from the syrup, your intake is less than 1700 kilojoules (405 calories) a day (when average intake is around 8700 kjilojoules or 2080 calories). This means it's a semi-fast. I don't recommend it, as it teaches you nothing about retraining your eating habits.

Juice-only cleanse

A juice cleanse sounds like the perfect way to 'start your detoxification, flush out toxins, hydrate your cells and leave you feeling better than ever', as many juice-only cleanses declare. But it's really a semi-fast. It can also be part of an intermittent fasting routine, but the juice doesn't fill you up the way solid food can.

During a juice cleanse you drink only juices (ideally made fresh each day in your juicer at home, but you can buy these pre-packaged in bottles) and eat no solid food in order to give your digestive system 'a rest'. You also avoid caffeine, alcohol and sugary drinks.

Ideally you should drink a variety of juices, focusing specifically on those plants traditionally praised by herbalists for their 'cleansing' properties, such as dandelion, cucumber, celery, lime, lemon and other citrus as well as chlorophyll-rich plants like parsley, kale, mint and spinach.

When you're on a cleanse, this usually refers to a period of three to 10 days when your diet consists mainly of juices. It's meant to help you lose weight quickly.

Certain people, including those with eating disorders or type 1 or 2 diabetes, should not embark on a juice-only diet, and really, there is no need for anyone to do so. It's no replacement for eating healthily and in moderation.

'YOU ARE
WHAT
YOU EAT,
SO DON'T
BE FAST,
CHEAP,
EASY OR
FAKE.'

UNKNOWN

7 Smart shopper

Food labelling is a mini-marketing machine that can drive you to make the decision to buy – but there's more to a label than meets the eye.

The 10 basics of a food label

Here is the compulsory information that *must* appear on every food pack sold in Australia and New Zealand.

1. Description or technical name
If the name of the food doesn't make it obvious what its true nature is, there must be a more detailed description that makes it meaningful. Sometimes it's semi-technical and hard to understand.

Remember, this is not the brand. For example, with the flavoured milk drink called Up and Go, you may recognise the brand with its colour and packaging, but its true technical name is 'Formulated Milk Drink'. This has a specification in the food code that allows it to carry added vitamins and minerals beyond the usual ones of calcium or vitamin D that are often added to milk.

2. Net weight
This is the actual weight or volume of the food and does not include the weight of any packaging. In canned foods, it includes any liquid – it is not the drained weight.

3. Date mark
This indicates the time of best eating quality by means of a 'Best-before' or 'Use-by' date. Food standards released by the Australian government state that certain foods do not need to have a date mark. These include food that lasts over two years, such as white sugar or flour; individual portions of ice cream, such as ice creams on sticks; whole fresh fruit and vegetables; and sandwiches or filled rolls that are made and sold on the premises in front of the consumer.

4. Ingredient list, including additives
All ingredients must be stated in order from the most to least by ingoing weight. The ingredient in the highest proportion is listed first, followed by the second, the third, and so on. More on this on page 133. Additives are included here by their functional name, say 'preservative', followed by either their chemical name, say 'sodium metabisulphite', or by their code number (e.g. 223).

5. Nutrition information panel
This shows the energy in kilojoules, protein, fat (both the total and saturated), carbohydrate (both total and sugars) and sodium, in an average serving and in 100 grams of the food. Some labels also show fibre, potassium, monounsaturated fat, polyunsaturated fat, trans fat and other biologically active substances depending on whether they make a claim on the front.

6. Allergy warning
The presence of fish, shellfish, peanuts, eggs, milk, tree nuts, sesame, gluten, soybeans, lupins, added sulphite in high concentrations or royal jelly must be declared. You'll usually find it near the list of ingredients to help sufferers. Sometimes the allergens are shown **in bold** in the ingredient list.

7. Name and address
The name and street address of the manufacturer, packer, distributor or importer must be clearly identified for consumers (a PO box is not good enough). A telephone number, website or Facebook page is a nice extra.

8. Country of origin (Australia only)
This lets you know the country or countries in which the food was grown, produced, made or packed. In Australia, if the food is made from imported ingredients or from local and imported ingredients, this must be stated. New Zealand does not require country of origin labelling. If you like to buy Australian

products, here's what you need to know.

- 'Grown in Australia': This is for foods that are 100 per cent Australian, such as lettuces, milk or oranges.
- 'Produced in Australia': This tells you that 100 per cent of the ingredients and all major processing was performed in Australia, for products such as cheese, yoghurt or cereals.
- 'Made in Australia': This tells you that all major processing happened in Australia and lists the percentage of Australian ingredients via a gold-and-green ruler plus a kangaroo symbol – for instance, 'Made in Australia from more than 95 per cent Australian ingredients'.
- 'Packed in Australia': This tells you that the produce may have been grown elsewhere but has been packed or canned in Australia.

9. Storage instructions
For best quality and safe eating, follow the instructions on the label. For example, 'Keep refrigerated below 4°C', or 'Store in a cool dry place'.

10. Lot or batch number
Identification of the lot or batch number is required so a product can be recalled in the event of an accidental error.

Source: FSANZ website at www.foodstandards.gov.au

Decoding the nutrition panel

Once you know how to decode it, the nutrition information panel (or NIP) is an invaluable aid to assess any food and figure out how healthy it is. It's also a great way to double-check any nutrition claim on the front, such as 'high in protein' or 'no added sugar'. I use it all the time.

Nutrition figures are presented in a standard table format. At a minimum, this always shows three columns:

1. The first column lists the energy in kilojoules and sometimes in calories, followed by the four nutrients: protein, fat plus saturated fat, carbohydrate plus sugars, and sodium.
2. The second column shows the quantities of these components per serving.
3. The third column gives you the quantities per 100 grams of the food, or 100 millilitres if it's liquid.

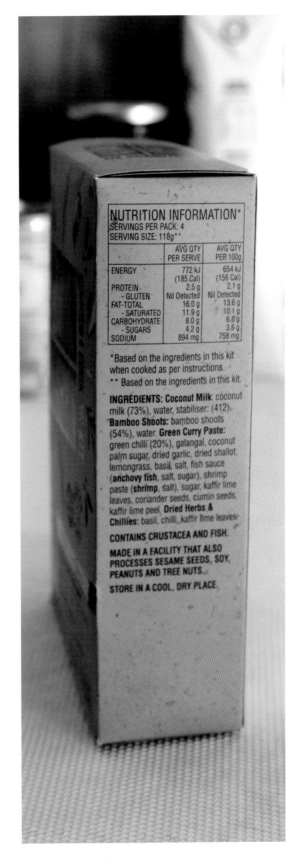

Serving size

At the top of the NIP, you'll spot the serving size, which must be defined, such as '75 grams' or '½ cup' and the number of servings in a whole package. This is often not the portion you eat but a weight or volume that's set by the manufacturer. Generally it represents the size likely to be eaten by their intended audience.

Per serving or per 100 grams – which to use?

Per serving column

The 'per serving' column is handy for estimating how much you should eat. You can quickly see how much fat, fibre, sodium or kilojoules you're getting from one serving. This may influence how much or how little you want to eat of it.

Per 100 g column

The 'Quantity per 100 g' (or 100 ml if liquid) information is handy to compare similar products with each other. For instance, which stock has the least sodium? Which cereal has the most fibre? Which yoghurt has the least sugar? I find it's the best way to compare different brands and to find the one with the lowest kilojoules, the lowest content of sugars, and the lowest sodium.

The figures in the 'Quantity per 100 g' column are the same as percentages. For example, if 20 grams of fat is listed in the 'Per 100 g' column, this means that the product contains 20 per cent fat.

Nutrition information panel

Example of a simple nutrition information panel from a can of chickpeas:

Servings per pack: 2 Serving size: 75 g Approx. ½ cup drained	Per serving	Per 100 g
Energy	399 kJ	532 kJ
	103 cals	125 cals
Protein	5.6 g	7.5 g
Fat, total	0.9 g	1.2 g
saturated	0.2 g	0.2 g
Carbohydrate,	13.1 g	17.5 g
total sugars	0.2 g	0.3 g
Sodium	209 mg	279 mg

Displaying calcium or any other nutrient

If the product's packaging makes any other claim, then they must give you extra figures. And the nutrition information panel is where you'll find those bits of additional information. You'll spot them at the end of the table.

For instance, a breakfast cereal may claim to be 'high in fibre' or claim to have 'no added salt'. By reading the panel, you can verify the nutrition number for fibre or sodium, as they must be over or under a set number in order to make the claim in the first place.

Using the recommended dietary intake

Sometimes the panel shows you how their food compares with the suggested intakes of certain nutrients such as folate, vitamin C, calcium, omega-3 or dietary fibre.

If they claim something on the front, companies are required to itemise these additional nutrients. Think of the ones you may have already seen such as cereal with added B vitamins, juices with added vitamin C, plant mylks with extra calcium and vitamin B12. The figure shows you what percentage of the overall day's recommended intake a serving will provide.

For instance, a carton of milk tells you that you'll get 308 milligrams of calcium from a 250 millilitres glass of this milk. For calcium, the recommended dietary intake (RDI) is set at an average of 800 milligrams a day. So 308 divided by 800 gives you 38 per cent of your RDI from one serving. This is a lot, over one-third of your total needs.

Understanding the list of ingredients

The list of ingredients is the most revealing thing on a food label. I use it in conjunction with the NIP to really find out what's what in that food.

Firstly, you have to understand a fundamental – all ingredients must be listed in decreasing order by ingoing weight, from most to least. The first ingredient at the beginning of the list is the largest, followed by the second, the third, and so on, right down to tiny quantities of salt and herbs. Water is listed in its order.

Second, any additives are included here and are listed by their functional name, say 'preservative', followed by either their chemical name, say 'sodium metabisulphite' or by their code number (e.g. 223).

Increasingly these numbers are being shown preceded by the letter 'E' as E numbers, which has been adopted from Europe. So you may also see 'preservative (E223)'.

Pay attention to the first three ingredients

Why three? These three are the 'biggies' and are usually responsible for the overall nutritional value of a food. For example, in a muffin, the first three ingredients are flour, sugar and some type of fat (oil, baker's shortening), which tells you that this is a baked good and is not going to be high in nutrition.

How to interpret an ingredient list

It's easier to use an example. Here is one from a popular breakfast cereal:

Wholegrain wheat (97%), raw sugar, salt, barley malt extract, vitamins (niacin, thiamin, riboflavin, folate), mineral (iron).

From this list of ingredients, you can see that wheat is the first and main ingredient out of nine, with whole grains of wheat making up the bulk at 97 per cent (which is pretty high). Then there's the rest that make up the remaining 3 per cent – a little sugar, a little salt followed by some barley malt extract for flavour. Finally you get down to the minor ingredients, being the four vitamins and iron. You can work this out, as you know that all the ingredients are in decreasing order.

Tip: Anything after salt is usually present in very small quantities.

Tip

If you're starting out, go for the simplest nutrition information panels, often on canned vegetables or generic private-label foods. These give you the bare minimum required and are the easiest to understand.

The first three ingredients of popular products

Fruit yoghurt – milk, cream, milk solids

Whole wheat breakfast biscuits – wholegrain wheat, sugar, salt

Sultana bran breakfast cereal – whole wheat, sultanas, wheat bran

Bran Flakes, All-Bran – whole wheat, wheat bran, sugar

Can of corn niblets – sweet corn, water, salt

Can of tomatoes – tomatoes, tomato juice, food acid (citric acid)

Bottle of tomato pasta sauce – tomatoes, onion, sugar

Can of tomato soup – concentrated tomatoes, sugar, onions

Tomato sauce – tomato puree (water, tomato paste), sugar, salt

Claims on the pack: what the label says versus what it really means

There is a multitude of claims designed to attract your attention (in the less than three seconds as you whiz by) and appeal to whatever is trendy at the moment. From 'high in protein' to 'no added sugar', there are claims on the front of the pack but they can all be verified on the nutrition panel on the back.

While most claims help consumers to interpret technical information, many are easy to misinterpret, misunderstand or simply misread – and lead us to buy a product we otherwise would not have! Read on for help sorting out claims such as 'lite', 'all natural', '97% fat-free', 'no artificial colours', 'no cholesterol', 'high-fibre' or 'no MSG'.

Lite or Light

'Lite' or 'Light' does not always mean that a food is low in kilojoules or fat, as many dieters often believe. Light potato crisps are lightly salted and thinly sliced (but still have about the same amount of fat as ordinary crisps); light beer is lower in alcohol; light olive oil has a blander flavour; light cheese has less fat and salt; light cake has a lighter, fluffier texture.

Any light food must state the characteristic that makes the food light. And the food must also fit the criteria for low-fat or low-salt, if applicable. Light foods are not automatically low in sugar, despite popular belief.

The spelling 'lite' is simply a variant of the standard word 'light'. It is often used as part of a brand name, such as 'Lite White'.

Examples: milks, yoghurts, cream, sour cream, olive oils, beers, muffins, chocolate bars, probiotic drinks, cordial, iced teas

97% fat free

This one catches a lot of people. It's just the reverse of the way figures are usually presented. Really '97% fat free' means that the food contains 3 per cent fat, but saying it the other way around somehow makes it sound better for you! It's a pretty common way to attract shoppers who are looking for weight reduction, as 'fat' can mean fat in food as well as body fat. However, in trying to achieve the same mouth feel and texture with little fat, many processed foods end up being high in sugar or in refined flours such as corn starch. Just be aware of this when you see this claim. It's amazing how often sugar turns up in savoury foods when you'd least suspect.

What's in a name

Other names that mean added sugar

Sucrose (the chemical name for sugar)	Golden syrup
	Treacle
Honey	Agave
Fructose (fruit sugar)	Rice malt syrup
Fruit juice concentrate	Maple syrup
Malt/maltose/malt extract	Golden syrup
	Panela
Glucose	
Dextrose (another name for glucose)	

Other names that mean fat

Vegetable oil	Dripping
Vegetable shortening	Triglycerides
Ghee	Coconut oil
Lard	Copha
Suet	

Other names that mean sodium

Monosodium glutamate (MSG)	Chicken salt
	Sodium bicarbonate, baking soda
Disodium guanylate	
Disodium inosinate	Sodium salts of citrate, nitrate, phosphate or lactate
Kosher salt	
Himalayan salt	
Murray River pink salt	Soy sauce
Maldon salt	Teriyaki sauce
Celtic salt	Hoi sin sauce
Rock salt	Fish sauce
Sea salt	

Watch for the words 'soda' or 'sodium' anywhere on the list.

Only low-fat foods with 3 per cent fat or less are supposed to make this claim. It also applies to '98% fat free' (which is really 2 per cent fat) and '99% fat free' (which is 1 per cent fat). See how they suddenly sound less fattening?

If you do spot a food shouting 92% or 93% fat free, it's not complying with the food code and should be reported to the food authority in your state. In NSW, for example, I would report this to the NSW Food Authority at www.foodauthority.nsw.gov.au.

Look for their contact form or info on how to make a complaint. Each state has its own relevant body.
Examples: milks, yoghurts, juices, savoury crackers, crispbread, instant soups, jellies, jubes and barley sugar (sugar lollies)

No cholesterol or Cholesterol-free

Pay *no* attention to this claim. It really is meaningless. Cholesterol from food isn't the worry. It's the saturated and trans fats that you need to cut back on if your blood cholesterol is too high. You'll spot this one on heaps of foods, ranging from avocados to potato chips.

It's a hangover from the 1980s when cholesterol was the big health concern and was believed to set the scene for heart attack and clogged arteries.

What's more, 'No cholesterol' does not mean no fat – which is what many falsely believe. Many foods such as oils, margarines, nuts, avocado and snack foods can be free of cholesterol but remain high in fat.

All plant-derived products are free of cholesterol anyway; only animal foods like meat, dairy and eggs have significant cholesterol. And even these are no longer a worry – since 2011, the Heart Foundation says you can eat six eggs a week (about one a day, up from their former limit of two a week) even if you have high cholesterol.

Examples: oils, avocados, eggs, meats, savoury crackers, margarines (mono- and polyunsaturated types), nuts, peanut butter

Low-fat

As above, don't be caught out by low-fat – it's not the ultimate choice for overall health. For a start, to qualify, the food must contain less than 3 per cent fat for every 100 grams of the food (or 1.5 per cent for liquids like milks, which is pretty low). But the food can still have lots of refined starch or added sugar or even natural sugars (think juice), so it's not necessarily all that healthy for you.

Examples: milks, cottage cheese, yoghurts, muffins, slices, bliss balls and frozen meals

High in fibre or Good source of fibre

High fibre can only appear when the food has at least 4 grams of dietary fibre in each serving. Check the 'Per serving' column to verify this.

Examples: wholegrain breakfast cereals, bran breakfast cereals, oats, multigrain breads, baked beans, brown rice, crackers, pasta, muesli bars, breakfast drinks

Salt free or No added salt or Low salt

Low-salt foods by definition must contain no more than 120 milligrams of sodium per 100 grams, which you can double-check on the nutrition panel. The panel must also list the potassium content, which is the chemical opposite to sodium. Generally these are unsalted products like unsalted butter or margarine.

Examples: low-salt canned tomatoes, no-added-salt tomato paste, salt-free baked beans, salt-free margarine, unsalted butter, salt-free sauces

Salt-reduced or Lite salt

Salt-reduced foods must have at least 25 per cent less sodium than in the same quantity of an original (reference) food. The nutrition information panel must also list the potassium content. The chemical name for salt is sodium chloride and figures on food labels are always given in milligrams of sodium.

Examples: salt-reduced soy sauces, reduced-salt chicken stocks, canned legumes, savoury snacks, low-salt baked beans, low-salt margarines, reduced-salt sauces and gravies.

Baked not fried

This claim often appears on snack foods and implies that the food is low in fat. For some snacks, like pretzels, this is true (i.e. they have less than 3 per cent fat) but for others, like biscuit snacks, it means they are low*er* in fat (around 25 per cent less) but not necessarily low in fat. 'Baked not fried' sounds healthier but still could have as much fat as fried items, so check the label. What's more, check to see how much of the fat is saturated!

Examples: snack foods (pretzels), biscuit snacks (Shapes, rice crackers), rice snacks (Sakata)

No artificial colours or flavours

This is a key selling point with consumers, but is often over-used and put on food labels where artificial colours and flavours are not permitted anyway, such as breads and breakfast cereals. They can still contain natural colours (like beta-carotene or caramel) or flavours, but you can spot these on the ingredient list. Ditto for 'natural' and 'real'.

Examples: breads, cereals, muesli bars, custards, canned vegetables, canned tomatoes, pasta, confectionery without artificial colours

Good source of protein

This means that a food must have at least 10 grams of protein per serving.

Examples: breakfast cereals, nut bars, flavoured milks, protein shakes, protein bars

No added sugar

This applies to foods that do not contain added cane sugar or any honey, agave, rice malt syrup, panela, glucose, fructose, malt, malt extract or maltose. These alternative sugars are just as high in natural sugars as cane sugar and provide similar kilojoules. Fruit juice concentrate is often used to sweeten products, but has as many kilojoules as ordinary sugar. Think of it as juice with the water removed!

Examples: fruit juices, fruit leather, canned fruit, sugar-free lollies, sugar-free chewing gum

Omega-3

Source of omega-3

This means that a food has at least 200 milligrams alpha-linolenic acid if plant-based *or* at least 30 milligrams total eicosapentaenoic acid (EPA) plus docosahexaenoic acid (DHA) per serving (the two main types of omega-3 fatty acids).

In addition, for foods other than fish, they also must contain less than 28 per cent of the total fat content as saturated and trans fatty acids or no more than 5 per cent of the total.

Good source of omega-3

This relates specifically to the long-chain omega-3 fatty acids, such as EPA and DHA, found in fish. It means that a food must contain at least 60 milligrams in total of these two fatty acids per serving.

Examples: canned sardines, eel, tuna and salmon, muesli bars and cereals with linseed, omega-enriched eggs

Vitamin C

Source of vitamin C
This means that one serving of the food provides 10 per cent or more of the recommended dietary intake (RDI) for the average adult. This means 4 milligrams or more.

Good source of vitamin C
This means that one serving of the food provides at least 25 per cent or more of the recommended dietary intake (RDI) for the average adult. This means 10 milligrams or more.
Examples: enriched breakfast cereals, baby foods, juices, juice drinks, cordials, vegetable juices, smoothies

Label decoder example

What to look for when buying breakfast cereal
- Ideally look for a percentage of whole grains (anything over 50 per cent is good), high fibre, little or no added sugar, little or no added salt
- Compare brands
- Health Star Rating: 4 or higher

Nutrient	Amount per 100 g
Fat	No criteria
Saturated fat	< 1.5 g
Sugars	< 5 g
	< 10 g if dried fruit is present as well
Dietary fibre	> 10 g
	Or > 50% of whole grains
Sodium	< 400 mg ideal, but can be < 600 mg

Additives – how safe are they?

In our complex food distribution system, food additives perform many useful functions. They extend the storage life of products, especially without refrigeration; improve the stability of food over time; and make food taste and look better. For instance, a common emulsifier like lecithin (322) ensures that mixtures of oil and water, like salad dressings and mayonnaise, do not separate into layers. A humectant like glycerol (422) stops foods like icings, soft tortillas and muesli bars from drying out and tasting stale. Yet

How low is low?

If you're trying to cut back on fat, salt and added sugar and eat plenty of fibre, here's an easy guide to what figures you should check out on the nutrition information panel in the 'Per 100 g' column.

Ingredient	Per 100 g
Fat	3 g (3%) or less
Sugars	5 g (5%) or less
Sodium	120 mg or less
Fibre	10 g (10%) or more

additives are feared enormously by shoppers.

All food additives must have a specific use and must have been assessed by Food Standards Australia New Zealand (FSANZ). They must be used in the lowest possible quantity to achieve their purpose – something that's consistent with good manufacturing practice. No one wants to use more than we need!

Australia's additive numbers correspond to an international system used to identify additives that starts with an E, as code numbers such as 282 or 621 are often easier to remember than a long complex chemical name. Numbers are short and take up less space on a food label, which was their original

purpose. This matters a lot for small-sized packets like muesli bars, dried fruit or sauces.

You can find a list of all the additives on the FSANZ website at www.foodstandards.gov.au.

10 everyday additives

While over 300 additives are permitted for use in food, in reality less than 50 are widely used. Here are 10 common additives with their use and code number.

Additive	Purpose	Code
Caramel	Colour	150a
Beta-carotene	Colour	160a
Sulphur dioxide	Preservative	220
Sodium nitrate	Preservative	251
Lecithin	Emulsifier	322
Citric acid	Food acid and antioxidant	330
Calcium propionate	Preservative/ bread mould inhibitor	282
Xanthan	Gelling agent	415

Know your additives

Additives can be divided into 11 major categories, each used for a different purpose. I have listed them here in alphabetical order.

1. Acidity regulators (also called food acids)

These give food a sharp or sour taste, producing a pleasing tart flavour that balances out any sweetness, and help maintain a constant acid level in food. They are sometimes used to prevent oxidation such as browning or deterioration. Acidity regulators are harmless; they are identical to what's in nature and what you most likely already eat. For instance, citric acid (330), which is added to canned tomatoes and fruity beverages, is the same as the citric acid found naturally in lemons and other citrus fruit. Other common examples are tartaric acid (334) from grapes and wine, and acetic acid (260) from vinegar.

2. Anti-caking agents

Anti-caking agents help dry foods flow freely when sprinkled and prevent particles clumping together. They absorb excess moisture. You'll find them in sachets of sweeteners or salt. Examples are sodium aluminosilicate (554) and magnesium carbonate (504).

3. Antioxidants

Antioxidants prolong the life of food by slowing down the process of oxidation and so preventing fats from turning rancid and food from going brown.

> Antioxidants prolong the life of food by slowing down the process of oxidation.

Vitamin E (tocopherols, 306–309) is a natural antioxidant that keeps oils and margarines from turning rancid. Another is vitamin C (ascorbic acid, 300), which keeps wine and cider from discolouring. As sodium ascorbate (301), it is used in cured meats, fruit salad and vinegars.

Butylated hydroxyanisole (BHA, 320) is one of the widely used antioxidants for fats and oils as well as foods made from them, such as snack foods, biscuits, cakes and muesli bars. It is often used in conjunction with a gallate like propyl gallate (310).

4a. Artificial colours

These are used to add or restore colour lost during processing and so make the food more appealing and enjoyable. However, there is some debate as to whether some artificial colours in high dosages can provoke adverse effects, such as asthma, mood changes and skin issues like hives. For this reason, you may want to avoid these as much as possible. Think of the yellow tartrazine (102); Sunset Yellow FCF (110); amaranth (123); the red Ponceau 4R (124); Brilliant Blue FCF (133). These colours are found in many soft drinks, cordials, energy drinks, sports drinks, electrolyte drinks and powders; lollies and confectionery; cakes, sweet buns and icing on cakes.

4b. Natural colours

These have the same purpose as artificial colours but are usually extracted from natural sources.

Caramel (150a), a dark-brownish colour, is the most widely used. It's made by heat treatment of carbohydrates in a process called caramelisation. It has an odour of burnt sugar and a slightly bitter taste, which many like. Beta-carotene (160a) imparts a yellow–orange hue and is found in carrots, pumpkin, mango and other orange produce.

Other natural colours are titanium dioxide (171), a whitish pigment; turmeric or curcumin (100); vegetable carbon (153); paprika oleo-resin (160c); chlorophylls (140 and 141); lycopene (160d); Beet red (162) and anthocyanins (163).

You'll spot them in soy sauce, oyster sauce, canned sauces, natural soft drinks, cordials, cola drinks, whiskey, breads, biscuits, coloured breakfast cereals, natural pickles, instant noodles, confectionery and yeast extract.

5. Emulsifiers

Emulsifiers ensure that oil and water mixtures stay combined and do not separate into layers. They are needed in salad dressings, mayonnaises, margarines and ice creams. Lecithin (322), a substance occurring in soybeans and egg yolk, is an emulsifier frequently used in salad dressing, margarine, chocolate, cake mixes, pastry and confectionery. Others include sorbitan monostearate (491) and mono- and di-glycerides of fatty acids (471). Emulsifiers are closely related to fats and are digested the same way, so can be considered quite safe.

6. Flavour enhancers

Flavour enhancers improve the existing flavour of a food but contribute no flavour of their own. They appear in many savoury foods such as savoury biscuits; gravy powders, stock powders, sauce mixes; instant noodle sachets; and ready-made meals. The best known is monosodium glutamate (MSG) (621) but you'll also see disodium guanylate (627) and disodium ribonucleotides (635) used. There has been a lot of controversy about MSG causing multiple symptoms, such as headaches and nausea, in the past. The main

Unmasking the additives in a salad dressing

This typical store-bought salad dressing has 12 ingredients, including four additives (in bold), all of which perform different functions to ensure the dressing looks attractive, tastes as it should and remains edible during its 12-month shelf life.

Sunflower oil (60%), water, vinegar (8%), salt, sugar, **food acid (330)**, **vegetable gum (415)**, spice, herbs, garlic (1%), **colour (102)**, **antioxidant (320)**.

Here's my explanation for what they do:

Food acid (330) is citric acid, a common additive that adds a pleasant tang with a 'bite' of acidity. You can readily buy citric acid powder at pharmacies or garden shops.

Vegetable gum (415) is xanthan, which thickens the dressing.

Colour (102) is tartrazine, which gives a golden hue to the dressing. It is an artificial yellow colouring and can be a problem for those with food sensitivities. Most food companies are now phasing it out.

Antioxidant (320) is butylated hydroxyanisole (BHA). As this dressing is not refrigerated, it needs an additive like this to stop it going off: the BHA prevents it from deteriorating before its best-before date. It's right at the end of the ingredient list, so is present only in minute amounts.

Take-home message: a shop-bought dressing needs these additives, but they do not always make it unhealthy. The dressing may have undesirable fats and too much added salt, which reduces its nutrition. If you make your own dressing at home (it's easy), you won't get any additives and you can control the type of oil you use and the amount of salt. A much healthier option.

component of MSG is glutamate, which can be found naturally in protein-containing foods, such as meat and aged cheeses. The ingredient has now been cleared and for the vast majority, it poses no harm.

7. Gelling agents (also called gums)

Gelling agents are a large group of compounds used to

set and thicken foods like sauces and custards. Most are derived from plants, like guar (412), pectin (440) or xanthan (415), while some are extracted from seaweed like agar (406), carrageenan (Irish Moss) (407) and alginate (401). There is nothing sinister about these.

8. Humectants
Humectants are used in icings, cakes, soft tortillas, dried fruit and muesli bars to help maintain moistness and to prevent foods drying out. Humectants include polydextrose (1200), sorbitol (420), and glycerol or glycerin (422).

9. Mineral salts
Mineral salts are used to enhance the texture of foods such as processed meats like ham, bacon, sausages, hot dogs, salamis, liverwurst/pâté, which might otherwise lose juices. Various phosphates, chlorides and carbonates are examples, such as sodium phosphate (339), calcium chloride (509) and sodium carbonate (500).

10. Preservatives
Preservatives are used to retard the growth of bacteria, yeasts and moulds, preserve colour and flavour, and prevent oxidation, so they lessen food spoilage and help keep food safe to eat.

Common examples are potassium sorbate (202) in cordials and fruit drinks; sodium benzoate (211); sulphur dioxide (220) in wines and pickled onions and other pickled vegetables; calcium propionate (282) in breads; potassium nitrate (252) in sausages and deli meats.

You need to weigh up what is important – the choice is often whether you want to reduce the risk of

a deadly food-poisoning bacteria thanks to a tiny 200 parts per million of a carefully regulated preservative or whether you want a potentially dangerous product with a 'clean' label.

11. Thickeners
Thickeners thicken foods such as soups, simmer sauces, flavoured milks, drinking yoghurts and toppings, and give a smooth uniform texture. Similar in function to the cornflour or arrowroot used at home, they include a number of starches (1400–1405) and modified starches like acetylated distarch adipate (1422) or hydroxypropyl distarch phosphate (1442).

Less-used additives
You may spot one or more of these other additives from time to time. They are less common than the ones already listed but are approved and considered safe by the food standards authorities. As with any additive, they must tell you their full chemical name or a code number:

- Anti-foaming agents stop excessive frothing when boiling or reduce the formation of scum.
- Colour retention agents ensure that the colour stays true and doesn't fade or change.
- Glazing agents give a shiny appearance or add a protective coating to foods.
- Propellants are gases used in aerosol sprays to expel the contents.
- Raising agents release gases that allow a dough to rise.
- Sweeteners (stevia, acesulfame K, aspartame, erythritol) replace the sweetness normally provided by sugar or honey in foods like diet chewing

gum and diet soft drinks without contributing significantly to their kilojoule content.
- Enzymes are protein-based compounds that speed up the rate of chemical reactions in food manufacture. They are used in very small quantities.
- Flour treatment agents (also called bread improvers or dough conditioners) are a diverse group of compounds that assist the yeast in rapid-fermentation baking and improve the workability of gluten during the mixing and shaping of the dough. The best known is cysteine monohydrochloride (920) but there's also alpha-amylase (1100).

Flavours

Flavour additives restore the flavours lost during processing and make food more palatable. These have no code number and are complex mixtures of many aroma compounds. Originally they were extracted from herbs or spices, but more recently they are synthesised in a lab to create the compounds responsible for the flavour. We have no way of knowing what's in a flavour: there is no legal requirement to spell this out. Flavours must be listed as 'Flavour' on the ingredient list, even if the flavour is a natural one.

Streamline your shopping

There are many factors to consider when deciding what to buy at the supermarket. Nutrition, taste, convenience, cost, and whether the family will eat it, all enter into your final choice. But, if you want a healthier daily diet, rank nutrition high up the scale. Here's how to improve your eating habits right from the start – when you buy your food.

1. Be prepared
Shop with a list; it will save you time and money, plus prevent impulse buys. Keep a pad on your fridge or cupboard to jot down things as you run out.

2. Never shop when you are hungry
Research shows you tend to buy more – particularly those things that you really don't need – when you shop on an empty stomach.

3. Don't take the kids
When you take the kids to the supermarket, be aware that supermarkets position lollies, biscuits, muesli bars and toys at their eye level to attract their attention. You can go for the confectionery-free

Mirror the shopping aisles

Write down what you need in categories that mirror your supermarket aisles. This saves backtracking and keeps you out of aisles you don't need to visit. Some supermarkets actually have maps of their aisles and an index of what product is in which aisle. Make use of them! Or shop online from your pre-defined list of healthy groceries.

checkouts to make that long wait less frazzling, but if you can, leave the kids with a friend while you do your shopping and then return the favour.

4. Buy in season
The smartest and cheapest way to eat healthily is to buy in season – seasonal produce is at its lowest price yet at its peak for quality and nutrition.

5. Food safety alert signs
Steer clear of damaged packaging such as dented cans, leaking cartons or torn packaging. With these, you can't guarantee the safety of the food inside.

6. Skip that aisle
If you don't need food from a particular aisle, don't visit it. This especially applies to the ultra-processed or 'junk food' aisles that include pre-made snacks like chips, biscuits, chocolates, sweets, nuggets, energy bars and carbonated sweet drinks. Really, any junk foods that are convenient, portable, shelf-stable, cheap and mess-free are best avoided.

7. Shop at the 'edges'
Shop around the perimeter of the supermarket when you need to grab a meal in a hurry. Here you'll find the meats, vegetables, dairy case (for yoghurts, custards and cheeses), deli, fishmonger, chilled meals, breads (skip the tubs of sweet biscuits and slices) and freezer cabinet for frozen vegetables.

8. Save the freezer until last
Don't buy items from the freezer until the end of your shopping trip. This minimises the time they will have to defrost and spoil. Bring an insulated cooler bag with you and pack frozen foods directly into it at the checkout ready for the trip home in the car.

How to use the Health Star Rating

The Health Star Rating (HSR) system ranks food products on a scale from half a star to five stars on the front of food packs. As with the energy rating you spot on fridges and washing machines, the more stars the better. Foods with five stars are the best nutritional choice within their group. As of 2019, there were over 4000 foods carrying this rating.

The HSR is designed to help us decide whether or not to buy a packaged food product like a bar, cereal, bread or meal base – use it to compare similar products, such as two breakfast cereals or two muesli bars. It's only meant for manufactured foods, not fresh foods.

The rating is worked out from an algorithm that takes into account kilojoules and three 'bad' or 'negative' nutrients – saturated fat, sugars and sodium.

These four aspects of a food are associated with an increase in the risk factors for chronic diseases like type 2 diabetes. This is balanced against its fruit, vegetable, nut or legume (fvnl) content. Visually, the HSR can also show one single 'positive' nutrient, such as protein or fibre.

I prefer the Health Stars over the earlier and more simplistic Traffic Light system, which had only the one set of criteria for all foods. You can't compare an oil with 100 per cent fat with a loaf of bread with only 3 per cent fat – they each need their own set of criteria for any guide to be meaningful.

What happened to the tick?

In 2015, after 26 years, the red tick managed by the Heart Foundation was retired in favour of the new Health Star Rating. I liked the tick, as it did work in highlighting healthier options – with less saturated fat and sodium, more fibre and whole grains and smaller portion sizes – for many categories.

What happened to the thumbnails?

The HSR tells shoppers more and is more meaningful than the older thumbnails, officially called the Percentage of Daily Intake or %DI. They were a graphic representation of how much one serve of a food contributed to an average day's intake.

Drawing their information from the figures from the panel on the back, the thumbnails were placed on the front of the pack in a graphic format. This made the numbers easier to interpret. A picture is faster to read than a table!

This was a voluntary scheme, developed by the Australian Food and Grocery Council, which

represents the major food companies. In it's heyday, in 2013, it appeared on over 7000 food packets. Some manufacturers chose to display only the %DI for energy (kilojoules) while others included energy as well as all seven nutrients – protein, fat, saturated fat, carbohydrate, sugars, fibre and sodium.

This was based on what a 'serve' was. And also based on an average person who consumes 8700 kilojoules per day. If you were a child, female or anyone overweight – all of whom need to consume fewer kilojoules than most males – the numbers wouldn't apply to you.

In the end, it was all too complicated. There were too many numbers to make it a simple at-a-glance check.

My concerns about these rating schemes

None of these ratings tell you everything about a food. For instance, they don't look at how many additives are present; they miss out on vitamins (say vitamin B12) or minor minerals (say selenium); how processed and refined a food is; whether it's locally grown or organic, or even whether it's a whole food or not. You don't get the whole story about a food's value. So it's only one tool to help you choose healthier packaged foods. Use your own judgement as well.

Just using energy (kilojoules) as a way of comparing foods ignores the overall nutrition of a food. It can make unhealthy foods seem like a good choice, as it is all about quantity, not quality. There's no judgement as to whether a food is good for you or not – it's left to the consumer to interpret.

8 Diets for health problems

Here's the latest on eating to help beat specific health problems, plus tips for cutting back or cutting out when you're following a medical diet.

Eat to beat cholesterol and heart disease

When your doctor tells you that your blood cholesterol levels are too high, it can be a bit of a shock. Often, you'll be advised to go on a type of medication called statins. These will reduce your cholesterol levels, but for some people they have side effects. So, is there anything you can do to reduce your levels to avoid taking medication? The answer is yes. Take a look.

Eat your way to lower cholesterol levels
It's not just a matter of buying skim milk and margarine. There is a whole range of foods that can actively drive cholesterol down. Some block its absorption into the body, while others help speed its exit so your blood levels drop. Here are nine steps you can take before your next blood test.

1. Consume plant sterols
Plant sterols reduce cholesterol reabsorption, which can reduce your cholesterol levels by up to 10 per cent. It's an easy dietary change to make but can be very effective.

Sterols already naturally occur in much of your food but, as it's hard to get enough, you'll need to boost your intake by consuming foods enriched with them. All you're after is a total of three serves, or 2 grams each and every day. It's often difficult to consume what's required from one food day after day, so I recommend having a variety. For example:
- If you use sterol-enriched margarine only, you will need to eat two teaspoons (10 grams, which is the

Reminder

Don't forget that you should always consult your doctor or, for nutritional aspects, an accredited practising dietitian (APD) for advice specific to your individual health problems.

What do plant sterols do?

Plant sterols (phytosterols) are a group of natural compounds that have a structure similar to that of cholesterol, yet they have the ability to inhibit its absorption from the digestive tract into the body. They are found in most plant foods, with the largest amounts found in vegetable oils and smaller amounts in nuts, legumes and grains. Enriched foods come and go at the supermarket, but you can usually find a sterol spread, milk or yoghurt, mayo or dressing, and breakfast biscuit or bar. Lower intakes are still effective for some people, especially if you're of small stature.

amount you'd spread on two slices of bread) per day to get the required 2 grams of plant sterols. That's hard to do.
- If you use sterol-enriched milk alone, you would need to consume two to three serves (500 to 750 millilitres) per day. Again, not that easy.
- If you choose to eat the cholesterol-lowering breakfast biscuits, you'd need to eat two. A little easier.

However, if you had a slice of toast with sterol-enriched margarine plus one cholesterol-lowering Weet-Bix with a sliced banana and sterol-enriched milk, plus the same milk in your tea over the day, then you're pretty close to the 2 grams you need.

2. Exercise more

Exercise will help reduce your cholesterol levels. The ideal is 30 minutes of brisk exercise every day, but if you're currently not exercising at all then any exercise will be better than none. Perhaps you can take a brisk 15-minute-each-way walk to the station instead of driving your car there and back. Or go for a walk at lunchtime or ride your bike when you get home from work. Not only will exercise help you drive down your cholesterol, but it will help you lose weight if you need to.

3. Add in fibre

Fibre is great in the fight against cholesterol. Both soluble fibre (found in legumes such as chickpeas and lentils, BARLEYmax™ and psyllium husks) and insoluble fibre (such as that found in wholegrain products like brown rice, wholegrain pasta and bread) are good.

4. Swap your coffee for tea

Tea contains substances called catechins, which research suggests may play a part in inhibiting cholesterol reabsorption.

5. Eat more oats

Oats contain a soluble fibre called beta-glucan, which can also lower your cholesterol. So make yourself some hot porridge with milk on colder mornings, or else soak oats in milk overnight in the fridge.

6. Eat more oily fish

Oily fish contain omega-3 fatty acids, which have been found to lower the bad cholesterol (LDL) and increase the good cholesterol (HDL). See pages 70–3 for more detail. If you don't eat fish, you can take fish oil or krill oil supplements.

7. Snack on nuts

Grab a handful of nuts such as almonds or walnuts. They contain fibre, plant sterols and heart-friendly fats. Good for those times you get hungry between meals and before dinner.

8. Say no to junk food

Steer clear of prepared and takeaway foods like pizza, burgers, fried chicken, ice cream, biscuits and chocolate, which tend to contain more saturated and trans fats (not good for cholesterol) and opt for more fresh and freshly cooked foods, including lean meats and vegetables.

9. Use the good oils

Cook with monounsaturated (olive, canola) and polyunsaturated oils (sunflower, hemp, rice bran) in your cooking and reduce your use of butter and frying fats.

And finally: stop smoking and reduce your alcohol intake.

Are you at risk?

Your risk of developing heart problems increases with the number of risk factors you have such as:

- Smoking
- High blood pressure
- High blood cholesterol (both the total cholesterol and the LDL) and having high blood triglycerides
- Having diabetes
- Advancing age (over 50)
- Heart problems in the family
- Being overweight (especially around the middle)
- Being sedentary

Work with your doctor

First consult your doctor before you undertake any diet or exercise regime, especially if you have other health problems such as diabetes or high blood pressure. If they have no objections, then try this way of eating for three months and then get re-tested.

Eat to beat metabolic syndrome

Metabolic syndrome is something we are hearing about more often, as it accompanies our 'obesogenic' lifestyle.

What is metabolic syndrome?

The term 'metabolic syndrome' refers to a cluster of risk factors that increase your risk for diseases such as diabetes, heart disease, and stroke. Studies are also examining links between metabolic syndrome and polycystic ovaries, gallstones, cataracts and certain types of cancer. Researchers originally coined it 'Syndrome X' but later renamed it after they worked out it centred on insulin resistance.

Muscles can't use the sugar in the blood to generate energy.

Insulin resistance means that the body produces insulin but the muscles don't 'recognise' it. In other words, the muscles become insensitive to insulin. The body then responds by making more insulin, and so levels build up in the bloodstream. Muscles can't use the sugar in the blood to generate energy, so the sugar ends up being processed by the liver and eventually converted into triglycerides (fats) and stored.

Are you a candidate?

You're most likely to have metabolic syndrome if you have two or more of these risk factors:
- Weight carried mostly around the middle (abdominal fat)
- High blood pressure
- Mostly sedentary lifestyle with little moving around or exercise
- Impaired glucose tolerance
- Type 2 diabetes or high blood sugar levels
- High fats in the blood (such as high LDL-cholesterol or high triglycerides)
- Smoke over 10 cigarettes a day

The two problems – resistance to insulin and a high level of circulating triglycerides in the blood – are related. No one knows for sure which comes first but either way, diet and exercise will help improve these indicators of metabolic syndrome.

How to manage it

The cornerstone of treatment is lifestyle – being more active and eating a healthy diet aimed at weight loss. Here are five ways to take control.

1. Eat less refined carbohydrates

Popular diet books claim that if you cut out all carbohydrates, your problems will disappear. Unfortunately it's not that simple. Rather than eliminating all carbohydrates, be selective. Get rid of the refined high-GI types such as white bread, white rice, pastries, biscuits, muffins and refined breakfast cereals and choose more 'slow' varieties such as wholegrain breads, rye crackers, wholegrain breakfast cereals, pasta, fruit and legumes.

2. Eat more fibre

People who eat more fibre-rich foods (fruit, vegetables, beans, wholegrain breads and bran cereals) have fewer risk factors.

3. Eat more lean protein

There's no need to follow a keto-style high-protein, high-fat diet, but boosting protein intake is helpful. Don't just eat noodles or toast. A serve of lean protein such as canned tuna, lean red meat or chicken at meal times will give you greater satisfaction for longer and demand less insulin. This means you will be less hungry between meals and have fewer swings in blood sugar.

4. Go for good fats

High blood fats and heart disease accompany metabolic syndrome and need special attention. Keep total fat intake down to help with weight control and make sure the fats you use are healthy. Choose vegetable fats such as olive, sunflower or canola oil and spreads made from these. Omega-3 fats from fish are also important, so include two fish meals a week (fresh or canned) and also try omega-enriched milks, breads and spreads.

5. Exercise daily

Exercise can prevent or reverse many of the unhealthy metabolic changes that contribute to this syndrome. Increase your general day-to-day activity by using the stairs, walking to the shops and getting up to turn the TV off. Invest in a pedometer or Fitbit and start counting your steps – your goal could simply be to walk 1000 more steps a day, or you could aim for the suggested 10,000 steps for weight loss.

Eat to beat type 2 diabetes

Rising rates of obesity, sedentary lifestyles, poor
diet and an ageing population are creating a 'hidden
epidemic' of diabetes, with an explosion in the
numbers of people with type 2 diabetes (the type of
diabetes that affects mainly older people, as opposed
to type 1, which affects mainly children and is not
caused by diet).

According to AusDiab, a national diabetes study
that began in 1999, almost one in four Australians now
has diabetes or elevated blood glucose or is at high
risk of developing diabetes in the next five to 10 years.
Obesity and type 2 diabetes are so intertwined that
researchers have created a new term, 'diabesity', to
embrace these twin conditions.

What is type 2 diabetes?

Diabetes is a breakdown in the body's ability to use
its blood glucose efficiently. The body fails to produce
enough of the hormone insulin or to make use of the
little insulin it does generate. Insulin is needed to
'transport' glucose into the muscles. Left untreated,
the glucose builds up in the bloodstream, resulting in
high blood sugar levels that increase the risk of serious
damage to the kidney, nerves, feet, skin and eyes.
Ideally it's wise to keep blood glucose within normal
levels of 4 to 8 millimoles per litre.

Are you a candidate?

You are more likely to develop type 2 diabetes
if you:
- Are over 50 and have high blood pressure
- Are over 50 and overweight
- Are over 50 and one or more members of your
  family has diabetes
- Had gestational diabetes while pregnant
- Have heart disease or have had a heart attack
- Have recorded a borderline blood sugar level
- Have polycystic ovary syndrome and are
  overweight
- Are over 35 years of age and are an Indigenous
  Australian or from Pacific Island, Indian
  sub-continent or Chinese cultural background
- Have metabolic syndrome (meaning any three
  of these: obesity, high cholesterol, high blood
  pressure, impaired fasting glucose, non-
  alcoholic fatty liver disease)

If you fit into any of these categories, it's time
to modify your lifestyle and speak to your doctor
or an accredited practising dietitian about
getting tested.

Healthy eating guidelines for diabetes

Having diabetes doesn't mean you need to buy 'special' foods. A healthy diet for diabetes is much the same as a healthy diet for all of us – one that is high in nutritious foods including fibre, whole grains and low-GI carbohydrates, while being modest in salt and added sugar, and low in bad fats. It should incorporate a variety of vegetables, fruits, nuts, legumes, lean meats, fish and dairy foods, preferably as whole foods that need chewing. Here's what to do.

Eat regularly

Have regular meals and snacks. Spread your carbohydrate throughout the day to give a steady supply of glucose to your muscles and organs (match it to your insulin dosing regimen). Don't skip meals, but eat something light if you're not that hungry.

Healthy weight

If you need to, lose your excess weight, especially if it's around your midriff. This can improve blood glucose and even lessen the number of tablets or injections you need each day. Even a reduction of 5 per cent of your weight can make a big difference. If your weight's fine, aim to maintain it as you get older.

Choose foods low in bad fats

People with diabetes have five to six times the risk of heart disease as the rest of the population, and often have high blood triglyceride levels, high blood pressure, and clotting and circulation problems. So it's essential to cut back in an effort to keep heart disease (one of the major complications of diabetes) at bay.

Go for the healthy fats

Include monounsaturated fats from olive and canola oils, avocados, almonds and other nuts or fats rich in omega-3s.

Increase omega-3s

Omega-3 oils from oily fish, seafood, canola oil, linseeds, chia and hemp seeds and walnuts help keep the blood freely flowing and reduce inflammation.

Fill up on fibre

Aim for plenty of fibre from vegetables, salads, baked beans and legumes. Eat moderate amounts of wholegrain bread, bran cereals, oats and other whole grains like barley.

Aim for plenty of fibre from vegetables, salads, baked beans and legumes.

The three types of diabetes

Type 1 diabetes

- Represents approximately 10 to 15 per cent of all cases
- Occurs when the pancreas gland does not produce enough insulin to convert glucose into energy
- Is one of the most common childhood diseases in developed nations
- Is not caused by obesity or lifestyle factors
- Is a genetic-led auto-immune disease and is linked to similar illnesses such as coeliac disease and Hashimoto's disease

Type 2 diabetes

- The most common type of diabetes – represents approximately 85 to 90 per cent of all cases
- Occurs when the pancreas is not producing enough insulin and/or when the body cannot use it effectively
- Is made worse by an unhealthy diet and lack of exercise
- Is closely linked to obesity and systemic inflammation
- Is more likely in people with a family history of type 2 diabetes

Gestational diabetes

- A form of diabetes that occurs in pregnancy and in most cases disappears after giving birth
- Occurs in around 15 per cent of pregnancies (where the mother does not have diabetes before pregnancy)
- May be as high as 30 per cent among Indigenous Australian and Maori women and those from high-risk ethnic groups such as Indian, Chinese, Asian and Pacific Islander
- Increases the risk of pregnancy complications and longer-term health outcomes for the child
- Indicates a 50 per cent chance of developing type 2 diabetes later

Do I have to avoid fruit?

No. You should aim to eat two serves of fresh, frozen or canned fruit a day. The sugars in fruit are natural fructose and glucose but come bundled with fibre, vitamin C, folate and beta-carotene, minerals such as potassium, plus bioactive substances. Skip juice, which has had the fibre removed and is often too easy to drink. Eat whole fruit and chew well. Fruit makes an easy snack or quick, refreshing dessert.

Eat to beat food allergy and intolerance

Are you sensitive to certain foods? Suspect a food allergy? We all need food to live on but for some people even a tiny amount of an allergen can prove disastrous. If you wonder if food is responsible for your health problems, whether they be skin rashes or tummy troubles, here's a good starting point for help.

Allergy or intolerance?

Although often described as 'allergies', food intolerances occur through a different biological mechanism. Symptoms often appear the same. But in order to get the best treatment, it's vital to understand the difference between them. For instance, stomach pains and diarrhoea could be due to an intolerance. But they could also arise from a gastric infection, food poisoning, coeliac disease or excessive fibre, which is why you need to be checked over first by a doctor. Here are the differences.

Allergy

A true food allergy provokes the body's immune system to produce antibodies to specific food proteins. It occurs within minutes, mainly in infants and young children, and involves only a relatively small number of foods, notably eggs, milk, peanuts, fish and nuts. Blood or skin-prick tests for detecting food antibodies are available.

One of the most severe forms of allergy is anaphylaxis, where the mouth, lips, tongue or throat swell, causing difficulty breathing and potentially fatal collapse. Peanuts are the food most likely to cause death from anaphylactic shock.

Choose 'better' carbohydrates that are wholegrain or slowly absorbed

These include slow-digesting carbohydrates like pasta, legumes, grainy breads, pumpernickel, yoghurts and certain fruit (apples, cherries, grapefruit, peaches, pears and plums). These low-GI foods demand much less insulin for their absorption and don't produce a high rise in blood sugar levels if you're having them in moderate amounts.

Move more

Regular daily exercise like walking or swimming is essential. Work towards at least 30 minutes a day for five days a week.

Should I use a sweetener?

If you need to lose weight, ideally you should lose that sweet tooth and go for sparkling mineral or soda water or else water flavoured with lemon rounds or tea. When you're out, the occasional diet soft drink is fine – but don't make it a daily habit or you'll lose the battle with your sweet tooth. (Ignore the claims that diet soft drinks cause cancer – they've been well tested and have passed with flying colours.)

Similarly, chewing gum with xylitol or other sweeteners is handy and refreshes the mouth without adding a heap of kilojoules. Again, fine once or twice a day, but don't chew a whole packet a day. And remember that swapping to a sweetener doesn't mean you'll automatically cut back on sugar or kilojoules. In fact, studies have found the opposite: people consume more of foods with artificial sweeteners. Don't fall into the trap of making up the deficit by eating more.

Allergens on labels

Allergy affects an estimated 5 per cent of infants, but only 1 to 2 per cent of children and less than 1 per cent of the adult population. Most children grow out of milk and egg allergies by the age of four or five. Allergies to peanuts and seafood generally last for life.

Intolerance or sensitivity

Food intolerances are harder to recognise as the reactions do not always occur immediately after eating and can be triggered by many different compounds, both natural and artificial.

Food intolerances are more common than allergy (affecting 5 to 10 per cent of the adult population), but tends to run in families who usually already suffer asthma, hayfever or eczema.

Generally it is dose related – the body reacts only when its threshold has been crossed after a number of chemicals have been consumed. Don't forget that anything with a strong fragrance – toothpaste, perfumes, deodorisers, flowers, petrol – also spells trouble for these 'super-sensitive' types.

Culprit chemicals

There are many problem chemicals in food – natural and added – that can upset sensitive people. Take a quick look at these examples.

Amines

Amines are compounds derived from the break down of protein or from fermentation. Large quantities are found in cheese, chocolate, yeast extracts, beer and wine. Lesser amounts are found in tomatoes, bananas, avocado and broad beans.

Symptom checklist

Salicylates

A large group of aspirin-like compounds, salicylates are found in citrus and most other fruit, many vegetables, herbs, spices, honey, tea, coffee, beer and wine. They are also present in mint flavours and eucalyptus oils, so they turn up in perfumes, aromatherapy oils, toiletries and toothpaste as well.

MSG and glutamates

Glutamates are responsible for the flavour of foods. High concentrations occur in soy sauce, cheeses

(Parmesan, blue vein and camembert), tomatoes, yeast extract and mushrooms. As flavour enhancer 621, MSG is added to stocks, gravies, Asian soups and snack foods. MSG generally causes no harm. But it can trigger wheezing or skin reactions in glutamate-sensitive people.

Sulphur preservatives

Metabisulphites 223 and 224 and their related compounds of sulphur dioxide 220 and sulphites 221, 222, 225 and 228 are used in wineries to destroy undesirable bacteria in wine storage vats. (In fact, sulphur has been used to preserve wine since the times of ancient Greece). They prevent the darkening of dried fruit and juices and are used to preserve soft drinks, pickled onions and sausages. In sensitive asthma patients, they can trigger wheezing and throat tightening, frequently within one minute after eating.

Benzoates

Benzoates occur in cranberries, bilberries and other fruit, vegetables, pepper, herbs, spices, peppermint and honey. Sodium benzoate 211 and potassium benzoate 212 are used as preservatives in soft drinks, cordials and fruit drinks. Both must be avoided by sensitive people.

Colours

Artificial colours like tartrazine, Sunset Yellow FCF, erythrosine, amaranth and Brilliant Blue FCF are linked to food sensitivity. Tartrazine, in particular, has been extensively investigated for its ability to induce hives and asthma in aspirin-sensitive asthmatics. Use of erythrosine is now limited. Many people blame sugar but it may well be the colours that sugar keeps company with in things like lollies, chocolates, ice creams, soft drinks, cordials and snack foods.

Fructans

Fructans are short chains of fructose sugars joined together. They are poorly absorbed and can trigger irritable bowel syndrome (IBS) symptoms, as do the galacto-oligosaccharides (GOS) – see page 153 for more detail. Humans do not produce any enzymes that can break the bonds between these sugars, so the fructans move through the gut unabsorbed. In IBS, when the gut is hypersensitive, you get bloating, abdominal discomfort and altered motility. Fructans are usually found in onion, leek, garlic and in wheat, rye, barley (when eaten in large amounts).

Eat to beat irritable bowel syndrome

A low-FODMAP diet is the best way you can take control of your gut health and improve the symptoms of irritable bowel syndrome (IBS).

What are FODMAPs?

FODMAPs are found in the foods we eat. A diet low in FODMAPs can help ease symptoms such as bloating and excessive wind. FODMAPs stands for:

- Fermentable
- Oligosaccharides (e.g. fructans and galacto-oligosaccharides)
- Disaccharides (e.g. excess lactose)
- Monosaccharides (e.g. excess fructose)

And

- Polyols (e.g. sorbitol, mannitol, maltitol, xylitol and isomalt)

These are complex names for a collection of molecules in food that can be poorly absorbed in the small intestine. When this happens, they then continue along their journey, arriving at the large intestine, where they act as a food source to the resident bacteria that normally live there. The bacteria then digest or ferment these FODMAPs, producing wind (gas) and bloating.

A low-FODMAP diet refers to a temporary eating pattern that has a very low amount of these windy compounds. The aim of this diet is to eliminate digestive symptoms by eliminating all FODMAPs, then reintroducing them one by one so you can work out which one is triggering the symptoms.

As well as IBS, this diet can be beneficial for managing symptoms in people who have other disorders, such as inflammatory bowel disease (IBD), functional gastrointestinal disorder (FGID) or small intestinal bacterial overgrowth (SIBO).

Where are FODMAPs found?

A few examples of food sources for each of the FODMAPs are listed below. The list is not complete. You need to see an accredited practising dietitian for more advice.

- Most legumes (e.g. baked beans, kidney beans, borlotti beans), lentils, chickpeas
- Artichokes (globe, Jerusalem), onion (brown, white, Spanish, onion powder), garlic (in large amounts), leek, spring onion (white part), mushrooms
- Wheat (in large amounts) such as bread (look

Irritable Bowel Syndrome – does this sound like you?

- tummy pain which is relieved once you have been to the toilet
- gassiness or flatulence all the time
- frequent bloating and abdominal discomfort
- irregular bowel movements
- frequent episodes of diarrhoea, often passing mucus as well
- diarrhoea alternating with constipation

for long-fermented breads or traditional sourdoughs that will have a reduced FODMAP content), pizza, breakfast cereals, pasta, crispbreads, rye (in large amounts)
- Apples, apricots, nectarines, pears, plums, prunes, mangoes
- Sugar-free chewing gum and confectionery made with sorbitol (420), mannitol (421) or xylitol (967)
- Milk, including goat's and sheep's, ice cream, custard, evaporated milk, milk powder, yoghurt, soft unripened cheeses (e.g. ricotta, cottage).
- Honey, high-fructose corn syrup, fructose, agave
- Inulin, fructo-oligosaccharides

FODMAP-friendly meal plan

Breakfast
- ½ cup cooked oats or porridge, topped with sliced strawberries and blueberries (about ½ cup total) and 1 tablespoon chopped walnuts

  Or
- An orange, cut into quarters, two-egg omelette filled with baby spinach, sliced red capsicum and cheddar cheese

Lunch
- Buddha bowl starting with a base of cooked brown rice, layered with chopped lettuce, cherry tomatoes and spring onions (green part only), topped with grilled chicken or prawns, and grated cheddar. Drizzle over a squeeze of lemon juice and olive oil for dressing

  Or
- Tuna lettuce wraps: tuna mixed with mayonnaise, splash of fresh lemon juice, ¼ celery stalk, sliced, and fresh dill, served in lettuce leaf cups, with a side of boiled rice

Dinner
- Grilled steak, roast potato, plus a mixed side salad with lettuce, grated carrots, cherry tomatoes and orange pepper slices with red-wine vinegar and olive oil dressing drizzled over

Snacks
- Rice cake spread with peanut butter and ½ ripe banana
- Rice crackers, cheese slice and small bunch of grapes
- Rice chips, handful of peanuts and a few baby carrots
- Carrot sticks and cucumber wedges with dip (blend ½ cup lactose-free cottage cheese with chopped dill and pepper in blender until creamy)

Eat to beat lactose intolerance

Can't drink milk? Get tummy pains and bloating when you eat dairy? Here's what you need to know.

What is lactose?

Lactose is a sugar naturally occurring in milk. It is made up of two simpler sugars, glucose and galactose, and is a natural component of the milk of all mammals, including cows, goats, sheep and also humans.

What is lactose intolerance?

Around one in every 10 Australians suffers from true lactose intolerance, a condition where they are unable to digest large amounts of dairy, mainly milk. If they drink too much milk, they end up with pain, bloating, wind and even diarrhoea.

Lactose intolerance occurs when there is too little of an enzyme in the small intestine that breaks down the sugar, so that it can be absorbed.

Around 90 per cent of Asian people, Indigenous Australians, Maori and Pacific Islanders, Middle

Where you'll find lactose in foods

Here's an easy guide to what figures you should check for on the nutrition information panel in the 'per serve' column

Foods and serve size	per serve (grams)
High lactose	
Milk, full-fat, 1 cup (250 ml)	15.8
Milk, evaporated, ½ cup (125 ml)	13.4
Milk, skim, 1 cup (250 ml)	12.5
Yoghurt, natural, low-fat, 200 g tub	10.6
Yoghurt, natural, full-fat, 200 g tub	10.0
Milk, goat's, 1 cup (250 ml)	9.3
Moderate lactose	
Buttermilk, ½ cup (125 ml)	7.0
Ice cream, vanilla, 2 scoops (100 g)	3.3
Low lactose	
Cottage cheese, 1 tablespoon	0.4
Cream, 1 tablespoon	0.4
Cream cheese, 1 tablespoon	0.4
Butter, 1 teaspoon	0.2
Cheese, cheddar, 1 slice	0.1
Cheese, edam, Swiss, gouda, 1 slice	negligible
Soy mylk, rice mylk, almond mylk	0

Source: Australian Food Composition Database 2019 from FSANZ.

Easterners and Africans are lactose intolerant. After childhood, they are unable to digest lactose in any large quantity. Their traditional diets reflect this. Any dairy products they consume are 'cultured' (such as yoghurts, kefirs, buttermilks and soft cheeses), as the live bacteria convert much of the lactose into a safer lactic acid.

Lactose intolerance is much less common in anyone of northern European descent, whose ancestors herded dairy cows for generations, continued to drink milk in adulthood and consequently retained the enzyme needed to split the lactose molecule.

However, it can also occur in the short term whenever the digestive tract is affected, say after a bout of gastroenteritis or in certain illnesses like coeliac disease or HIV infections.

Good news on milk

One of the most common misconceptions is that lactose intolerance means no more dairy. The good news is that milk and other dairy foods – important sources of protein, calcium and B vitamins – don't need to be completely eliminated. Research shows that even people with low enzyme levels can have up to two glasses of milk a day, best taken with food.

6 tips to manage lactose intolerance

1. Eat lactose-containing foods as part of a meal rather than on an empty stomach. Milk over your cereal with fruit may pose no problems but a large milkshake on its own can give you bloating and an upset tummy.
2. Reduce the amount of lactose-containing foods you eat at any one time. Eating a little often is likely to be better tolerated than a large quantity from time to time.
3. If you are really sensitive, stick to low- and moderate-lactose foods like firm cheeses and ice cream (see table on page 154). Also avoid milk and yoghurt.
4. Look for lactose-reduced milks, yoghurts and cheeses at your supermarket – or for plant mylks that have no lactose, such as almond or rice mylk.
5. Talk to your pharmacist about enzyme drops. You simply add a set number of drops to your regular milk and leave it for 24 hours in the refrigerator. This breaks down the lactose before drinking.
6. Yoghurt may be better tolerated than milk, as around 30 per cent of its lactose has been broken down to lactic acid and the friendly bacteria present actually produce the enzyme that splits lactose.

must be avoided. Even small quantities of flour or thickeners are a problem. Rice and corn are gluten-free and should substitute for gluten-containing grains wherever possible.

Oats are technically gluten-free but are not permitted to be labelled so in Australia (and many other countries) as they're generally grown near wheat and transported and stored in silos with wheat. Contamination with wheat means commercial oats usually contain some gluten, although there are moves to market pure 100 per cent gluten-free oats. In addition, some oat proteins can trigger reactions.

Don't go gluten-free without a diagnosis

If you don't have to avoid gluten for medical reasons, gluten-free foods will not help you lose weight or digest your food better or have more energy.

Despite the hype from sports stars and celebrities, gluten-free foods have around the same kilojoules, fat and carbs as regular products.

Gluten-free foods are not mainstream foods. They are special dietary foods to help treat medical problems. They are refined, low in fibre, high-GI and highly processed, which is the opposite of what's recommended for good health. They won't cause you harm but they're not necessary.

> Gluten-free foods are not mainstream foods. They are special dietary foods to help treat medical problems.

Gluten-free food tips

- At home, keep cornflour (corn starch) made from maize, rice flour, arrowroot or potato flour for thickening sauces, soups and making gravy.
- Make sauces and dressings from ingredients you are sure are free of wheat, e.g. oil, vinegar, garlic, pure herbs, grated lemon rind, eggs and butter.
- Use a commercial gluten-free pre-mix for baking bread or cakes. These work with the help of speciality fibres such as carboxymethyl cellulose or methyl cellulose along with stabilising gums such as xanthan or guar, which stop the cakey-ness and minimises the crumbliness.
- You can substitute a blend of ⅓ soy flour with ⅓ rice flour and ⅓ potato flour for wheat flour, but remember that you will need to vary the quantity of liquid needed.

Eat to beat coeliac disease

People with coeliac disease have a permanent intolerance to gluten. If left untreated, it damages the delicate inner lining of the bowel, preventing food from being absorbed properly. Symptoms most often reported are those relating to an 'irritable bowel' – bloating and tummy pain – as well as diarrhoea or loose motions, constipation, weight loss and fatigue. However, some individuals have no symptoms at all. If left untreated, coeliac disease can result in deficiencies of iron, calcium and other minerals and an increased risk of diseases such as lymphoma and osteoporosis. Here's a handy guide if you are unable to tolerate gluten.

Gluten – where you'll find it

Gluten is part of a protein found in wheat, rye, barley and triticale (a cereal that is a cross between wheat and rye). When mixed with water, gluten forms an elastic-like substance that expands when a dough rises and traps the gas. Gluten gives the structure to bread and cakes and enables pastry and biscuits to 'hold together'. Without gluten, most baked goods do not rise as well and so are flatter and less aerated.

Flour, bread, cereals, pasta, crackers and biscuits

- Cook Asian dishes like stir-fries and curries, based on rice.
- Stock up on rice, rice noodles, buckwheat, millet, amaranth and soy. Ancient grains such as farro, spelt and emmer are not free of gluten.
- Always remember, if in doubt, leave it out!

Alternatives to bread?

Bread is the food most missed by people with coeliac disease, and it's hard for children who like sandwiches or rolls for school lunches. Puffed rice cakes, corn thins and rice crackers can help. Keep a stock of bought gluten-free breads and muffins in your fridge or freezer. Or if you have a bread machine, you can bake your own using a commercial gluten-free bread mix.

For non-coeliacs with digestive upsets

Commercial dough today is routinely loaded with conditioners and agents designed to help the dough survive the pummelling it goes through with the machines that produce bread. Rapid fermentation transforms flour into soft, squeezable, packaged loaves in two hours. But it doesn't allow time for the yeast to break down those starches and proteins.

For those who don't have coeliac disease but do find that you experience digestive problems such as bloating and flatulence after eating sliced supermarket breads, maybe it's time to switch to a genuine sourdough that's been made the old-fashioned way – one that's been proofed for 18 hours (ideally), or at least 12 hours (overnight).

The fact that people with digestive troubles can find they have few problems after eating a genuine sourdough suggests that something in the commercial bread-making process is a critical factor. So give the genuine sourdoughs a try.

But don't buy anything merely labelled 'sourdough', as larger manufacturers have cottoned on and are creating a sourish taste with the addition of vinegar. Seek out trusted independent bakeries that specialise in a long ferment and are proud of their bread.

Avoiding deficiency problems

Avoiding most grains can leave you short on fibre and B vitamins. So try to include brown rice or rice bran (or Metamucil, psyllium or Benefiber maize fibre) and make sure you eat plenty of vegetables and fruit. Talk to your doctor about a calcium or iron supplement, particularly if you have had diarrhoea for some time.

How the label can help you

The presence of gluten in *any* food ingredient or component of an ingredient (including additives) must be declared on the label, no matter how small the amount.

Avoid any thickener that could be derived from wheat starch (additive codes from 1400 to 1450). Most manufacturers now use thickeners derived from tapioca, maize or potato. If it doesn't tell you, there should be a warning 'Contains gluten' on the label.

Foods labelled as 'gluten free' must not contain any detectable gluten (less than 0.003 per cent).

Foods labelled as 'low gluten' must not contain more than 0.02 per cent gluten.

Eat to beat anxiety and depression

Depression is estimated to affect 350 million people worldwide. It's usually treated with medications, but new evidence suggests certain foods and nutrients may also help. In other words, eating better can mean fewer depressive symptoms, fewer side effects and less time off work. Always check with your medical professional before making any changes to your treatment.

In other words, eating better can mean fewer depressive symptoms, fewer side effects and less time off work.

Depression and anxiety are the two most common mental disorders. But other less common conditions include schizophrenia, bipolar disorder, eating disorders (anorexia and bulimia), alcohol abuse disease and drug abuse disorders.

Here are four steps you can take to 'battle the blues':

1. Follow the Med

Adherence to a Mediterranean diet is associated with a reduced risk of depression. An Australian study showed that this diet can be modified (with fresh meat replacing traditional preserved meats like prosciutto) and still work. Interestingly it contains some of the foods now tested for easing mental problems (see below). Still plan to eat more vegetables, more whole grains, fresh fruit, dairy, olive oil, fish and legumes, and less discretionary items such as soft drink and chips.

2. Spice it up

Saffron

Saffron (*Crocus sativus*) may well be the world's most expensive spice, but there have been several well-designed studies using it to help treat depression or minimise the side effects of antidepressants. In fact, two studies found that saffron extract performs as a SSRI (selective serotonin reuptake inhibitor, like Prozac) in reducing depressive symptoms.

Turmeric

Turmeric (*Curcuma longa*) is well known for its anti-ageing and brain-boosting properties. But it now seems that it has clinical efficacy in ameliorating

depressive symptoms. Anti-anxiety effects were reported in three of the six trials thus far investigated into the use of curcumin (turmeric's active ingredient) as an antidepressant.

Nutmeg
Nutmeg (*Myristica fragrans*) may help prevent and/or treat anxiety and depression without the side effects of antidepressants. But this has only been shown in animal studies so far. Adding more to your diet is a great first step.

3. Try St John's Wort
St John's Wort (*Hypericum perforatum*) has been the traditional herb for depression. However, it is important that you speak to your doctor before you decide to start taking this herb, as it can interact with other medications including antidepressants.

It is important that you speak to your doctor before you decide to start taking this herb, as it can interact with other medications including antidepressants.

4. Try fish oil
Fish oil, especially EPA, is useful in treating severe depression. It seems to improve the effectiveness of antidepressants by up to 30 per cent. The effective dosage is thought to be more than can be obtained through food alone and must be supplemented, although eating fatty fish itself is strongly recommended too.

Ways to halt the clock

Food is just part of healthy ageing. Here are four other ways to halt the clock:

1. Physical activity improves blood flow to the brain, reduces insulin resistance, regulates glucose metabolism, maintains muscle, maintains bone mass, controls weight, lowers blood pressure, lifts the mood and decreases chronic inflammation.
2. Join a club, volunteer, mix with others. Have a lot of social contact so you have friends and someone to talk to.
3. Don't forget: crosswords, sudoku, brain gym exercises, jigsaws, puzzles and other memory games, and learning a new skill (like dancing or knitting) all train your brain.
4. Keep your weight steady. People who are obese in middle age have twice the risk of developing dementia as those who aren't. But at later age, weight loss causes muscle loss, so stay active and keep your weight stable.

Eat to beat ageing

What can you eat to hold back the clock? To minimise the loss of brain function and memory loss as you get older? Let's be realistic about this – you *can* look younger than your years. Maybe 10 years younger – but if you're 60, it's unlikely that you can look 30 again. We can't stop ageing, but can eat to enjoy more years of health and vitality. What you eat in the early and middle years of adulthood reduces your risk of chronic disease and dementia later in life. Here are some ways to protect your brain and provide nutrients that can slow the cognitive decline and memory loss that occurs with old age. Add them now to your daily diet.

This list is adapted from the MIND diet, a hybrid of the Mediterranean diet (to lower the risk of Alzheimer's disease and dementia) and the DASH diet (to reduce high blood pressure).

Principles

Adults over 70 have unique nutrition needs. At older ages, changes in the way the body works, including digestion, actually increase the need for protein and some nutrients, despite many people feeling less hungry than they once did. So they need a nutrient-dense diet to supply them with extra protein, B12, folate, vitamin D, as well as many minerals.

For example:

- As you get older, vitamin D gets harder to make – by the age of 80, there is a 60 per cent reduction in the ability of the skin to synthesise it from sunlight. Of course, some can be obtained through regular, time spent safely outdoors, with the rest coming from food plus supplements.
- Reduced absorption of vitamin B12 from food is common in older people due to a combination of lowered production of acid in the stomach plus the impact of medications.

How to meet your needs

Eat more protein

Older people need about 20 per cent more protein than younger adults. Extra protein stimulates protein synthesis and works to offset the usual muscle loss (known as sarcopenia) that happens with age.

In practice, it's best to spread protein intake over the day and not eat it all at dinner. Try to have 25 to 30 grams of protein at two to three meals a day, ideally from nutrient-rich choices such as fresh meat, poultry, fish, eggs, cheese or yoghurt, legumes or tofu. These provide other key nutrients required for good health such as iron, zinc, omega-3 and B vitamins. There is no need for protein powders or bars.

Eat plenty of green leafy vegetables (like spinach, silverbeet, fresh herbs, salad greens)
Green leafy vegetables supply lots of folate, vitamin C, minerals like potassium and magnesium, and fibre, as well as numerous phytochemicals. They also fill you up for fewer kilojoules.

Aim for a salad a day, plus at least one serving of cooked greens.

Go for berries
Blueberries and strawberries in particular have been shown to protect from memory loss. Plus berries are rich in vitamin C, folate and anthocyanins – all good for older bodies. Aim for two or more servings a week.

Go fish (fresh, frozen or canned)
Oily fish such as tuna or salmon gives you omega-3 fatty acids to strengthen the brain, preserve eyesight and maintain blood flow, plus a good dose of vitamin D. Aim for two servings a week.

Add some spice
Be generous with spices such as turmeric, which is now a well-researched anti-inflammatory that can lower whole-body, low-grade inflammation (via a mode similar to that of aspirin). This inflammation is thought to play a role in damaging brain cells and damaging the heart. Studies on turmeric originally focused on its anti-inflammatory benefits and its

ability to inhibit cancer growth. Now studies are looking at its potential for improving cognitive function. And don't forget saffron, cinnamon and many similar spices, plus those woody herbs like rosemary and sage, all of which have been shown to be beneficial to our health.

Eat to beat heartburn

Indigestion and heartburn is a weekly occurrence for about one in five of us. It's that burning, painful, uncomfortable feeling we get at the top of the abdomen after eating. Its technical name is acid reflux or GORD (Gastro Oesophageal Reflux Disease), which is a more scientific way to describe it.

Symptoms of heartburn include burning pain, irritation, nausea, coughing (or just clearing the throat, especially after eating), wheezing, asthma symptoms and eroded tooth enamel. Unfortunately, heartburn also increases your chances of oesophageal cancer.

Who's at risk?
People who are overweight or older tend to be affected more since abdominal fat interferes with oesophageal function. Plus, the oesophageal sphincter, which prevents the backup of acid, weakens with age. And heartburn tends to run in families.

How to cope

Here are eight things you can do to minimise it.

1. Avoid eating a huge, heavy dinner within two hours of going to bed. Aim to eat by 8 pm so you can head to bed around 10 pm.
2. Aim to eat 'small and often'. Be more of a grazer than having three large meals a day.
3. Stay upright for at least an hour after eating. This reduces the risk of acid creeping up your oesophagus. You also want to avoid bending over or lifting heavy objects.
4. Lose excess weight, as it will reduce the pressure around your stomach.
5. Steer clear of greasy, spicy and fatty foods, which can relax the sphincter between your stomach and oesophagus, allowing food back up.
6. Cut down on caffeine. Reduce your intake of coffee, tea and cola drinks, as they're all heartburn triggers, especially on an empty stomach. Have them half-strength.
7. Avoid carbonated drinks and anything acidic on an empty stomach, e.g. fizzy drinks and lemon-flavoured waters.
8. Raise the height of your bed if you're a night-time refluxer. When you lay flat in bed, your throat and stomach are at the same level, making it easy for stomach acid to cause heartburn. Use a thick, wedge-shaped pillow so it raises your entire upper body, not just your head. Or raise the top of your bed by placing 10 to 15 centimetre (4 to 6 inch) blocks or

bricks under the legs at the head end of the bed – your aim is to sleep at a slight angle downwards.

Eat to beat gallstones

Gallstones, small hard 'rocks' of cholesterol and calcium, can block the tubes that drain the gall bladder. Once this happens, you experience terrible pain. Here's what you can do to prevent or lessen their occurrence.

Gallstone symptoms

People with gallstones may experience indigestion or an upset stomach, often noticed after a rich or heavy meal. Many people, however, have gallstones but experience absolutely no symptoms at all. In fact, gallstones can exist for years without causing any problems. It's only when gallstones block the tubes that the problem begins. This blockage causes inflammation of the gall bladder (cholecystitis) or of the bile drainage tubes (cholangitis). Symptoms then escalate to include:

· Severe pain or colic
· Fever
· Jaundice (skin turns yellow)

Symptoms are usually treated by surgery to remove the gall bladder (cholecystectomy), often done by keyhole surgery to minimise a major abdominal disturbance.

It's only when gallstones block the tubes that the problem begins.

Two life situations – before and after

1. If you've got gallstones and are awaiting surgery
Eating particular foods will not make gallstones disappear but can certainly lessen your pain while you are waiting for your operation.

· Steer clear of fatty, oily or fried foods. These high-fat foods 'activate' the gall bladder to release bile (needed to digest the fat) and so make your symptoms worse.
· Avoid concentrated fats like oil, butter, margarine, coconut oil, fat on meat or avocado, but you don't have to eat completely fat-free. Often it's a case of trial and error while you work out how low in fat you need to go.
· Avoid alcohol.

2. Once you have had your gall bladder removed

Once removed, the bile that was formerly stored in the gall bladder will now flow directly from the liver to the small intestine rather than being stored in the gall bladder first. The gall bladder is an organ that people can easily live without.

This means you can return to your usual diet. Restricting fat is no longer necessary; however, it is healthier to avoid 'bad' fats and to eat plenty of fibre. Check with your doctor about when you can drink alcohol again.

How to prevent gallstones

Gallstones are estimated to affect around 10 per cent of people in Western countries, mostly older women. The classic gallstone patient is characterised by the '4Fs': being female, fat, fair and forty plus. Here are five factors that can increase your likelihood of developing gallstones:

1. Obesity
2. History of gallstones in the family
3. Eating too little fibre and vegetables
4. Diabetes
5. Extreme weight loss and/or prolonged fasting

Eat to beat traveller's diarrhoea

Traveller's diarrhoea is the most common affliction for those travelling overseas and is so named because the cause is often simply the change in food or water. Unfortunately, if you're in developing countries, you're also more likely to encounter food that is contaminated, harbouring dangerous bacteria and viruses such as *E. coli*, shigella, salmonella, rotavirus and giardia.

Symptoms

Wherever in the world you are, the symptoms are usually the same:

- Diarrhoea
- Abdominal pain
- Vomiting
- Nausea
- Fever

Treating tummy troubles

Keep the following six key food safety tips handy:

1. Remember the best treatment is simply to drink plenty of fluids, as fluid loss through the bowel is significant. Keep your fluid intake up. Little and often is better than big and once only, and make sure the fluids are safe to drink. Water that is either boiled or bottled is fine, but a rehydration drink such as Hydralyte or Gastrolyte is better, as it replaces lost electrolytes and is recommended for children.
2. You can make your own rehydration drink by dissolving 8 teaspoons of sugar and ½ teaspoon of salt in 1 litre of safe water. Alternatively, sip weak black tea, sports drinks, mineral water or well-diluted fruit juice or soft drink (1 part juice or lemonade to 4 parts water).
3. There's no need to starve yourself. If you feel like eating, try bland carbohydrate foods like boiled rice, oats, plain toast, banana, cracker biscuits, mashed potato, cooked cereals and cooked pasta.
4. Avoid or limit milk products, alcohol, and fatty and spicy foods.
5. There's usually no need to see a doctor unless the diarrhoea is severe or has not improved after two to three days. Antidiarrhoeals should not be taken unless you absolutely must (e.g. you have to get on a plane), as they can make things worse in the long run.
6. For further information and to obtain sachets of rehydration powder and antibiotics (as well as vaccinations), visit a traveller's medical and vaccination centre.

Where do I need to follow these tips?

They apply to developing countries, especially those with warm or tropical climates, like South-East Asia, Africa, the Middle East and South America. High-risk destinations are India, Nepal, tour boats on the Nile and poorer areas outside the main cities of any developing country.

The BRAT diet

The acronym BRAT stands for Bananas, Rice, Applesauce and Toast. These are the bland low-fibre foods to treat yourself with. Behind them all is the goal to provide electrolytes, fluids and starch in low-fibre form. Backpackers and frequent travellers swear by this BRAT diet. There are many variations. The BRAT diet is a sort of anti-diarrhoea first-aid treatment. If it helps, then medical treatment may not be required.

Sample meal plan

Breakfast
· Half a mashed banana on dry toast, no butter or margarine
· Weak black tea with half spoon of sugar or honey

Morning tea (or two hours after breakfast)
· Half a cup of applesauce or however much you can manage
· Diluted flat lemonade

Lunch
· Bowl of boiled white rice
· Rehydration drink

Afternoon tea (or two hours after lunch)
· Half a cup of applesauce or however much you can manage
· Diluted flat lemonade

Dinner
· Boiled or steamed chicken breast
· Bowl of boiled white rice
· Mug of clear chicken broth

In between meals
· Suck on ice blocks (assuming the water is clean)
· Frozen ice cordial
· Rehydration drink
· Boiled tea or herbal tea or water with sugar/honey

Eat to beat a hangover

Many people suffer the ill effects from excess alcohol in the form of a hangover – a pounding headache, a drier-than-dry mouth, loss of balance, nausea and fatigue. Hangovers have three causes:

1. Dehydration
2. Alcohol's interference with the body's chemistry
3. Substances that are present in alcoholic drinks called congeners, such as tannins, volatile acids, methanol and histamines

Researchers believe that it's these congeners that actually cause more headaches than the alcohol itself. Dark-coloured drinks like brandy, sherry and red wine (especially cheaper brands) have been shown to produce the most distressing headaches, followed by rum, whisky, beer, white wine and gin. The least effect is produced by vodka. Mixing different types of drinks can also produce hangovers.

Congeners are viewed as toxic substances in the alcohol.

Congeners are viewed as toxic substances in the alcohol, which, when you drink, are dispersed through your system. The level of congeners varies between different beverages. More expensive alcohol contains fewer congeners, as it undergoes a more rigorous distillation process that filters out a higher percentage of them.

Steps to avoid a hangover

1. Stay hydrated
Prevent dehydration and you stave off the worst of a hangover. Dehydration is responsible for most of the symptoms of a hangover such as the raging thirst, the throbbing headache and the dizziness. Alcohol is a diuretic, which means it 'pushes' water out from the body. So water is one thing to replace. Nausea and vomiting result from the direct action of alcohol irritating the delicate lining of the digestive tract.

2. Skip hangover tablets

Almost everyone you know seems to have a tablet or drink they swear will take away the bad effects of too much. But in reality, there isn't one that works!

Over-the-counter hangover remedies such as Alcodol, Chaser, Sob'r-K Hangover Stopper, RU-21 and Rebound usually contain some type of sugar (fructose, glucose) along with vitamins B or C, minerals or a herbal liver tonic such as milk thistle, artichoke, taurine or dandelion.

You pop a couple of these before you start drinking, before you go to bed and the next morning 'if required'. Some are based on charcoal granules or clays such as bentonite, which claim to 'filter' out any impurities while passing out undigested. Don't believe the hype about these so-called 'miracles' – the herbs are not there in sufficient quantity to do much, while the charcoal and clay are unproven. The vitamins and minerals are meant to top up what gets washed out in the urine by alcohol's diuretic action.

A 2005 study published in the *British Medical Journal* of eight trials assessing eight different products reported there was 'no compelling evidence to suggest that any conventional or complementary intervention is effective for preventing or treating alcohol hangovers'. Again it's the water you drink with them that does the job.

No hangover cure has ever been proven. Hangover remedies may work when your drinking is light but become ineffective if you go on a huge binge.

Hangovers and B1

Effervescent hangover remedies such as Berocca and Hairy Lemon extol the benefits of thiamin (vitamin B1) to counteract the excesses of alcohol. You drop the tablet in a glass of water and allow it to dissolve before drinking the lot or simply rip open a ready-to-drink bottle – ideally before you go to bed at the end of a big night.

In theory, this makes sense as alcohol depletes the body's thiamin for its own metabolism. However, there is no real scientific evidence to support a super-quick effect for this B vitamin on preventing hangovers or for curing them the morning after. Many supplements and drinks have huge amounts of thiamin so their label looks good – in excess, they're not harmful and the water you drink while getting them down helps you get over the dehydrating effect of alcohol.

The best ways to avoid a hangover

Not drinking is the best form of prevention ... but let's be realistic! Here's what else you can do:

1. Have something fatty to eat before you start – that traditional glass of milk or a wedge of cheese fits the bill.
2. Drink plenty of fluid during and after to counteract the dehydration. Alternate alcohol drinks with water or fizzy soda; aim to match the volume of alcohol you drink with something non-alcoholic.
3. At the start, quench your thirst with a large non-alcoholic drink to slow down how much you drink.
4. Beware fizzy drinks such as champagne. The bubbles 'push' the alcohol into the body more quickly, so high blood alcohol levels are rapidly reached.
5. Pace yourself – binge drinking does the worst damage, so try to restrict alcohol to around meal times or after 6 pm in the evening.

Eat to beat iron-deficiency anaemia

If you're tired all the time with little energy, it's worth paying a visit to your doctor for a blood test to check whether you have iron-deficiency anaemia. They will send your blood to a lab to do an analysis of the markers of iron – your ferritin (a measure of your body's iron stores) or transferrin (the main iron transporting protein in the circulation).

Iron deficiency is the most common nutrition problem in the world.

Iron deficiency is the most common nutrition problem in the world, affecting around 35 per cent of people in developing countries and 8 per cent in affluent countries. Because it is not life-threatening and mainly affects women and children, iron deficiency never receives the attention it deserves.

Symptoms
The symptoms of iron-deficiency anaemia are:
- Lack of energy
- Poor capacity for exercise/stamina
- Pale skin
- An inability to concentrate
- Greater susceptibility to infections
- Feeling the cold often
- Delayed psychomotor development in children

3. Skip greasy foods
Greasy eggs and bacon are a popular hangover cure. They fix the 'munchies', particularly if you've been dancing or have otherwise burned off heaps of energy, but it's wise to hold off the greasies if the nausea and vomiting are bad. Light fare such as toast, fruit (fresh or canned), flat lemonade, weak black tea with sugar, clear soup or boiled rice go down better on a delicate stomach. Eat small amounts often.

Eggs – both cooked and raw – may have some evidence behind them. Egg yolks are rich in cysteine, a component amino acid of protein that scientists believe can break down acetaldehyde, one of the major end-products of alcohol metabolism. Cysteine supplements are sold at pharmacies for this reason.

4. Sleep it off
Time is the best way for your body to break down the alcohol. Sleep, or at least rest, for as long as you can. The effects of a hangover last about 24 hours, so be patient. Neither strong coffee, vigorous exercise nor cold showers speed the rate of alcohol breakdown in the body, but fructose (fruit sugar) has been found to do so and is often sold for just this reason to help sober up. Unfortunately the amounts needed to work are quite large and would make you feel unwell.

The 6 groups who are commonly iron deficient

1. Women need almost double the iron requirements of men due to the monthly blood loss through menstruation (especially women who have heavy periods).
2. Teenage girls require more iron to meet the demands of rapid growth and the onset of menstruation.
3. Vegetarians have a lower iron status than meat eaters. Although there is abundant iron in green vegetables and grains, it is not as well absorbed.
4. Young children under the age of two are growing fast and can be fussy eaters.
5. Athletes lose out on iron due to the heavy pounding of exercising, plus a greater muscle mass. 'Sports anaemia' is well documented in professional female athletes and can affect their capacity to train to peak levels.
6. Poor absorbers can be at risk if your body can't absorb iron efficiently. For example, many people with coeliac or Crohn's disease don't absorb the iron they ingest, as their inner bowel is inflamed or atrophied and so unable to do its job properly.

What to eat

Red meat is the best source of iron, and it's well-absorbed by the body. Generally, the redder the richer, so enjoy that steak or lean lamb rump. Even if you only eat meat occasionally (which I recommend), small amounts (such as a few strips of beef in a vegetable stir-fry) can improve your iron absorption from the vegetables in your meal. The iron in grains, vegetables, legumes, nuts and eggs is not absorbed as well as it is from meat.

Ways to boost your iron absorption

Here are two ways to boost the iron you absorb:

1. Add vitamin C. Adding a glass of fruit juice or some tomato or capsicum (all rich in vitamin C) to a meal increases the amount of iron delivered by grains or lentils. Most vegetarian meals, with their emphasis on vegetables and fruit, would automatically contain much vitamin C.
2. Watch what you drink with meals. Relative to water, orange juice doubles iron intake, while milk decreases it by 50 per cent and tea by 75 per cent. Best to save tea and coffee for between meals.

When an iron supplement can help

The body's iron is in delicate balance – too little leads to problems, but so can too much. Ideally it's best to obtain iron as nature intended: from food, rather than rely on supplements.

A US study of 60 females who exercised moderately found that the iron in meat was better absorbed than that from an iron supplement. The researchers calculated that only 2.2 milligrams of iron was finally absorbed from a 50 milligram controlled-release iron capsule.

When body iron stores are low, an iron supplement can help. But it pays to choose carefully. The most common form of iron in supplements is slow-release ferrous sulphate, but this tends to cause constipation, dark stools and nausea. Ferrous gluconate, ferrous fumarate and chelated forms of iron are more readily absorbed and may cause fewer problems. All, however, are non-haem forms of iron, which are subject to the same poor bioavailability as that in vegetables. So, take an iron tablet on an empty stomach, i.e. before breakfast, as food can inhibit absorption by up to 50 per cent. In addition, take one every second day as this is less likely to produce the unpleasant side effects.

Eat to beat constipation

Constipation is a common problem – almost one in five people over the age of 30 has constipation at some stage during their life. Often it is mild, occurring after surgery, childbirth or any bowel procedure. Straining to pass small, hard stools causes a build-up of muscular pressure in the bowel. Eventually, constant pressure causes weak spots or 'blow-outs' in the wall, which can become inflamed and painful.

Many people rely on laxatives in the form of powders, granules, tablets, chewables, syrups, suppositories or enemas. While they're okay for a week or two, apart from the expense, laxatives (whether bulking agents, stool softeners, osmotic agents or stimulants) can become habitual and may even be harmful over a long period of time.

Long term, I recommend you forget laxatives, and get your system regular with a high-fibre diet. A bowel motion each day is not essential, but it is important that your stools are easy to pass. Straining should be avoided – aim for a soft consistency rather than regularity!

Fibre offers the safest, simplest solution to relieve constipation. It increases the bulk of the stool, giving the faeces the correct soft consistency so they can be eliminated without effort. When you eat lots of fibre your bowel motions are passed more easily and more frequently and it also helps enrich your microbiome so you stay healthy.

Tips to help

Food and exercise first, laxatives second:

- Drink plenty of water. Fibre absorbs a lot of water (around 70 per cent of the weight of bowel motions is water).
- Substitute high-fibre foods for any low-fibre choices you now eat. The easiest food to start with is breakfast cereals, where I suggest you buy a bran cereal or one labelled 'high in fibre'. Look for one with more than 10 grams per 100 grams of fibre. Or just sprinkle 1 tablespoon of wheat bran or ½ cup bran pellet cereal over your favourite cereal.
- Add cooked or canned beans or lentils to a mince dish or slow-cooked curry. Or eat a small can of baked beans on toast.
- Forget fruit juice, which lacks fibre. Instead drink water or weak tea and eat a piece of fresh fruit, preferably with the skin on. For example, instead of a glass of juice, eat a whole apple, cut into quarters. You'll get double the fibre.
- Exercise helps maintain bowel tone and internal muscles. Walking is all you need to do.
- When you need to pass a motion, allow yourself enough time to relax and have privacy on the toilet.
- Try prunes, prune juice, dried figs, raisins, liquorice, liquorice tea, senna pod tea or dandelion tea. These foods contain naturally occurring compounds that have long been known to have a laxative effect (ranging from mild to strong) and can be worth trying before resorting to laxatives.

9   The top 20 superfoods

Here at last is good news – foods that you can tuck into regularly that are not only nutrition superstars but can be valuable weapons in the war against a host of ailments.

Catherine Saxelby's top 20 superfoods

1. Almonds
2. BARLEYmax™
3. Blueberries and other berries
4. Cabbage and other cruciferous vegetables
5. Chillies
6. Cinnamon
7. Eggs
8. Green leafy herbs such as basil and parsley
9. Linseeds (flaxseeds)
10. Salmon
11. Garlic
12. Lamb
13. Lupin
14. Mushroom
15. Oats
16. Oranges and other citrus
17. Spinach, silverbeet, Asian greens and other green leafy vegetables
18. Tea
19. Wheatgerm
20. Yoghurt

Almonds

Include these nutrition-packed nuts in your diet regularly and you'll make a good investment in your heart's health, so latest research suggests. Over a dozen studies now point to almonds, walnuts, cashews, Brazil and other nuts as being heart-protective. We all know that a handful of nuts a day (anywhere from 30 to 50 grams) is on the list of must-eat foods for heart health.

Crunchy, flavoursome and very more-ish, almonds are a concentrated food. Around half their weight is natural oils, which gives them a high kilojoule count. But the good news is that their fat is 72 per cent monounsaturated and 20 per cent polyunsaturated, but only 8 per cent saturated – a profile that matches olive and canola oils. The oil occurs in its natural state, so you can eat almonds as a natural, intact source of 'good' fats.

Almonds boast a rich content of vitamin E, fibre and arginine (an amino acid) – three factors that lower the 'harmful' LDL cholesterol or prevent oxygen from damaging it. They also have good amounts of a number of B vitamins and minerals such as calcium and magnesium.

Their protein ranges from 7 to 20 per cent, making them an important protein source for vegetarians. Like all nuts, their carbohydrate is quite low.

Almonds stand out for their high calcium content – ⅓ cup (50 grams) offers 125 milligrams of calcium, as much as from half a glass of milk.

Almonds have been cultivated since ancient times and are a close relative of the plum and the peach. They are available whole, split, slivered, chopped and ground (also known as almond meal) and feature in confectionery, muffins and pastries, particularly those of European origin, like marzipan.

BARLEYmax™

Developed by CSIRO scientists in the late 1990s, BARLEYmax™ barley grain contains twice the fibre and four times the resistant starch of regular barley. It works to improve health by delivering high levels of resistant starch, soluble fibre and insoluble fibre – the three components of fibre.

BARLEYmax™ contains 70 per cent more beta-glucan than oats, and has a low GI. It is used as the basis of high-fibre breakfast cereals, porridge, breads, wraps and muesli bars.

The resistant starch in BARLEYmax™ does four things. It:

1. Has a mild laxative effect, which, like insoluble fibre, can increase the bulk of the stool
2. Supplies fuel for the friendly bacteria in the bowel, which encourages their growth so they can reproduce and outnumber or 'dominate' the bad bacteria to keep you healthy
3. Produces compounds called short-chain fatty acids (in particular butyrate), which is good for your bowel
4. Maintains steady blood glucose levels by increasing the body's sensitivity to insulin

I like that we are eating another grain that's not wheat. With its hefty dose of fibre, as well as protein, B vitamins, phosphorus and other minerals, this is one grain that is going to make a difference to your digestive health. Plus you'll be boosting your wholegrain intake.

Blueberries and other berries

Blueberries are the nutrition powerhouses of the fruit world. Not only are they low in kilojoules, but they also happen to taste juicy and sweet.

Researchers at the USDA Human Nutrition Center rank blueberries as number one for antioxidant activity when compared to other fresh fruits and vegetables. Anthocyanins – the pigments that give the berries their blue–red colour – are believed to be responsible for this health benefit. These anthocyanins act as antioxidants and slow down the ageing of the brain. They have been shown to boost memory and brain function as we age, as well as protect the eyes from cataracts and glaucoma.

Anthocyanins have also been shown to enhance the effects of vitamin C, improve the strength of capillaries and stabilise collagen (the ground

> Anthocyanins have also been shown to enhance the effects of vitamin C.

substance of all body tissues), improve the circulation and protect the heart.

Like other berries, blueberries are good-to-excellent sources of vitamin C – half a small punnet (75 grams) supplies 10 milligrams of vitamin C, which is 25 per cent of your average daily requirement – and fibre (both insoluble and soluble fibre, like pectin), which adds to their superfood status.

They also offer beta-carotene (which gets converted into vitamin A once in the body); vitamin E; and B vitamins such as folate (which helps prevent birth defects in babies) and niacin (which releases energy from food), as well as lesser amounts of a number of essential minerals like manganese, potassium, magnesium and phosphorus.

All this for very few kilojoules. Half a punnet supplies a mere 165 kilojoules (39 calories) so makes a guiltless indulgence for anyone concerned about weight loss. And it's low GI. Add a squeeze of orange juice and serve with berry yoghurt or ice cream and you have the ideal light dessert, low in kilojoules and light on fat – not to mention absolutely yummy!

Cabbage

This nutritional superfood is a must-eat, providing over twice your daily requirement of vitamin C from an average serve. Plus it's top of the list for beta-carotene (the precursor of vitamin A), folate, vitamin E plus several B vitamins and minerals like iron and calcium. With hardly any kilojoules, as anyone who has tried the cabbage soup diet can testify, cabbage is a winner all round.

People who eat large helpings of cabbage or its cruciferous cousins, cauliflower, brussels sprouts, broccoli and kale, show a reduced risk of several cancers, especially cancer of the colon. Their active ingredients are sulphur compounds known as indoles

and isothiocyanates, which seem to 'switch on' cancer-fighting enzymes and block potentially dangerous carcinogens in the food we ingest. The sulforaphane in broccoli is the best known of these, but they're in all cruciferous vegetables.

Cabbage is also high in fibre, another dietary factor that keeps the bowel healthy (and has given it its reputation as a 'windy' vegetable). This soluble fibre also makes it bulky and filling – good for appetite control – and can lower blood cholesterol. Half a cup of raw shredded cabbage (70 grams) has only 31 kilojoules (7 calories). See more on raw versus cooked cabbage on pages 78–9 (sauerkraut).

Chillies

Chillies pack a mighty punch in nutrition terms. They have a strong concentration of vitamin C, around two to three times greater than citrus fruit, and are high in fibre, minerals like potassium and some of the B vitamins. But as the quantities of chilli consumed are fairly small, their overall contribution ends up being minor (although for chilli aficionados, it may be significant).

Red chillies, which are at a more mature stage of ripeness than green, offer plenty of beta-carotene, a prominent antioxidant and precursor to vitamin A. Dried chilli flakes have less vitamin C than fresh, but are still rich in beta-carotene, other related carotenoids and minerals.

Thanks to their capsaicin, chillies are known to raise the metabolic rate, one of the reasons why a curry often warms you up (known as a thermogenic effect). This has been promoted as an advantage to dieters, as a body with a 'super-speed engine' burns fuel faster. In any case, chilli and chilli sauces can certainly pep up an otherwise bland diet meal.

Cinnamon

If you only have room for one spice in your kitchen, cinnamon should be it! I love it for its aroma, but research has revealed that small amounts of cinnamon taken each day can lower blood sugar levels in those with diabetes. Good news.

For instance, researchers in Pakistan took 60 men and women with type 2 diabetes and supplemented their diets with 1, 3 or 6 grams of cinnamon a day. Over the 40 days of the study, their blood sugar levels dropped on average by 20 per cent compared to those in the control group who were given a placebo (a similar-looking powder without any cinnamon).

The amount of cinnamon found to be effective was around half a teaspoon (3 grams) a day. Surprisingly, levels stayed low 20 days after the cinnamon was stopped, and blood triglycerides and cholesterol also showed a decrease.

So you can be generous with the cinnamon in your

desserts such as creamy rice, baked custard, apple crumble, apple strudel and stewed pears as well as porridge and smoothies.

Cinnamon is probably not the only spice with such good news. Other spices like cloves and nutmeg may well turn out to have similar benefits. Already we know that most spices are extremely rich in nutrients such as beta-carotene, certain B vitamins and natural phytochemicals. But in the tiny amounts used in cooking, they are not usually significant sources of nutrition.

Eggs

Eggs are great to cook and have elite nutrition qualities. As one of nature's best convenience foods, they travel with us from cradle to grave. Babies love their soft texture as a weaning food (the yolk can be introduced after six months, while the white is usually held back until after nine months to minimise the possibility of allergy).

Older folk appreciate their high protein and ease of use. A dozen eggs, stored in the refrigerator, is the most convenient of protein foods, always on hand to create a quick omelette, frittata or simply served scrambled on toast.

An egg is a compact package of nutrition. For a very modest 355 kilojoules (85 calories), it gives you a host of essential minerals, and every vitamin except vitamin C. Worth mentioning is vitamin B12, which is hard to obtain on vegetarian diets, and folate, a B vitamin that can help minimise birth defects.

Eggs are a surprising source of two carotenoids, lutein and zeaxanthin, natural compounds related to the beta-carotene of carrots and usually found only in vegetables and fruits. These two phytochemicals are now under study for their role in preventing macular degeneration of the eye, a common cause of blindness in older folk.

If your risk of heart disease is low, then an egg a day poses no problem.

If your risk of heart disease is low, then an egg a day poses no problem. And eggs are not high in saturated fat. A medium 60-gram egg has only 6 grams of total fat. Of this, less than 2 grams is saturated, with the remaining 4 grams being healthy monounsaturated fat plus polyunsaturated fat.

Garlic

Long hailed as 'nature's penicillin', garlic was used as a medicine by the ancient Egyptians, Vikings and Chinese. The slaves who toiled to build the Great Pyramid kept their strength up with a ration of garlic and onion each day. Fresh cloves of garlic are better than other forms of garlic, such as dried garlic and aged extract, and can slow the growth of bacteria and fungi if you are seeking its antibacterial or antiviral qualities.

Both fresh and dried garlic have been shown to lower LDL cholesterol, lower high blood pressure and help dissolve clots, although not all studies agree. The dose required is quite large for most of us – 10 to 20 grams of fresh garlic (2 to 4 cloves) a day, or 600–900 milligrams of powdered garlic. Garlic's pungent odour comes from allicin and other sulphur compounds, which at present are credited with being its active agents – odourless garlic tablets are not as effective.

You can use plenty in your stir-fries and curries. A couple of cloves has hardly any kilojoules and adds fibre, starch and protein.

Green leafy herbs

Let's not forget that those culinary herbs such as parsley, basil and coriander that grace our meals can make a sizeable contribution to our nutrition intake – if we eat enough of them.

All fresh herbs are rich sources of a number of minerals – potassium and magnesium, with smaller

amounts of iron and calcium – as well as vitamin C, folate, vitamin B1 and vitamin K. They also score high for fibre.

For instance, on a weight-for-weight comparison, basil and parsley have almost twice as much vitamin C as oranges. Dill has six times more beta-carotene than rockmelon or pumpkin.

But we consume at most only 1 or 2 grams of any herb while we happily tuck into 120 grams of an orange. So it's easy to see why herbs have been deemed 'insignificant' in the vitamin stakes.

But this wouldn't be the case if we made a herb-rich dish like tabouleh every night.

But this wouldn't be the case if we made a herb-rich dish like tabouleh every night. With a couple of bunches of parsley in every bowl along with mint, cracked wheat, garlic and tomato, this is a delicious way to prove how herbs can really boost your nutrient intake. Ditto for pesto sauce – lots of basil (or you can use coriander instead) blended with toasted pine nuts, olive oil and garlic. Maximum flavour, maximum vitamins.

Herbs are surprisingly rich in beneficial phytochemicals. Rosemary, thyme and oregano have been found to be rich in polyphenols, one type of compound that may cut the risk of heart disease. Mint, basil and parsley are high in monoterpenes, which are thought to have cancer-delaying properties, especially with mammary tumours.

Parsley is also high in coumarins, noted for their anticoagulant and antibacterial effects, while extracts of rosemary are being used as a natural food-grade preservative. If you're trying to cut back on salt, use herbs freely to boost the flavour of your meals.

Lamb

A roast leg of lamb was once regarded as the best food on offer. Despite a huge drop in consumption over the last 60 years, lamb remains a popular meat, accounting for around one-third of all red meat eaten in Australia.

Lean lamb, trimmed of visible fat, makes an important nutrition contribution to our diet. It offers high-quality protein with all the essential amino acids required by the human body; the minerals iron, zinc and potassium; and a range of B vitamins, including thiamin, niacin, vitamins B6 and B12.

Nutritionally, lamb – like all red meat – is most valued for its iron, which occurs as haem iron, the type most easily absorbed by the body. Iron is important for healthy blood, the development of our brain, the functioning of our immune system and for work performance. It is somewhat ironic that women, who have the greatest nutritional requirement for iron, are the smallest consumers of meat and so deprive themselves of the best form of iron from food.

Look for the expanded range of lean cuts of lamb such as boneless leg roasts, lamb strips, fillets, steaks, cubes and cutlets, which offer a healthier alternative – a far cry from the fatty chops of yesteryear. And lamb portions are smaller, in line with lighter-style meals. Lambs are largely grass-fed, not barn-raised, and killed young so don't accumulate any heavy metals or potential toxins.

Linseeds (flaxseeds)

Small, shiny, dark brown seeds about the size of sesame seeds, linseeds (also called flaxseeds) are a storehouse of omega-3s. They're the richest plant source of one particular fatty acid called alpha-linolenic acid (ALA), which is the building block of all the same omega-3 oils found in fish.

Linseeds are also rich in lignans, a type of plant oestrogen that lowers female oestrogen levels, helps minimise the unpleasant side effects of the menopause like hot flushes, lowers blood pressure and has anti-tumour properties.

In the plant kingdom, there aren't many foods where you'll find omega-3s. So linseeds are an important food for vegans who eat no eggs or fish and may run the risk of going short on omega-3s. One or two tablespoons is all it takes to boost your intake. Add this to your muesli, yoghurt or smoothie. Or make up a nutrient-packed sprinkle – grind together 1 cup of walnut pieces with ½ cup of linseeds.

Lupin

Lupin has a nutritional scorecard that shines, boasting fibre and protein as its highlights. Scientists developed this sweet, Australian legume as an alternative to the more bitter European lupin back in the 1960s. Now it is a significant crop grown in Western Australia. The flakes are small and hard (rather than thin and light), with a distinctive yellow colour and a mild fibrous smell, but nothing too off-putting. Surprisingly it is low in carbohydrates (only 4 per cent), which makes it stand out from quinoa, barley, brown rice and other high-carb grains.

As lupin is a legume, not a grain, it is free of gluten and so is suitable for those with coeliac disease or gluten intolerance. It's low in sodium, at 42 milligrams per 100 grams. Lupin has more fibre than most other legumes (double the fibre in chickpeas) and grains (roughly four times more than quinoa).

It's quick and versatile to use, acting as both a legume and grain substitute in recipes. Finally, it's grown in Australia, so it's good news for our farmers and it has low food miles (unlike quinoa).

Mushrooms

Mushrooms – dubbed the 'meat of vegetarians' – are known to be a good source of many of the B vitamins (including B2, B3, B5, B12 and biotin), plus the minerals copper, chromium, selenium and potassium, as well as fibre and protein. Plus, thanks to their high level of natural glutamates, they have a delicious savoury flavour classified by the Japanese as 'umami'.

Mushrooms are an abundant source of ergosterol, which can readily be converted to ergocalciferol (the active form of the vitamin known as vitamin D2) through the action of sunlight.

Mushrooms have virtually no fat and, while they lost this status for a little while, mushrooms are again regarded as a source of B12. If the mushrooms are farm cultivated, they add a modest quantity of the same type of vitamin B12 found in meats and seafood.

Mushrooms are healthy, versatile, easy to prepare and delicious. Toss them into salads, stir-fries, risottos, frittatas, omelettes and soups; cook them on the barbecue or simply serve on thick crunchy toast. They extend the flavour of meat and, in many recipes, subbing in half the weight of mushrooms for minced meat lowers the kilojoules without altering the flavour.

Mushrooms come as buttons, cups and flats (portobellos). But you'll also spot shiitake, which have a surprising meaty flavour that imparts a richness to Asian-style soups and stir-fries, oyster mushrooms, Swiss browns, with a rich flavour and firm texture characteristic of European dishes, and enoki, which look like clusters of tiny white plants with small heads on long stems.

Oats

Oats are a winner among all grains, being nutrition all-rounders. Wholegrain oats have a medium GI, so their carbohydrate is more slowly absorbed into your system. Their fibre is the soluble type that prevents the breakdown products of cholesterol from re-entering the system via the intestine. Plus they contain beta-glucan. The result is less cholesterol being made in the body.

Oats are one of the few grains to be free of gluten (although most oat crops are often contaminated by stray wheat grains and so are unsuitable for gluten-free diets). They carry small amounts of good fats, more than wheat or rice. And they are packed with nourishment, giving you B vitamins and vitamin E as well as protein and minerals.

Half a cup of cooked porridge oats (weighing 130 grams) supplies – because it's largely water – 2 grams of protein, 1 gram of fat, 11 grams of starch, a little dietary fibre and 260 kilojoules (60 calories).

Oat bran is the outer high-fibre component of the oat grain. It soared to celebrity status in 1987 with the publication of Robert Kowalski's *The New 8-Week Cholesterol Cure* but then has 'died' as a health food.

Oranges and other citrus

Oranges get the thumbs up from every nutritionist. Like other citrus, oranges are packed full of vitamin C, providing an entire day's needs in just half an orange. This vitamin can enhance iron absorption, speed up wound healing, keep gums healthy and reduce the risk of an infection.

Containing little in the way of fat, added sugar or protein, oranges are high in water (over 85 per cent of their flesh is water) with natural fruit sugars. Oranges give us sizeable quantities of soluble fibre, including the gelling fibres pectin and several gums – a fact well known to home marmalade makers.

They offer much potassium and smaller amounts of other minerals as well as vitamin B1, making them a nutritional all-rounder. Few other fruit can match this overall nutrition profile.

To top it off, they contain natural compounds such as limonene (a monoterpene) that research shows can

help prevent colon cancer and reduce the risk of lung cancer in smokers.

Even the peel contains nutritional 'goodies' that lower cholesterol or ward off cancer, so use it wherever you can in desserts or as a marinade.

Ideally go for whole oranges. Freshly squeezed orange juice is heavenly but lacks the original fibre and is concentrated in kilojoules. A 250 millilitre glass of juice is equivalent to four whole oranges in kilojoule value – a trap for anyone on a diet.

Salmon

Low in saturated fat, rich in protein, zinc and iron, and a great source of long-chain omega-3s – there are plenty of good reasons to eat salmon, tuna, trout, mackerel, herring and other oily or darker fish.

Salmon is full of minerals from the sea like iodine, potassium and prostate-protecting zinc. Few other fish show salmon's versatility – it can be eaten fresh, smoked, frozen or canned.

Oily fish are the best source of omega-3 fats, unique polyunsaturated fatty acids which can prevent stickiness of the blood, steady the heart's rhythm and lower blood pressure.

Omega-3s are crucial for our brain function (fish truly is brain food!). One omega-3 called DHA plays a key role in the development of babies' brains and eyesight. It is abundant in breastmilk and many cultures have traditionally fed fish to new mothers to increase their milk. All types of fish carry some omega-3, but the oily cold-water varieties like salmon have around double that of temperate-water fish.

The small edible bones of salmon, softened and made digestible in the canning process, yield an important source of calcium, a mineral generally derived from milk. A small 100-gram can of salmon provides 200 to 230 milligrams of calcium, which represents 25 per cent of the recommended daily intake for calcium.

Spinach, silverbeet and other green leafy vegetables

If you're not adding spinach to your meals, you're missing out on one of nature's true superfoods. It's chock-full of vitamins, minerals and plant compounds – yet supplies few kilojoules.

It's an excellent source of vitamin C, folate, beta-carotene (converted to vitamin A in the body) and vitamin E. An average serve of 60 grams provides 10 milligrams of vitamin C, 25 per cent of the recommended day's intake.

It offers many phytochemicals but is one of the best sources of lutein and zeaxanthin. These two phytochemicals can help protect our eyes as we age, so keeping macular degeneration at bay.

Well known for its high iron content (which was made famous by the cartoon *Popeye*), spinach's iron is unfortunately not well absorbed. It's present but doesn't get into the body in great amounts.

Regardless of whether you make a salad with baby spinach leaves or cook spinach as a base for eggs (think of Eggs Florentine), spinach won't disappoint. Plus you can add a handful of spinach leaves to finish off any curry or stir-fry.

Tea

Black or white, strong or weak, with or without sugar, tea is the world's favourite hot drink. It has been drunk for thousands of years – since the time of ancient China.

Tea leaves contain protein, B vitamins and the minerals potassium, phosphorus, calcium, magnesium and iron. When drunk as an infusion, however, tea is not especially rich in any single nutrient, except for fluoride, which protects against tooth decay.

Both green tea and black tea are rich in

Both green tea and black tea are rich in phytochemicals known as catechins.

phytochemicals known as catechins, shown to be more potent than the well-studied beta-carotene or vitamin E. One of these catechins, called EGCG, has been extensively studied and can inhibit the growth of tumours in animals.

Many studies have examined the link between tea and heart disease and reported that people who drink it regularly have a significantly lower risk of heart issues than those who don't. It seems that the catechins in tea help maintain heart health by decreasing inflammation, lowering the tendency for clotting (an early factor in heart attacks) and by keeping the arteries more 'elastic'.

The addition of milk or lemon has no effect on the absorption of these catechins. As black and green are derived from the same plant, *Camellia sinensis*, their caffeine count is about the same.

Best of all, if you take it black with no milk or sugar, tea has no kilojoules and has the ability to both relax and revive you.

Yoghurt

Yoghurt has been viewed as a superfood ever since the early 1900s when the longevity of Bulgarian peasants was attributed to their high intake of thick yoghurt.

Packed with calcium, protein and B vitamins (especially riboflavin, a B vitamin needed for healthy skin and eyes), yoghurt offers the nutrients of milk but in a more concentrated form. For example, in terms of calcium, a 200 gram carton of yoghurt – plain or fruit – is equivalent to drinking a 250 millilitre glass of milk. For women and teenage girls, who need plenty of calcium to build strong bones, yoghurt is a must-eat food.

In addition, yoghurt is more easily digested and absorbed than milk due to its 'partial pre-digestion' by its lactic acid bacteria. Studies show the protein, fat and lactose it contains are better absorbed and the calcium is more available than from milk.

People with lactose intolerance are more likely to tolerate yoghurt than milk. During yoghurt making, the bacteria partly break down the milk sugar lactose, turning it into lactic acid, which imparts yoghurt's sour taste.

On top of that, the carbohydrate in yoghurt is slowly absorbed, producing only a modest rise in blood glucose levels, which makes it a filling low-GI snack or dessert for anyone with diabetes. A 200 gram carton of plain low-fat yoghurt supplies 10 grams of protein, a trace of fat, 16 grams of sugars, no starch or fibre and 566 kilojoules (135 calories).

Many yoghurts advertise that they contain probiotics. This refers to special live bacteria that can help us stay healthy. These probiotics may well be the key to yoghurt's healthy properties.

While all yoghurts contain acidophilus and bifidus bacteria (known simply as a/B cultures), if you're really serious about probiotics, you'll need to buy one of the well-researched types like Yakult. These show that their particular strain(s) of bacteria is able to survive the journey through the upper digestive tract in sufficient number and reach the large intestine where it can then multiply and thrive.

Wheatgerm

If you feel tired and run down, wheatgerm is the natural way to top up your diet and give yourself a boost of almost all the B vitamins, plus some vitamin E, a healthy dose of phytochemicals and many minerals – all in one.

Wheatgerm is in fact the 'embryo' or developing new plant of the wheat grain and is amazingly rich in fibre and many nutrients, but particularly the B vitamins. It's a pity that it's usually discarded or fed to animals via stockfeed.

As a group, the B vitamins (thiamin, riboflavin, niacin, folate and pyridoxine) function to release energy from food, especially carbohydrates. Your body can't perform at peak without them. Definitely the 'must-have' topping for your daily morning cereal.

Index

A
acesulfame K 46
acidity regulators 138
activated charcoal 51
additives 137–41
    less used 140–1
aflatoxin 105
African olive tree 103
agave 43
ageing, diet to beat 160–1
alcohol 39–40
    cons of 40
    kilojoules in 109
    nutrition in 40
    during pregnancy 68
    pros of 39
    and weight loss 108–9, 112
allergens on food labels 151
almonds 170
Alternate Day Fasting (ADF) 123
amaranth 53
amines 151
amino acids 17
anti-caking agents 138
antioxidants 138
anxiety, diet for 158–9
artificial colours 138–9, 152
aspartame 46
Atkins diet 10
avocados 11–12

B
BARLEYmax™ 170–1
beetroot 57
benzoates 152
berries 171
beta-carotene 58
birch syrup 42–3
blueberries 171
BRAT diet 165
bread, alternatives 157
breads, lower-carb 113–14
burgers 24

C
cabbage 171–2
cafe culture 80
caffeine 33–5
    cutting down on 35
    downsides 34
    in drinks 35
    and guarana 35
calcium 89
    and pregnancy 89, 90
    vegetarian diets 90
carb-free diets 10
carbohydrates 7–10
    complex vs simple 8
    cutting carbs 10
        for weight loss 113, 116–17
    lower-carb foods 113–14
    refined 9
    and weight loss 107
cauliflower 54
chewing 124
chia seeds 55–6

chickpeas 56
chillies 172
cholesterol, diet for 144–5
cinnamon 172–3
citrus fruits 177–8
clean-eating diet 122–3
    for weight loss 122–3
cleanse, juice-only 127
coconut oil 52
coconut sugar 45, 52
coeliac disease, diet for 156–7
coffee 33–5
    alternatives 35
    fairtrade 98
    substitutes 35
    types of 33–4
collagen 57
colours, artificial 152
constipation, diet for 168–9
cooking vegetables 5
copper 59
cravings, managing 110
cyclamate 48

D
dairy 15
dandelion 103
dandelion root 35
DASH diet 160
decaf coffee 35
depression, diet for 158–9
detoxing 127
diabetes
    diet for type 2 148–50
    types of 149
diarrhoea
    symptoms 164
    treating 164–5
dieting 106–8
    see also diets, weight loss
diets
    to beat ageing 160–1
    for anxiety and depression 158–9
    Atkins diet 10
    BRAT diet 165
    cabbage soup diet 171–2
    carb free 10
    for cholesterol and heart disease 144–5
    clean-eating diet 122–3
    for coeliac disease 156–7
    for constipation 168–9
    DASH diet 160
    for diabetes, type 2 148–50
    diet trends 115–22
    fasting diets 123
    for food allergy and intolerance 150–2
    for gallstones 162–4
    gluten-free diet 121–2
    for health problems 144–69
    for heartburn 161–2
    high-protein diet 19, 107
    high-protein low-carbohydrate diets 18
    for iron-deficiency anaemia 167–8
    for irritable bowel syndrome (IBS) 153–4
    keto diet 10, 107, 113, 116–18
    for lactose intolerance 154–5

    lemon detox diet 127
    low-FODMAP diet 75, 153–4
    MAOI diet 79
    Mediterranean diet 11, 85, 86–7, 158, 160
    for metabolic syndrome 146
    MIND diet 160
    no-sugar diets 116–18
    nutrient-dense diet 108
    Paleo diet 107, 113, 115–16
    raw diet 118–21
    see also dieting, vegan diet, vegetarian diet, weight loss
Dirty Dozen 101
doughnuts 81

E
eating out 84–7
    Italian 86–7
    Japanese 84–5
    Middle Eastern 85–6
    Vietnamese 87
eating seasonally and locally 97–8
edible weeds 103–4
eggs 173
emulsifiers 139
erythritol 46–7
exercise 110–11
    aerobic 111
    benefits of 110–11
    and protein 17
    and weight loss 110–11

F
fairtrade 98
farmer's friend 103
fast food
    basics 23
    vs junk food 25
    problems with 26
    salad bars 82
    sandwiches 84
    wraps 84
    see also junk food, eating out
fasting diets 123, 127
fat
    in dairy 15
    facts 15
    on food labels 134
    good fats 11
    saturated 15
    terminology of 12
fermented foods 76–9
    vitamin B12 in 65
fibre 9
fidgeting 111
fish
    canned 69
    mercury in 69, 105
    oily 14
    during pregnancy 68, 105
5-(vegetables)-a-day 4, 5
flavour additives 141
flavour enhancers 139
flaxseeds 175–6
FODMAPs
    FODMAP-friendly meal plan 154

low-FODMAP diet 75, 153–4
folate 68
    during pregnancy 68
food additives 137–41
food allergy and intolerance
    diet for 150–2
    symptom checklist 151
food labelling
    allergens on 151
    claims and what they really
        mean 134–7
    decoder example 137
    decoding the nutrition information
        panel 131–3
    gluten on 157
    the 10 basics 130–1
    understanding the ingredients list 133
food miles 97
food shaming, ending 126
food waste 96–7
foods, fermented 76–9
foraging 103–4
fries and chips 25–6
frozen vegetables 5
fructans 152
fructose 45

G
gallstones
    diet for 162–4
    preventing 162–4
    symptoms of 162
garlic 173
gelling agents 139–40
genetically modified (GM) foods 102
ginger 52–3
glucose 45
glutamates 151–2
gluten
    gluten-free diet 121–2
    gluten-free tips 156–7
    in foods 156
    what is 121
gluten-free diet 121–2
golden syrup 44
grains, whole 7
guarana 35
gut vs microbiome 74

H
hangovers 165–7
    avoiding 165–7
    and B1 166
Health At Every Size (HAES) 125
health problems, diet for 144–69
Health Star Rating (HSR) 143
heart disease, diets for 144–5
heartburn, diet for 161–2
hemp 51
herbs, green leafy 173–5
high-protein diet 19, 107
high-protein low-carbohydrate
    diets 18
honey 42
hormones 102
humectants 140

I
insects 54
intermittent fasting 123
iron 65–66
    boosting iron absorption 168
    deficiency 65
    and fatigue 65
    during pregnancy 68
    sources of 66
    supplements 66, 168
    vegetarian and vegan diets 88–92
iron-deficiency anaemia
    diet for 167–8
    symptoms of 167
irradiation 101–2
    pros and cons 101
irritable bowel syndrome (IBS), diet
    for 153–4

J
juice-only cleanse 127
junk food 22–6, 108
    vs fast food
    see also fast food

K
kale 51
kebabs 26
kefir 77–8
    making 78
keto diet 10, 107, 113, 116
kimchi 79
kombucha 76–7
    benefits of 77
    homemade vs bottled 76–7
    how to make at home 76–7
Konjac (shirataki) noodles 114

L
labels see food labelling
lactose in foods 154
lactose intolerance
    diet for 154–5
    managing 155
    and milk and dairy 155
lamb 175
lemon detox diet 127
linseeds 55, 175–6
listeria 68, 104
    avoiding 104
    during pregnancy 68
losing weight see weight loss
lupin 176

M
manganese 59
MAOI diet 79
maple syrup 42
matcha 49–51
Mediterranean diet 11, 85, 86–7, 158, 160
mercury in fish 69, 105
metabolic syndrome, diet for 146
microbiome 74–5
    benefits of a healthy biome 74–5
    vs the gut 74

milk, raw 105
MIND diet 160
mindful eating 124–5
mineral salts 140
molasses 44
monk fruit 47–8
MSG 151–2
mushrooms 176–7
    vitamin B12 in 65
    vitamin D in 63

N
natural colours 139
New Year's resolutions 107
no-sugar diets 116–18
Non-Exercise Activity Thermogenesis
    (NEAT) 111
noodles, Konjac (shirataki) 114
nuggets 24–5
nutrient-dense diet 108
nutrition in alcohol 40
nutrition information panel, decoding 131–3
nuts and nut butters 12

O
oats 177
oils 11
    coconut oil 52
    in vegetarian diets 93
olive tree, African 103
omega-3 70–3
    benefits 70–2
    on food labels 136
    omega-3 rich foods 72–3
    vegetarian and vegan diets 90
oranges 177–8
organic certification and practices 98–9
overweight kids, helping 126

P
Paleo diet 107, 113, 115–18
panela 44–5, 52
pasta, high-fibre pulse 114
pea protein 57
pesticides 99, 100–1
    residue in fruit and
        vegetables 99, 100–1
phytochemicals 58–61
    vs antioxidants 59
    boosting 59
    in food 60–1
pigface 103
pizza 25
potatoes, lower-carb 114
prebiotics 75
pregnancy
    and alcohol 40
    and caffeine 34
    and calcium 89, 90
    and diet 67–73
    and fish 105
    and omega-3 70
    and vegetarian diets 89
    and vitamin B12 65, 89
    and vitamin B12 deficiency 65
preservatives 140

probiotics 74–9
    'good' bacteria 75
protein 17–20
    daily intake 18–19
    after exercise 17
    how much do we need 17–18
    on food labels 136
    pea protein 57
    processed 20
    protein-rich foods 18–19
    for vegans 20
protein shakes and powders 20
purple foods 7, 53

R
Rainforest Alliance 98
raw diet 118–21
raw milk 105
raw treats 52
raw vegetables 5
resistant starch 9, 75, 171
rice malt syrup 43–4, 52

S
saccharin 48
salad bars 82
salicylates 151
salmon 178
salt 36–9
    on food labels 134, 135
    in foods 38
    mineral salts 140
    on packaging 36–7
    reducing 38–9
    types of 37
sauerkraut 78–9
seafood, canned 69
seeds 14
selenium 58
shame-free body zones 125
shopping 130–43
    streamlining 141
silverbeet 178–9
smart carbs 7
snacking, healthy 80–2
sodium see salt
sorbitol 47
spinach 178–9
stevia 47
sucralose 46
sugar 28–31
    alternatives 42–6
    coconut sugar 45
    cutting back on 31
    daily intake 30
    on food labels 134, 136
    in foods 29
    forms of 30
    and health 30
    no-sugar diets 116–18
sulphur preservatives 152
sun exposure 63

superfoods
    foods with a nutrition buzz 49–57
    top 20 170–80
supplements, iron 66
sweet syrups 42–4
sweeteners 46–8
syrups see sweet syrups

T
takeaway 109
tea 179
teff 53–4
thickeners 140
treacle 44
treats, raw 52
turmeric 49

U
ultra-processed foods 84

V
vegan diet 20, 55, 57, 64–5, 88–90, 176
    benefits of 88
    nutrients likely to be in short
      supply 89–90
    protein in 20
    substitute for honey 43
    what you should eat 90
vegetables
    cooking 5
    5-a-day 4, 5
    frozen or fresh 5
    green leafy vegetables 178–9
    nutritional value of 7
    raw or cooked 5
    what is a serve 4
vegetarian diet 56, 64–5, 88–93, 106, 168,
    170, 173
    benefits of 88
    for children 90–2
    getting started 92
    how not to go vegetarian 93
    nutrients likely to be in short
      supply 89–90
    and pregnancy 89
    types of 88–9
    what you should eat 90
vitamin B12 64–6
    absorption 64
    deficiency 65
    in fermented foods 65
    in foods 64
    during pregnancy and childhood 65
    vegetarian and vegan diets 89
vitamin C 58
    on food labels 137
vitamin D 62–3
    and bones 62
    deficiency 62
    in foods 62–3
    in mushrooms 63
vitamin E 58

W
warrigal greens 103
weight loss 106–13
    clean eating for 122–3
    common traps 106–7
    cutting carbs 113
    fundamentals 107–8
    helping overweight kids 126
    the healthiest way 106–7
    see also dieting, diets
wheatgerm 180
wholegrains 7, 8
wraps 84

X
xylitol 47

Y
yoghurt 180

Z
zinc 59, 89
    in vegetarian and vegan diets 89